Trial Court & Appeal: False Arrest, Imprisonment, and Civil Rights Violations By L.A. County

Complaint, Discovery, Court Forms & Motions, Appellate Briefs, and Writs of Mandate

Dumas v. Los Angeles County Board of Supervisors et al. 45 Cal. App. 5th 348

By

Paralegal Publishing Group©

Trial Court & Appeal: False Arrest, Imprisonment, and Civil Rights Violations By L.A. County
Dumas v. Los Angeles County Board of Supervisors et al. 45 Cal. App. 5th 348

PARALEGAL PUBLISHING GROUP©

Copyright. © 2021 Paralegal Publishing Group.

Copyright. © 2021. Paralegal Publishing Group.

All rights reserved. No part of this publication may be reproduced or transmitted in any form or by any means, electronic or mechanical, including photocopy, recording or any other information storage and retrieval system without prior permission in writing from and of the publisher, except in the case of brief quotations embodied in secondary or post-secondary educational papers and for certain other noncommercial uses permitted by copyright law. For permission request please contact the publisher at the email address with "Attention: Permission Request", at the address below.

ISBN: [see publisher]

Library of Congress Control Number: [see author]

Front cover design and image by Luke Ink™.

Printed by Paralegal Publishing Group™.

First Edition. 2021.

Distributor:

ProgressivePublishingCo@gmail.com

Copyright. © 2021. Paralegal Publishing Group.

Table of Contents

Foreword	12
Chapter 1	14
Complaint	14
Chapter 2	41
Case Management Statement	41
Chapter 3	47
Form Interrogatories	47
CHAPTER 4	113
Statement of Disqualification of Judicial Officer	113
Case No.: BC618191	115
PLAINTIFF IN PRO PER'S VERIFIED STATEMENT OF DISQUALIFICATION OF ASSIGNED JUDGE GREGORY KEOSIAN	115
STATEMENT OF FACTS PERTINENT TO THIS VERIFIED STATEMENT OF DISQUALIFICATION	129
THE JUDGE KEOSIAN ALLOWS OFFICERS OF THE COURT TO LIE IN THEIR DECLARATIONS IN ORDER TO PROVIDE THEM WITH UNLAWFUL COURT ORDERS	131
THE JUDGE KEOSIAN ALLOWS OFFICERS OF THE COURT TO OBSTRUCT LAW BECAUSE HE IS PREJUDICED AGAINST MEXICAN-AMERICAN MALES IN PRO PER AND IN FORMA PAUPRIS	133
THE DECLARATION OF W. SCOTT MCINTOSH WAS A SHAM DECLARATION AND NOT TRUTHFUL, BUT THE JUDGE KEOSIAN SUPERIOR COURT PERMITTED MR. MCINTOSH TO PLAY FAST AND LOOSE WITH THE DISCOVERY PROCESS AND SHOWING PREJUDICE AGAINST THE PLAINTIFF IN PRO PER	136
THE JUDGE KEOSIAN TENTATIVE RULING WAS A CLEAR ABUSE OF DISCRETION AND NOT ONE SINGLE WORD FROM THE PLAINTIFF IN PRO PER'S PLEADINGS WERE CITED; THE JUDGE KEOSIAN ABUSED ITS DISCRETION IN FAVOR OF THE LOS ANGELES COUNTY BOARD OF SUPERVISORS	141

Copyright. © 2021. Paralegal Publishing Group.

THE DEFENDANT COUNTY GOVERNMENT'S OPPOSITION TO PLAINTIFF'S GOOD FAITH MEET AND CONFER REQUESTS TO MR. JOHN M. COLEMAN ESQ. WAS BASED ON A SHAM DECLARATION BY HIS ASSOCIATE COUNSEL OF RECORD MR. WILLIAM SCOTT MCINTOSH ESQ. 141

THE DECLARATION OF LUKE EDWARD DUMAS ESTABLISHED GOOD FAITH ATTEMPTS TO "MEET AND CONFER" WITH THE DEFENDANT COUNTY GOVERNMENT'S COUNSEL OF RECORD BUT WAS DISREGARDED BY THE JUDGE KEOSIAN SUPERIOR COURT IN FAVOR OF THE DEFENDANT COUNTY GOVERNMENT 144

THE JUDGE KEOSIAN SHOULD HAVE DISCLOSED IF HE HAD RECIEVED UNLAWFUL COMPENSATION FROM THE DEFENDANT COUNTY 144

JUDGE KEOSIAN INTENTIONALLY FAILED TO READ AND PROPERLY CONSIDER AND WEIGH EVIDENCE BECAUSE OF HIS PREJUDICE AND THE PLAINTIFF IN PRO PER CANNOT RECEIVE A FAIR TRIAL 146

The Judge Keosian has miscarriaged justice in favor of the Defendant .. 147

THE PLAINTIFF CANNOT RECEIVE A FAIR AND IMPARTIAL TRIAL FROM JUDGE KEOSIAN 148

THE JUDICIAL DISQUALIFICATION OF JUDGE KEOSIAN 148

COURT RELIEF REQUESTED: 149

VERIFICATION 150

MEMORANDUM OF POINTS AND AUTHORITIES 151

PLAINTIFF'S REQUEST FOR COPIES – LOS ANGELES SUPERIOR COURT FORM 154

Case No. B283557 155

Related Case No. B286369 155

PETITION FOR WRIT OF MANDAMUS, PROHIBITION, OR OTHER EXTRAORDINARY RELIEF 155

Certificate of Interested Persons 156

TABLE OF CONTENTS 157

TABLE OF AUTHORITIES 161

State Cases 161

California State Constitution	165
Statutes	165
Court Rules	166

VERIFIED PETITION FOR WRIT OF MANDAMUS AND/OR PROHIBITION OR OTHER APPROPRIATE RELIEF 168

I. INTRODUCTION 168
- A. The Parties to this Verified Petition for an Extraordinary Writ 169
- B. The Basis for Writ Review for the Denial of Discovery 169
  - i. In Propria Persona 172
  - ii. Confidential Medical Condition & Disability Issue 172
  - iii. The Petitioner is in Forma Paupris 172
- D. The Limitation of relying on Clerk Copies 173
- D. Authenticity of Exhibits Volume 1 & Volume 2 174

II. FACTS & PROCEDURE 174
- A. Chronology of Pertinent Events to this Petition for a Writ 174
- B. Absence of Other Remedies 175
- C. No Prejudice to Opposing Party in Issuing a Writ 176
- D. An Alternative Writ of Mandate can be used to seek Compliance with the Petitioner's Statutory Right to obtain Truthful Answers to Official Interrogatories 177

III. LEGAL DISCUSSION 178
- A. The Respondent Superior Court had a duty to Act in accordance with The Civil Discovery Act 178
- B. Case of First Impression? 180
  - 1. Judicial Council Form Interrogatories 181
  - 2. Pro Per Litigants 181
  - 3. The County of Los Angeles 181
- C. The Basis for Relief, Beneficial Interest of the Petitioner, and the Capacities of the Respondent Superior Court and the Real Party in Interest County of LA 182

D. The Petitioner's Motion to Compel Further Discovery Responses to Judicial Council Form Interrogatories was completely disregarded by the Respondent 184

E. The Declaration of Luke Edward Dumas established good faith attempts to "Meet and Confer" with the Real Party's Counsel of Record but was disregarded by the Respondent Superior Court in favor of the Real Party in Interest County of LA..185

F. The Declaration of W. Scott McIntosh was a sham declaration and not truthful but the Respondent Superior Court permitted Mr. McIntosh to play fast and loose with the discovery process and showing prejudice against the Petitioner...186

G. The Respondent Tentative Ruling was a Clear Abuse of Discretion and not one Single Word from the Petitioner's pleadings were cited; the Respondent abused its discretion in favor of the Real Party in Interest County of LA..189

H. The Real Party's Opposition to Plaintiff's Good Faith Meet and Confer Requests to Mr. John M. Coleman Esq. was based on a sham declaration by his associate Counsel of Record Mr. William Scott McIntosh Esq.....190

RELIEF REQUESTED: 192

MEMORANDUM OF POINTS AND AUTHORITIES 193

I. INTRODUCTION...193

II. THE STANDARD OF REVIEW...195

A. Writ Review is proper for the denial of the discovery of Official Form Interrogatories 195

III. A CASE OF FIRST IMPRESSION?...197

A. Pursuant to the Judicial Council's rule-making power, are "Form Interrogatories" primary authority in and of itself, and generally "Objection-Proof" notwithstanding the instructive and statutory legal exceptions?..197

IV. ARGUMENT 199

A. The Respondent's abuse of discretion resulted in the denial of discovery with no legal justification..199

B. California Judicial Council Form Interrogatories are inherently primary authority thus commanding a proper and complete response to each unanswered interrogatory...200

C. The Separate Statement Rule Does Not Limit the Respondent's Discretion to Compel Further Answers & Responses Notwithstanding even in its absence 202

D. The Petitioner is Entitled to Propound and Obtain Lawful Discovery Responses by using Judicial Council's Official Form Interrogatories 204

E. The Petitioner has a broad right to obtaining lawful discovery from the Real Party in Interest County of LA using the Judicial Council Form Interrogatories 205

F. The Real Party was using Boilerplate Objections to Evade Lawful Discovery via Judicial Council Form Interrogatories and the Respondent abused its Discretion in denying the Petitioner's Motion to Compel Further Discovery Responses 207

G. The Real Party's Objections must be deemed waived by Operation of California law and the Respondent abused its Discretion in not Considering the Petitioner's Evidence 208

H. The Respondent abused its discretion and deprived the Petitioner a Statutory Right to Lawful Discovery via Judicial Council Form Interrogatories on its face 209

I. The Respondent has failed to perform a mandatory duty by California Law and the Respondent has not Acted in the Spirit of California Law and should be Mandated to do so or the Petitioner will be harmed at the upcoming jury trial 210

V. CONCLUSION 212

VERIFICATION 212

CERTIFICATE OF WORD COUNT 212

(Cal. Rules of Court, rule 8.204(c)(1)) 212

Case No. B288554 213

APPEAL FROM FINAL ORDER OF DISMISSAL AND SUBSEQUENT ORDERS FOR ABUSE OF DISCRETION, DENIAL OF DUE PROCESS, & DISQUALIFICATION 213

TABLE OF CONTENTS 216

TABLE OF AUTHORITIES 217

Federal Constitution 217

California Court Rules 218

Additional Citations 218

Copyright. © 2021. Paralegal Publishing Group.

APPEAL FROM FINAL ORDER OF DISMISSAL AND SUBSEQUENT ORDERS FOR ABUSE OF DISCRETION, DENIAL OF DUE PROCESS, & DISQUALIFICATION 219

INTRODUCTION 219

II. GOOD AND JUST CAUSE EXISTS FOR THE LEGAL REASONS OF WHY THE FINAL ORDER DISMISSING PLAINTIFF'S CASE SHOULD BE REVERSED & ASSIGNED A NEW JUDICIAL OFFICER 220

III. PLAINTIFF IS ENTITLED TO DUE PROCESS OF LAW & THE TRIAL COURT ABUSED ITS DISCRETION THROUGHOUT THE LEGAL PROCESS OF THIS CASE 221

IV. SUMMARY OF FACTS AND PROCEDURAL HISTORY 222

V. The Court Order dismissing the Plaintiff's Case against the Defendant County Government Should and or Must be Reversed and Remanded 223

VI. The Trial Judge Made a Harmful Error by not Disqualifying himself and or for Calendaring a Hearing before the Presiding Judge 225

VII. The Trial Court made a Harmful Error by sustaining the Defendants Demurrer to the Plaintiff's Complaint, the final Order must be reversed, and is null and void 226

VIII. The Trial Court made a Harmful Error by Sustaining the Defendant's Motion to Strike and a Disqualified Judge's Order is null and void 228

IX. The Trial Court made a Harmful Error by Failing to Disclose his Potential Conflicts of Interests involving the County of Los Angeles 229

X. The Trial Court's Order Violated the Plaintiff's right to privacy in his medical records, the trial court violated the Plaintiff's Rights in disclosing medical information to the Government and police, whom are now using and misusing his medical conditions against him 231

XI. CONCLUSION 232

CERTIFICATE OF WORD COUNT 233

Court of Appeal No. B288554 234

Superior Court No. BC618191 234

APPELLANT'S MOTION FOR JUDICIAL NOTICE 234

TABLE OF CONTENTS 235

TABLE OF AUTHORITIES 236

APPELLANT'S MOTION FOR JUDICIAL NOTICE 237

I. INTRODUCTION 237

II. EXHIBITS TO BE JUDICIALLY NOTICED 237

III. ARGUMENT 238

IV. CONCLUSION 240

Court of Appeal No. B288554 241

Superior Court No. BC618191 241

APPELLANT'S MOTION TO AUGMENT THE RECORD 241

TABLE OF CONTENTS	242
I. INTRODUCTION	243
II. ARGUMENT	243
A. The administrative record should include all papers in the case	243
B. Good cause exists to grant the augmentation the legal papers to be part of the appellate record	246
III. CONCLUSION	247
LIST OF EXHIBITS	248
Case No. B288554	**249**
APPELLANT'S REPLY TO RESPONDENT'S REPLY BRIEF	249
I. INTRODUCTION	250
II. ARGUMENT	250
1. THE TRIAL COURT ABUSED ITS DISCRETION AND DISREGARDED CALIFORNIA LAW BY GRANTING THE DEMURRER	250
III. APPELLANT'S REQUEST FOR JUDICIAL NOTICE	257
1. Evidence of Two Separate Trials on the Exact Same Day	257
IV. PLAINTIFF HAD REASONABLE EXPECTATION OF PRIVACY IN HIS MEDICAL AND OR EMPLOYMENT RECORDS	259
1. Appellant Request this Reviewing Court to take Judicial Notice of Writ or alternatively to Augment Record of Writ	259
V. APPELLANT MOTION TO AUGMENT THE CLERK'S TRANSCRIPT OR ALTERNATIVELY REQUEST FOR JUDICIAL NOTICE	260
1. Evidence of Plaintiff and Appellant's Objection to the Defendant and Respondent's Deposition Notice	260
VI. CONCLUSION	260
VII. CERTIFICATE OF COMPLIANCE	262

Trial Court & Appeal: False Arrest, Imprisonment, and Civil Rights Violations By L.A. County

Dumas v. Los Angeles County Board of Supervisors et al. 45 Cal. App. 5th 348

MORE FROM
PARALEGAL PUBLISHING GROUP©!

Edward Dumas

The Playbook of Business Law: Legal Forms, Documents, and Research for Lawyers, Paralegals, & Self-Represented Litigants

#1 New Release in Legal Education Writing

Format **Paperback**

Criminal Self-Defense for Misdemeanor Trial in the Los Angeles Superior Court & Federal Civil Rights Lawsuits Against the Police: Pro Per Sample Legal ... Motions, Civil Rights Complaints, and More! Paperback – February 9, 2021
by Edward Dumas (Author), Paralegal Publishing Group (Contributor)

Have you ever wanted to defend yourself in court but did not know how? Couldn't afford a lawyer? But wanted to type your own legal forms but did not know how? Then in this publication you will find real court documents in a misdemeanor trial regarding a single charge that is sophisticatedly styled in a paralegal format. The style of legal writing and non-pleading format is up to date. The legal documents published are the following: Pro Per Sample Legal Forms for Demurrer, Informal Discovery Requests, Motion to Compel Discovery, Motion to Suppress Statements to Law Enforcement, Motion to Dismiss, Motion for Inspection of Third-Party Property, Memorandums of Points and Authorities, Declarations, Federal Civil Rights Complaint & Appeal. For students and self-represented litigants, this is a useful tool when researching California criminal law and civil rights law together. Political activists may find it useful when litigating civil rights against police brutality, harassment, and illegal surveillance. This publication does not substitute the advice of a licensed attorney. True Story. Real Case.

Copyright. © 2021. Paralegal Publishing Group.

Foreword

This is a true story. There are no fictional characters.

The names in this book are real, as are the incidents, events, and legal rights violations by the Government for the "County of Los Angeles". The Los Angeles County Government has spent millions of tax dollars against Luke Edward Dumas ever since he first filed his claims against the Los Angeles County Board of Supervisors and the Los Angeles County Sherriff's Department.

This publication includes legal research, actual case, writs, and appeal numbers, plus the exhibits docketed in the California Courts. All of these lodged legal documents are also in the Government's databases, computers, and websites.

In this legal case against the L.A. County Government for false arrest, imprisonment, discrimination, and other civil rights violations, the overt denial of fundamental legal rights does prove how institutionally racist and corrupt the judicial and political system is in the California Courts, especially L.A. County.

As Dumas' civil rights were violated and still are to this date of publishing, the Government has sabotaged, suppressed, and stalked Mr. Dumas (along with his family) ever since he filed his claim of damages with the Los Angeles County Board of Supervisors. Since the filing of Mr. Dumas' first Government Claim presented to the L.A. Board of Supervisors in 2015, pursuant to the **Government Code**, this lawful civil case resulted with an illegal criminal response by the County Government toward Mr. Dumas by a group of possible "white supremacists" and crooked cops working in Los Angeles County Sherriff's Department (and military) with the aid of some politicians in the County and State Government.

Copyright. © 2021. Paralegal Publishing Group.

Trial Court & Appeal: False Arrest, Imprisonment, and Civil Rights Violations By L.A. County

<u>Dumas v. Los Angeles County Board of Supervisors et al.</u> 45 Cal. App. 5th 348

The 2nd Court of Appeal for the State of California bears the final responsibility for the denial of civil rights in this published case. Fact, under Presiding Judge Nora Margret Manella and a judge by the name of Gregory Keosian had initially denied Dumas' fundamental civil rights. Greg Keosian has been a judge for about two decades and is a registered "democratic judge" for the State of California. Judge Greg Keosian is no ally to the civil rights movement for American ethnic minorities in the State of California. Mr. Keosian proved, along with Mrs. Manella, and their judicial colleagues are in fact professional discriminators and racists against Mexican-Americans.

The Superior Court that Mr. Keosian institutionalizes his racism and corruption at the Stanley Mosk Courthouse and Mrs. Manella at the 2nd Court of Appeal. In Mr. Dumas' opinion, he believes that Mr. Keosian, as the initial judge, was on the "take". That means he was most likely taking a bribe or may have taken a bribe and then was blackmailed by the crooked cops at the Los Angeles County Sherriff's Department. Or perhaps Judge Keosian just hated Mr. Dumas for litigating for civil rights as a Mexican-American in pro per.

As judges are just men and women in black robes, they are elected politicians and have absolute power over the legal case presented before them. The California courts are plagued with racists judges. Judges like Gregory Keosian and Nora Manella made sure that Mr. Dumas' legal rights would be further suppressed, and this is how the Judicial System works to institute racism against Mexican-Americans, therefore change the law, change the system.

Copyright. © 2021. Paralegal Publishing Group.

Chapter 1
Complaint

Before filing a "government complaint" with any State, City, County, agency, department, and or bureau, anyone who has been aggrieved by the "Government" must "file" a claim of damages according to each State's code or guidelines. For example, in my State, the State of California, the Government Code requires that a formal presentation of a "claim" against the "State" must be presented and filed in writing in accordance with the law, within six months of the date of injury. Generally, personal injury claims pursuant to the California law must be filed within two years with the Court, in contrast to a "government claim". Be conscious that the Government has given itself 'special immunity' for lawsuits against themselves such as time limits and liability. The immunity doctrine is very unfair, undemocratic, and contributes to the culture of government corruption.

So, in this journey about how to file a lawsuit against the government begins with a letter to the government presenting a claim for damages. Some agencies or States have their own form, and some do not. Check with that relevant agency for their own forms or their policies on how to file a claim. You will find online many good examples and references on how to write and describe your own or your client's claim.

And please note that some agencies and departments of the United States and other States require claims to be made within shorter timelines. In addition, as always, consult at least three different attorneys regarding the incident(s) immediately.

Copyright. © 2021. Paralegal Publishing Group.

Sometimes attorneys may agree, and some may have different views about the incident(s). It is better that you do not inform them you got previous legal advice, so it does not result in "group think". Bottom line and lessoned learned, therefore it is better to go into court with an attorney than without, just make sure that they are professional. Best of luck.

This publication does not substitute for the advice of an attorney at law.

Nothing in this publication solicits or offers legal advice.

This publication is designed primarily as a research tool for civil rights activists, students, paralegals, and lawyers.

Luke E Dumas

Plaintiff In Pro Per

CONFORMED COPY
ORIGINAL FILED
Superior Court of California
County of Los Angeles

APR 26 2016

Sherri R. Carter, Executive Officer/Clerk
By Cristina Grijalva, Deputy

SUPERIOR COURT OF THE STATE OF CALIFORNIA

COUNTY OF LOS ANGELES

BC 618191

Luke E Dumas, an individual,

Plaintiff,

v.

Los Angeles County Board of Supervisors, a public entity;

the Los Angeles County Sherriff's Department, a public entity;

Sheriff Jim McDonnell, a public official;

and DOES 1-10, inclusive, Defendants.

Case No.:

COMPLAINT FOR DAMAGES

1) False Arrest & False Imprisonment under Government Code 820.4
2) Denial of Civil Rights & Discrimination
3) Violation of Cal. Const. Art. 1, Sec. 1
4) Gross Negligence
5) Failure to Discharge Mandatory Duty under Government Code 815.2 & 851.5
6) Delay in Processing & Releasing
7) Malicious Prosecution
8) Conspiracy
9) Unruh Civil Rights Conspiracy

COMES NOW, Plaintiff, in propria persona, and hereby alleges the following:

THE PARTIES

1. The Plaintiff is Luke Edward Dumas, an individual and citizen of the State of California, whom is domiciled in Los Angeles County, California, is over the age of 18 and has standing.

2. The Defendants are the Los Angeles County Board of Supervisors (herein "County"), a public entity and political subdivision and governmental authority, and employer for law

enforcement services in and around Los Angeles County California. The Defendant County is and at all times herein mentioned herein is political subdivision of the State of California, known as "Los Angeles County", duly organized and existing under the laws of the State of California.

3. The co-Defendant is the Los Angeles Sheriff's Department (herein "LASD"), also a public entity and specifically a governmental law-enforcement public agency and law enforcement public service provider for the Defendant County. Defendant LASD is at all times herein mentioned, the law enforcement agency for the political subdivision of "Los Angeles County", also employed by Defendant County as the law enforcement services provider, and in doing the things hereinafter alleged was acting within the course and scope of their employment.

4. The other co-Defendant is duly elected Los Angeles County Sheriff Jim McDonnell (herein "Defendant McDonnell"), a public official and entrusted with the mandatory duties of safeguarding and administering California Constitution, Statutes, and Ordinances; not limited to U.S. Constitutional law.

5. Plaintiff is ignorant of the true names and capacities of the other Defendants sued herein as "Deputy Murren", and DOES 1 through 10, inclusive, and therefore sues these Defendants by such fictitious names.

6. Plaintiff will amend this Complaint to allege their true names and capacities when ascertained. Plaintiff is informed and believes and thereon alleges that each of the fictitiously named Defendants is responsible in some manner for the occurrences herein alleged, and that the Plaintiff's injuries as herein alleged were proximately caused by their conduct.

7. Defendant LASD at all times herein mentioned were the agents and employees of their co-Defendant County, and in doing these things hereinafter alleged; all Defendants were acting within the course and scope of Defendant County and Defendant LASD, jointly and severally, and with the permission and consent of each other.

STATEMENT OF FACTS

8. On Saturday, April 25, 2015, the Plaintiff was traveling on the Metro transit blue line train from Long Beach to Los Angeles. The Plaintiff was harassed and threatened by several unknown African American males and one or more of them had a gun and or weapon in his

pocket. Plaintiff believes that he was harassed and threatened because of his ethnicity, race, color, and or disability.

9. The Plaintiff was in panic and fear because one of these assailants stated that they were going to use their "heater" against the Plaintiff.

10. So the Plaintiff stood his ground, attempted to defend himself and or others, and then immediately got off the train to go wait for the bus.
Defendant DOE 1, whom may be associated with the assailants, had falsely reported to Defendant LASD that Plaintiff had a gun on his person.

11. Defendant DOE 1 intentionally mislead the Defendant LASD to believe that Plaintiff had perpetrated a crime. Defendants knew or should have known that Plaintiff had the right to self defense of himself and or others.

12. Defendant Doe knew or should have known that Plaintiff did not have a gun on his person nor did Plaintiff say he ever had one.

13. Defendant Doe 1 knew or should have known that Plaintiff was being harassed and threatened because of his ethnicity, color, race, and or disability.

14. Moments later, near the bus stop, the Defendant LASD approached Plaintiff and pointed a gun to his head and commanded him"...to drop to his knees and lie face down on the ground!".

15. With complete compliance by Plaintiff, after said Defendant LASD commanded Plaintiff to the ground; the Defendant LASD forcibly seized and grabbed Plaintiff's body and hands from his back against Plaintiff will and without his consent and over his State and Constitutional Rights.

16. Then the Plaintiff was handcuffed while on the ground and surrounded by several more Defendant LASD deputies who at all times mentioned were wearing official uniforms, insignia, and badges of the Defendant LASD.

17. The Plaintiff's backpack was immediately taken off him, and searched while he was still on the ground. The Plaintiff was then placed in a patrol car with a Hispanic male deputy without consent of, and no Miranda warning reading, to Plaintiff.

18. While Plaintiff was in the patrol car, Plaintiff was not informed that he was he told he actually was "under arrest" nor given a full reading of the Miranda warning while in

handcuffs and forced to sit in the back of Defendant's patrol vehicle.

19. The search did not reveal any incriminatory or dangerous contraband or articles. The Defendant LASD found a lawful hunting knife in a black sheath made by Winchester. The Plaintiff informed Defendant LASD that he had seen and heard the assailants say they had a "heater" in his pocket and in fear, and in anticipation of defense of himself and others, he put his lawful hunting knife on his belt during the commotion.

20. The Defendant LASD was falsely informed by Defendant DOE 1 that Plaintiff had a gun or dangerous weapon and knowingly gave false information to Defendant LASD to conspire an arrest of Plaintiff.

21. The Defendant LASD deputy was talking with other deputies and knew or should have known that the information was false because no firearm or "gun" was found on Plaintiff nor in his backpack after they fully searched and seized it.

22. The Defendant LASD knew or should have known that the alleged information was false because the Defendant LASD claimed that the "k-9 was searching for a gun around the tracks" and never found any "gun" for that matter.

23. The Defendant LASD knew or should have known that the information and alleged witness was unreliable and the information provided to them was not verifiable and contradictory.

24. Shortly thereafter, the Defendant LASD instituted a common design and implied understanding to conspire and allege a false arrest of the Plaintiff because of his race, ethnicity, ancestry, age, sex, and or gender.

25. As the Plaintiff was in a Hispanic deputy's custody, an African American supervising deputy for Defendant LASD (herein "DOE 2"), took hold of the Plaintiff and placed him in the immediate custody of a Caucasian deputy for the Defendant LASD known as "Deputy Murren" (herein "Defendant Murren").

26. At Defendant DOE 2 direction, the Defendants grabbed, forcibly seized, and pushed the Plaintiff into their patrol car without any legal reason or notice of "under arrest" nor still not given a reading of his Constitutional rights under the Miranda warning for such acts of Defendants because of his race, ethnicity, ancestry, age, sex, and or gender.

27. As the Plaintiff was now in a different patrol vehicle, Defendant DOE 2 and Defendant Murren were talking amongst themselves and conspiring to falsely arrest and imprison Plaintiff.

28. The Defendant LASD deputies had began to conspire to deprive Plaintiff of his constitutional rights and to violently damage his personal property in his backpack.

29. Defendants knew or should have known that the Plaintiff had expensive property in his backpack such as his computer laptop.

30. Defendant LASD deputies that searched and handled Plaintiff's backpack had also stolen his medication, money, rare pocket utility knife, and lighters to be converted to their own property in violation of State and Federal regulations.

31. The Defendant LASD, Defendant County, and Defendant McDonnell are responsible for the Defendants' policy of stealing and robbing hardworking and taxpaying American citizens such as Plaintiff because of his race, ethnicity, ancestry, age, sex, and or gender. Defendant DOE 2 and Deputy Murren talked amongst themselves and then begin to intentionally damage the contents of the Plaintiff's backpack such as his expensive computer laptop because of his race, color, age, ethnicity, gender, and by retaliatory motivation and corrupt police practices by Defendants.

32. While the Plaintiff was still inside the back of the Defendant Murren's patrol car; DOE 2 was constantly banging, in a violent manner, and intentionally damaging the computer laptop in Plaintiff's backpack because of his race, ethnicity, color, gender, sex, and for retaliatory purposes.

33. Defendant Murren told Plaintiff in the patrol vehicle that he owns a lot of knives and likes to play with knives, and was okay to "stand your ground".

34. Defendant Murren and the DOE 2 for Defendant LASD then went to go discuss among themselves again what they were going to do with Plaintiff and knew or should have known that he did nothing unlawful but they were conspiring to charge Plaintiff with a crime. Deputy Murren knew or should have known that he was writing a false police report against Plaintiff because there was no evidence that Plaintiff had committed a crime.

35. Deputy Murren had knowingly falsified his written police report against Plaintiff in order to make it look like he committed a crime because of his race, ethnicity, ancestry, age, sex, and

or gender.

36. Defendants had continued to talk outside of the patrol vehicle in order to conspire to deprive the Plaintiff of his constitutional rights, fabricate a false police report, and to falsely arrest Plaintiff with the intent to never allow him to call an attorney, relative, bail bond company, nor even a magistrate bail judge because of his race, ethnicity, color, sex, gender, and or for retaliatory motive by way of police corruption; so they hauled Plaintiff off to a jail right next to the Willowbrook/Rosa Parks station.

37. The Defendants then had talked amongst themselves and conspired to deny Plaintiff his constitutional and statutory rights by telling him that he would be able to make a phone call to the bail judge pursuant to Penal Code Section § 851.5 et seq.

38. Plaintiff contends that the Defendant LASD had a common design to deprive Plaintiff of his due process rights and to falsely imprison him until they saw fit to release him.

39. The Plaintiff repeatedly requested to deputies of the Defendant LASD that he wanted to call a lawyer, and Defendant Murren told the Plaintiff that "...this is not like a movie...".

40. The Plaintiff even wrote down on a document that he desired and needed to contact and gave the paper back to the Defendant Murren.

41. Now in a jail cell, the Plaintiff was still uninformed as to what he was being charged with, and asked Defendant Murren as to what he is being charged with?

42. Deputy Murren told Plaintiff that he was being charged with a misdemeanor knife possession, and was instantly mislead by Deputy Murren and later by another Deputy of Defendant LASD during the booking process to believe that he would be "cited out" for the erroneous knife charge.

43. Before the booking procedures, the Defendants knew that they were going to charge Plaintiff with a felony he did not commit but stated to Plaintiff that he was being charged with a misdemeanor.

44. Then Defendant Murren went to go speak to Defendant DOE 2 and they had conspired to deny him his rights under Penal Code Section 851.5 et seq. because of his race, ethnicity, color, age, sex, gender, and for retaliatory motives by way of police corruption.

45. Then the Plaintiff informed Defendant DOE 2 standing behind Defendant Murren

of the Defendant LASD that Plaintiff wanted to call a lawyer. Defendant DOE 2 of Defendant LASD nodded his head but stayed silent and looked away.

46. Then both deputies of the Defendant LASD left the Plaintiff in a jail cell and prohibited him from exercising his statutory rights under Civil Code § 51.5 et seq. because of his race, color, ethnicity, sex, gender, age, and for retaliatory motives.

47. Plaintiff kept repeatedly asking during his imprisonment to Defendant LASD for his right to call a lawyer and bail bond company.

48. At the direction of said Defendants, Plaintiff was booked on the false charge of possession of carrying a concealed dirk or dagger under Penal Code Section § 21310 and he was compelled to the booking procedures such as to submit to fingerprinting, DNA swabbing, and photographing of his person and body by personnel in the employment of the Defendant LASD.

49. During the entire course alleged above, said Defendant LASD deputies pulled, pushed shoved, cursed, yelled at Plaintiff; like an animal in a cage, in a very un-American and un-Constitutional way with complete disregard or his rights vested in the California and U.S. Constitution; similiar to a Nazi or Communist Police-State, Defendants did and have not acted in the American way.

50. The Defendant LASD set aside Plaintiff's State Constitutional rights for no lawful reason, for corrupt and illegal purposes, with the intent to cause distress and unemployment of Plaintiff because of his race, ethnicity, color, age, sex, gender, and for retaliatory motives.

51. Plaintiff suffered injury to his reputation, person, and lost the privilege of his full time employment due to Defendants false arrest, malicious prosecution, and false imprisonment, and governmental corruption.

52. The Defendants acted with malicious intent of humiliating, intimidating, discriminating, and mentally torturing Plaintiff because of his race, ethnicity, color, age, sex, gender, and for retaliatory motives and police corruption by Defendant LASD.

53. During the booking procedures Plaintiff kept asking to call for a lawyer or to make bail and one deputy of Defendant LASD stated that sometimes they will "cite people out for a charge like this", misleading him to believe he would be released soon that day. After booking the Plaintiff never seen that specific deputy ever again.

COMPLAINT

Copyright. © 2021. Paralegal Publishing Group.

54. Defendants issued to Plaintiff and alleged that a "pin" number would enable him to call out to a third party but the "pin" number provided never worked; this was misleading and with an intent to falsely imprison Plaintiff because of his race, ethnicity, color, age, sex, gender, and for retaliatory and corrupt motives by Defendant LASD.

55. Plaintiff continuously requested from Defendants to be allowed to call his relative and an attorney but Defendants with malice and gross negligence did not perform any of their Constitutional and mandatory legal duties to allow Plaintiff to exercise his rights under California law and the United States Constitution because of his race, ethnicity, color, age, sex, and gender.

56. On Saturday night by midnight, Plaintiff was transferred to the Los Angeles County Men's Central Jail located at 441 Bauchet St, Los Angeles, CA 90012, and he continuously requested that he be allowed to call an Attorney and the Defendant LASD and their employees intentionally ignored Plaintiff's constitutional and legal requests under Penal Code Section § 851.5 et seq.

57. The deputies of Defendant LASD often looked at Plaintiff with anger and rage, in order to cause intimidation, fear, humiliation, and deprivation of his civil rights because of his race, ethnicity, color, age, sex, gender, and for retaliatory motives.

58. The Defendants did not adhere to, nor respect California statutory laws nor even the U.S. Constitution because of his race, ethnicity, color, age, sex, gender, and for retaliatory motives.

59. As Plaintiff would continuously plead with Defendants to allow him to call his attorney, or relative, and or bail magistrate judge; Plaintiff was constantly told no, to shut up, "don't say sh*t", "I don't know" by Defendant LASD deputies.

60. Plaintiff, as an innocent person, was unable to barely eat, bath, go to the bathroom, and was treated less than a human being without dignity by Defendant LASD employees.

61. The Defendant LASD had no respect for Plaintiff's constitutional and statutory rights including the right to due process by said Defendants because of his race, ethnicity, color, age, sex, gender, and for retaliatory motives.

//

62. At all times mentioned herein Plaintiff was denied his right to telephone call pursuant to Penal Code Section § 851.5 et seq. because of his race, ethnicity, color, age, sex, gender, and for retaliatory motives by Defendant LASD.

63. On April 27, 2015, the arraignment judge ordered the Defendants to release Plaintiff on his own recognizance but the Defendants failed to do so because of his race, ethnicity, color, age, sex, gender, and for corrupt motives.

64. The Defendants kept Plaintiff falsely imprisoned and held hostage in order to further cause Plaintiff harm, humiliation, loss of income, and to deprive him of his constitutional and statutory rights under California law.

65. On April 28, 2015, the Defendants still did not allow nor permit, and with malicious intention, barred the Plaintiff to make any telephone call to a private attorney, relative, nor release him as he was ordered to be on his own recognizance because of his race, ethnicity, color, age, sex, gender, and for retaliatory and corrupt motives by the Defendant LASD.

66. On April 29, 2015, the Defendants began to process the Plaintiff in a large group of inmates and made him submit to more fingerprinting.

67. While in this process the Defendants were yelling at Plaintiff using curse words and making outrageous remarks. For example, one Caucasian deputy of the Defendant LASD kept making rude and demeaning comments to Plaintiff such as "Thank you for committing crime, thank you for helping me pay for my mortgage, and please go out and commit more crime because you are all paying for my children's private school, thank you for this overtime... I am making a lot of money, now go out and go out and commit more crime".

68. The Defendants have and harbor anti-American and anti-Constitutional practices against Plaintiff because of his race, ethnicity, color, age, sex, gender, and for retaliatory motives and police corruption by Defendants.

69. The Defendants did show police corruption and no respect for Plaintiff's constitutional rights under the law nor professional policy of the "Los Angeles County Sherriff's Department", nor even for the United States and California Constitutions as supreme laws of the land.

//

70. The Defendants intended to falsely arrest and imprison Plaintiff in order to create a fraudulent workload so the Defendants, acting corruptly with police power, could make more money in overtime as in fact they did state it as fact incorporated by reference herein.

71. The Defendants intended to act with fraud, oppression, and malice to wrongfully imprison Plaintiff in violation of the Own Recognizance Judicial Order and California law.

72. The Defendants, while processing the fingerprints of the large group of prisoners, told Plaintiff that they were not going to let him out until the last prisoner's fingerprints were readable for the computer, thus unlawfully justifying their false imprisonment policy or rule.

73. The Caucasian deputy of the Defendant LASD kept yelling at Plaintiff and the group of ethnic minorities that were segregated, "damn it", "this is all going to be your guys fault", and "you will not get released until this guy's fingerprints go through!".

74. Defendants acted with malice and with intent to cause harm to Plaintiff, with an intent to maintain their false imprisonment of Plaintiff because of his race, ethnicity, color, age, sex, gender, and for retaliatory and corrupt motives by the Defendants.

75. The Defendants' process took an unreasonable amount of time, with intent to delay, and was meant to deprive Plaintiff of his constitutional rights, and cause tensions between the Hispanic prisoners and African American prisoners; the Caucasian deputy of Defendant LASD was keeping Plaintiff falsely imprisoned with an intent to cause racial disparity and racial tension in the processing room, as is the Defendant LASD's policy throughout the jail.

76. Plaintiff was made to wait in a holding cell in where one or two inmates were released earlier than Plaintiff and was purposely made to be imprisoned further with the intent to oppress, defraud, and induce entrapment through mistreating Plaintiff as a prisoner for the sake of inflicting additional punishment.

77. Plaintiff was told to line up by a Caucasian deputy that was constantly using curse words such as "shut the f**k up when I am talking", "stand in this f***ing line", "no one say sh*t or you are going back to a jail cell", and kept looking at the Plaintiff with anger and rage because of his race, ethnicity, color, age, sex, gender, and for retaliatory motives and the culture of corruption for Defendants.

78. The Defendants constantly treated Plaintiff like he was guilty and with contempt for the U.S. and California Constitution, and Penal Code mandates, referenced herein. The Defendant County allows, permits, turns a "blind eye", and authorized the false arrest and imprisonment, theft and conversion of Plaintiff and his property because of his race, ethnicity, color, age, sex, gender, and for retaliatory motives.

79. The Plaintiff was finally provided his clothes and a Caucasian deputy came into the room and spoke sarcastically and angrily toward Plaintiff by stating "I don't want to violate your constitutional rights...", spoke with more sarcasm and yelled, then looked at Plaintiff with anger and rage.

80. Plaintiff was finally released on April 29, 2015, around 4:00PM, two days after the arraignment judge ordered Defendants to release Plaintiff on his own recognizance on April 27, 2015, at around 1:00PM.

81. Plaintiff never did not attempt to flee or physically resist the Defendants. Plaintiff had not committed any crime against Defendants nor anyone else, and Defendants knew of Plaintiff's innocence since first contact on April 25, 2015.

82. Plaintiff is informed and believes and thereon alleges that at the time of any of the above-described events, and at all other pertinent times, Defendants had no warrant for the arrest of Plaintiff or other times, Defendants had no warrant for the arrest of Plaintiff or other verifiable facts or reliable information that constituted actual probable cause that Plaintiff had ever committed or was about to commit a crime so as to prove grounds for a lawful arrest.

83. Nor did Defendants have any facts or information that constituted a reasonable suspicion that Plaintiff was involved in any unlawful activity, so as to provide ground for any detention, restraint, or search whatsoever against Plaintiffs freedom of money and property; and that Plaintiff arrest, search, and seizure was in fact unlawful.

84. Defendants willfully, maliciously, and falsely denied Plaintiff his constitutionally protected rights and privileges, such as free and equal access to the metro transit train and law enforcement services because of his race, ethnicity, color, age, sex, gender, and in retaliation for filing citizen complaints against the Defendant LASD's corrupt practices.

85. Defendants arrested Plaintiff without probable cause or warrant; failed to provide criminal bail proceedings before a bail magistrate judge, never promptly released him from the jail upon Court Order; all for the purposes of intentionally discriminating, intimidating, humiliating, and causing Plaintiff's damage to his reputation by providing false arrest information to his prospective employer(s).

86. On the day of April 25, 2015, Plaintiff was seized and arrested by Defendant LASD, whom maliciously and without warrant or order of commitment or any other legal authority of any kind because Plaintiff had not committed any crime or public offense.

87. Defendant accused Plaintiff of committing the offense of carrying a concealed dirk or dagger under Penal Code Section 21310, but in fact the offense had not occurred, nor did Defendant have probable cause to believe that it had occurred, nor did Defendant have probable cause to believe that Plaintiff had committed it.

88. As a proximate result of the acts of Defendants herein alleged, Plaintiff was denied his right to bail and secure his release by bail or bond, for which Plaintiff was never allowed to obtain even one phone call to a bail bond company for his release on money which he had available for bail.

89. Although formal charges were brought against Plaintiff under Penal Code § 21310, the Defendant County by way of the District Attorney Office of Los Angeles County acted with malicious prosecutorial authority for approximately four months.

90. Then after Plaintiff submitted a proposed motion to dismiss the criminal complaint against him pursuant to the opinion of the Prosecutor, the Court dismissed the single charge.

PLAINTIFF FILED A TIMELY CLAIM AND HAS A RIGHT TO PETITION GOVERNMENT FOR GRIEVANCES AGAINST DEFENDANT COUNTY & LASD

91. On October 27, 2015, in a letter with postage prepaid, per mailbox rule, Plaintiff presented a lawful claim; showing his name, dates, and place that gave rise to this claim.

92. The Plaintiff submitted his mailing address with the claim for notices to be sent; Plaintiff also emailed the Defendant County a copy of the letter with the attached booking information.

93. Plaintiff presented this lawful claim in an unspecified amount of this unlimited claim to Defendants, which is the amount of the compensatory damages sought in this action.

94. On October 28, 2015, the claim for injuries, losses, and damages suffered and incurred against the Plaintiff by reason of the above described events, all in compliance with the requirements of § 905 of the Government Code. in which Defendant County did send untimely notices on December 31, 2015; January 6, 2016; and February 12, 2016.

95. The Plaintiff's claim provided the circumstances that gave rise to this claim; a general and brief description of the indebtedness, obligation, injury, damage, and loss that incurred so far as it was known at the time of the presentation of the claim.

96. Plaintiff did not know the true names of the public employees causing the injury, damages, and losses of Plaintiff. No dollar amount was provided because the claim exceeded ten thousand dollars and is an unlimited civil case.

97. On or about December 31, 2015, Defendant County sent Plaintiff a postcard stating that it is conducting an investigation and will contact Plaintiff in 60 days. The postcard, as acknowledgement and receipt of Plaintiff's claim was issued after 65 of days from the date of his valid claim.

98. The 60 days elapsed into 71 days and the Defendant wrote Plaintiff a letter dated January 6, 2016.

99. Pursuant to Government Code Section § 910.8 the Defendant County on February 12, 2016, alleged that the Plaintiff's claim which was presented had failed to comply with the requirements of Government Code Section § 910 and § 910.2; and this notice was sent first on February 12, 2016, and the so called rejection letter was **not within** 20 and or 45 days proscribed by law; before the claim was presented to Defendant County on October 27, 2014.

100. The Defendant never gave any written notice of any alleged insufficiency with Plaintiff's claim, nor did Defendants allege any defects nor asserted any omissions therein.

101. No notice was given in the manner prescribed by Government Code Section § 915.4.

102. Plaintiff further contends that the presentation of his claim was valid and in substantial compliance with California law and with his United States Constitutional right to petition his government for grievances; and any dismissal of this claim would be a violation of Plaintiff's rights under the Constitution.

103. A copy of this claim is attached as Exhibit A and made a part hereof.

DEPRIVATION OF CIVIL RIGHTS, PRIVILEGES AND IMMUNITIES

104. Furthermore, Defendants' acts violated the following California State laws such as the Cal. Const. Art. I, § 31, Penal Code § 422.6, § 422.7 and Civil Code Sections § 51, § 51.5, § 51.7, § 52, which prohibited conspiracy, violence against property, threat of violence, discrimination, intimidation, interference, or oppression based on race, color, sex, gender, ancestry, age, ethnicity, or disability.

105. Under Penal Code Section § 836(a), which prohibited arrest of Plaintiff for alleged misdemeanor not committed in the presence of the arresting Defendants; Government Code § 820.4, which prohibited false arrest and false imprisonment; and Penal Code § 851.5, which prohibited the denial of Plaintiff's constitutional and civil rights under California law.

SUPERVISORY & MUNICIPAL LIABILITIES OF DEFENDANT COUNTY, LASD, & SHERIFF JIM MCDONNELL

106. Defendant County, Defendant LASD, and Defendant McDonnell are responsible for supervision, instruction, training, discipline, restriction, control, promotion, hiring and/or firing of individual coDefendant DOES 1 to 10, and knew or in the exercise of due diligence should have known that the conducts of said co-Defendants were likely to occur.

107. Plaintiff has presented a oral and written complaint of the misconduct of Defendants to the supervising Defendants mentioned above, but they totally refused and failed to conduct a proper investigation, and intentionally and maliciously authorized, justified, tolerated, ratified, and adopted every co-Defendants' misconduct as an institutionalized practice, even theft of personal property.

108. These supervising Defendants were deliberately indifferent to the State and Federal Constitutional rights of Plaintiff in their hiring, promotion, retention, training, supervision, instruction, discipline, restriction and control of their co-Defendant employees.

109. The Defendants failed to enforce rules and regulations, ensure that their employees obey the laws of the State of California and of our God Blessed United States, and take corrective actions with respect to misconduct of their employees.

110. The Defendants authorized, tolerated as institutionalized practices, and ratified the misconduct and decisions herein alleged by approving both the decisions and the basis for them.

111. The Defendants failed to forward to the office of the District Attorney evidence of criminal acts committed by their employees. The office of the District Attorney for the Defendant County had ignored, disregarded, and covered up the Defendants criminal acts with absolute immunity.

112. The Defendants failed to establish and/or assure the functioning of a bona fide and meaningful departmental system for dealing with complaints of employee misconduct, but instead responding to such complaints, with bureaucratic power and official denials, the Defendants have calculated this information to mislead the public.

113. Public entity Defendants County and LASD are also liable under the doctrine of Respondent Superior for these valid State law claims.

114. Defendant McDonnell campaigned in Los Angeles County to change the culture of corruption by the Defendant LASD and its employees.

115. Defendant McDonnell stated during his election campaign for Los Angeles County Sheriff stated:

"I bring a fresh perspective from the outside. I'm not encumbered by internal alliances. I didn't grow up with people in the organization. I don't owe anybody anything."; from the LA Times article "Jim McDonnell cites fresh perspective as L.A. County sheriff candidate", by Cindy Change, May 28, 2014.

116. Plaintiff contends that Defendant McDonnell has not changed the culture of corruption of Defendant LASD and is liable for the failure to ensure that Plaintiff's State and Constitutional rights were not violated by their employees.

BREACH OF DUTY OF CARE

117. The above-mentioned State laws imposed upon any person a legal duty to use due care. Especially, Defendant LASD had the fundamental duty to obey and carry out the laws of the State of California irrespective of their source, be it a constitution, statute, or duly promulgated regulation, order or judgment.

118. In addition, every Defendant owed a legal duty of care imposed by the rules, regulations and policy of both the County of Los Angeles and the Sheriff's Department to Plaintiff.

119. Moreover, as government employees and public servants, each Defendant owed a special duty of care to the public and Plaintiff not to harm, intimidate, discriminate, or retaliate.

120. Furthermore, every person, including Defendants, owed the general duty to use ordinary care and to avoid "unreasonable risk" of danger to others, including Plaintiff, in activities from which harm might reasonably be anticipated and the breach of the care consists of actively careless conduct [4 Witkin Cal.Proc.4th Pleading § 541 to 543, 630, to 632].

121. At all times herein mentioned, each of the Defendant LASD had the power and duty restrain the other Defendants and prevent them from violating the law and the rights of Plaintiff, but each of the Defendants failed and refused to perform that duty, failed and refused to restrain the other Defendants, and thereby became a party to the injuries inflicted upon Plaintiff.

122. Defendants failed to exercise duty of care and breached that legal duty.

123. Defendants, and each of them, knew, or should have known, that their failure to exercise due care would cause Plaintiff severe emotional distress. The injury to Plaintiff was foreseeable.

124. Therefore, the acts of Defendants, each of them, herein alleged also constituted gross negligence and carelessness under California State law.

PLAINTIFF'S FIRST CAUSE OF ACTION AGAINST ALL DEFENDANTS
FOR FALSE ARREST & FALSE IMPRISONMENT WITHOUT WARRANT
(Gov. Code § 820.4)

125. Plaintiff was wrongfully arrested by Defendant LASD. Defendant LASD arrested the Plaintiff without a warrant, the Plaintiff was harmed and Defendant LASD was a substantial factor in causing that harm to Plaintiff.

126. Defendant DOE 1 knew that she was authorizing, assisting, and directing the Defendant LASD to procure an unlawful arrest of Plaintiff. Defendant DOE 1 had knowingly given Defendant LASD false information and knew that it would lead to a false arrest of Plaintiff.

127. The Defendant lied about Plaintiff having a "gun" and falsely stated to Police that Plaintiff said he had a "heater", meaning an illegal gun or street slang for a firearm, and caused Plaintiff to be falsely arrested.

128. During the search of Plaintiff, the Defendant LASD never found a "gun" on Plaintiff, nor did Plaintiff ever have a gun. The facts and evidence demonstrated that Plaintiff was credible in his report to the Defendant LASD about him not having a gun.

129. The Defendant LASD knew or should have known that DOE 1 was not only uncredible and unreliable, but was in fact lying about the Plaintiff having a gun on the metro train.

130. The Defendant LASD knew or should have known that there was no probable cause for arrest of Plaintiff for possession of a dangerous weapon such as a firearm on his person nor in his backpack.

131. The Defendant LASD conspired to falsely arrest Plaintiff by writing a false police report about Plaintiff having a "heater".

132. Defendant LASD knew or should have known that the hunting knife in Plaintiff's backpack was lawful and legal under California law pursuant to People v. Pellecer (2013) 215 Cal.App.4th 508 [155 Cal.Rptr.3d 477].

133. The Defendants conspired through a common design and implied mutual understanding that they were going to falsely arrest Plaintiff for a crime he did not commit.

134. The preliminary hearing judge was either appeasing the Defendant County's prosecutors with the malicious prosecution of Plaintiff; or the judge erred in that it should have been found that no probable cause actually existed.

135. Defendant Murren had no reasonable grounds to believe that Plaintiff committed a felonious crime not in his presence nor even a misdemeanor in his presence.

136. The facts known to Defendant LASD were that Plaintiff did not have a dirk or dagger in violation of Penal Code Section § 21310.

137. Plaintiff incorporates herein the allegations of paragraphs 1 through 136, inclusive. As alleged above, Defendants, and each of them, subjected and caused to be subjected, Plaintiff to be arrested and imprisoned for five days without probable cause and under

fraudulent pretenses.

138. As a proximate result of Defendants' false arrest and false imprisonment, Plaintiff has suffered, continues to suffer and will suffer general and special damages and is entitled to exemplary and punitive damages as alleged in, and incorporated herein, paragraphs 1 through 137, inclusive.

PLAINTIFF'S SECOND CAUSE OF ACTION FOR DENIAL OF CIVIL RIGHTS AND DISCRIMINATION UNDER CIVIL CODE §§ 51, § 51.5, § 51.7, § 52

(Civil Code §51, §51,5, §51.7, §52)

139. Plaintiff incorporates herein the allegations of paragraphs 1 through 138, inclusive. As a proximate result of Defendants' denial of civil rights and discrimination, Plaintiff has suffered, continues to suffer and will suffer general and special damages and, in addition, is entitled to exemplary and punitive damages under Civil Code Section § 52(b)(1), as alleged in, and incorporated herein, paragraphs 1 through 106, inclusive.

140. Defendant is a business establishment for the purposes of the Unruh Civil Rights Act, Civ. Code § 51 et seq.

141. The Plaintiff is free and equal, no matter what his ethnicity. sex, race, color, gender, sex, age, and or disability to have been entitled to the full and equal accommodations, advantages, facilities, privileges, or services in the business establishment of the Defendant.

142. Civil Code Section § 51.5(a) provides that no business establishment of any kind whatsoever shall discriminate against, boycott, or blacklist, or refuse to trade with any person in this state on account of any characteristic listed or defined in subdivision (b) or (e) of Civil Code Section § 51.

143. On April 25, 2015, Plaintiff was refused full and equal advantages, privileges, and services because of his sex, race, color, medical condition, genetic information, and sexual orientation by Defendant.

144. Defendant's actions violated the Unruh Civil Rights Act, Civ. Code § 51 by not providing him full and equal access to governmental services that are readily available to Plaintiff such as legally mandated telephone services.

145. The Defendants acted with discriminatory intent by denying him equal access because of his race, ethnicity, color, age, sex, gender, and for retaliatory motives.

146. As a proximate result of Defendants unlawful discriminatory actions, Plaintiff suffered great shame, humiliation, inconvenience, and suffering, all to Plaintiff's general damages. As a proximate result of Defendant's unlawful discriminatory actions, Plaintiff suffered special damages.

147. Defendants violation of Unruh Civil Rights Act, Civ. Code, §51 entities Plaintiff to recover statutory damages of a maximum of three times the amount of actual damages or a minimum of $4,000.00.

148. An actual controversy exists between Plaintiff and Defendant as to the application of the Unruh Civil Rights Act, Civ. Code § 51, and whether Defendants actions violate the Act. The correct interpretation of the Act is that is applies to Defendant and prohibits Defendant's discriminatory actions.

149. Plaintiff is entitled to recover up to a maximum of three times the amount of actual damages and in no case less than $4,000 for each and every offense, in the total sum of $40,000.00 USD, as provided in Civil Code section § 52(b)(2).

150. As a proximate result of the wrongful acts of Defendants, Plaintiff is further entitled to recovered entitled to recover a statutory civil penalty of $25,000 for each and every offense, in the total sum of $25,000 for each and every offense, in the total sum of $25,000, as provided in Civil Code Section § 52(b)(2).

151. Furthermore, Plaintiff is entitled to attorney's fees, if applicable, as provided in Civil Code Sections § 52(a), 52(b)(3).

PLAINTIFF'S THIRD CAUSE OF ACTION AGAINST DEFENDANTS FOR VIOLATING CALIFORNIA CONSTITUTION ARTICLE 1, SECTION 31

152. Plaintiff incorporates herein the allegations of paragraphs 1 through 151, inclusive. The California Constitution Article 1, Section 31 (a) states that the State shall not discriminate against, any individual or group on the basis of race, sex, color, ethnicity, or national origin in

the operation of public contracting. Section (g) proves that the remedies available for violations of this section shall be the same regardless of the injured party's race, sex, color as otherwise available for violation of then-existing California antidiscrimination law.

153. Violation of Civil Code Section § 43 states besides the personal rights mentioned or recognized in the Government Code, every person has, subject to the qualifications and restrictions provided by law, the right of protection form bodily restraint or harm, from personal insult, from defamation, and from injury to his personal relations."

PLAINTIFF'S FOURTH CAUSE OF ACTION FOR GROSS NEGLIGENCE UNDER GOVERNMENT CODE SECTION § 815.2

(Against all Defendants)

154. Plaintiff incorporates herein the allegations of paragraphs 1 through 153, inclusive. As a proximate result of Defendants' breach of mandatory duties and gross negligence, the Defendants are liable for injury to Plaintiff proximately caused by an act or omission of the employees of the Defendant County and LASD within the scope of all their employment. Plaintiff has suffered, continues to suffer and will suffer general and special damages, and is entitled to exemplary and punitive damages as alleged in and incorporated herein paragraphs 1 through 111, inclusive.

PLAINTIFF'S FIFTH CAUSE OF ACTION FOR FAILURE TO DISCHARGE MANDATORY DUTY UNDER GOVERNMENT CODE SECTION § 815.6

(Against all Defendants)

155. Plaintiff incorporates herein the allegations of paragraphs 1 through 154, inclusive. As alleged above, Defendants had the mandatory duties imposed by the Constitution, Statutes, Rules, and Regulations that were designed to protect against the risk of false arrest, imprisonment, unlawful search and seizure, conspiracy, cruel and unusual punishment, retaliation, discrimination, intimidation, deprivation, and oppression, but the Defendants had failed to discharge the duties [Gov. Code §§ 815.6, § 815.2].

156. As a proximate result of Defendants' breach of mandatory duties and gross negligence, Plaintiff has suffered, continues to suffer and will suffer general and special damages and is

entitled to exemplary and punitive damages as alleged in and incorporated herein paragraphs 1 through 155, inclusive.

PLAINTIFF'S SIXTH CAUSE OF ACTION FOR UNNECSSARY IN PROCESSING & RELEASING PLAINTIFF

157. Plaintiff incorporates herein the allegations of paragraphs 1 through 156, inclusive.

158. Plaintiff was wrongfully confined by Defendant LASD. Defendant LASD held Plaintiff in their custody and there was an unnecessary delay in releasing Plaintiff. Plaintiff did not consent to the delay; the Plaintiff was harmed and through the loss of employment, the Defendant LASD was a substantial factor in causing Plaintiff's harm and economic loss.

PLAINTIFF'S SEVENTH CAUSE OF ACTION FOR MALICIOUS PROSECUTION

(Against all Defendants)

159. Plaintiff incorporates herein the allegations of paragraphs 1 through 159, inclusive.

160. The prosecuting officer for the Defendant County relied on the Defendant DOES 1 to 10, Defendant Murren, and Defendant LASD in making the complaint. The Defendants did not make full honest disclosure about the Plaintiff res of all the important factors known to the district attorney for Defendant County.

161. Prosecuting attorney for Defendant County knew or should have known that the information was false, unreliable, and inaccurate; and the prosecuting attorney for Defendant County acted with malice and with an intent to maliciously prosecute the Plaintiff based on false and inaccurate information because of his race, ethnicity, ancestry, age, sex, and or gender.

162. The Defendants were actually involved in causing the Plaintiff to be maliciously prosecuted and in causing the continuation of the prosecution of Plaintiff. The Defendants acted with the sole purpose other than bringing the Plaintiff to justice. The Defendants conduct was a substantial factor in causing harm to Plaintiff.

163. Plaintiff alleges that he was falsely prosecuted by Defendant County because of his race, ethnicity, color, ancestry, age, sex, political affiliation, and or gender.

164. "The elements of a cause of action for malicious prosecution are (1) the institution of an action (2) without probable cause and (3) with malice, (4) termination of the action favorable

to the Defendant, and (5) resulting damage by way of attorneys' fees incurred in defense, mental distress, and/or injury to reputation or social standing pursuant to Harbor Ins. Co. v. Central National Ins. Co. (1985) 165 Cal.App.3d 1029 [211 Cal.Rptr. 902].

165. "The malice required in an action for malicious prosecution is not limited to actual hostility or ill will toward Plaintiff; it may exist when proceedings are commenced primarily for an improper purpose, as was such herein. See Camerena v. Sequoia Ins. Co. (1987) 190 Cal.App.3d 1089 [235 Cal.Rptr. 820].

166. In the case of Harbor Ins. Co., "Favorable termination thus serves to confirm the element of lack of probable cause, the focus of the wrong is upon the institution of the suit, with malice and without such probable cause. The cause of action does not accrue until favorable termination of the malicious action".

167. "A termination...is favorable when it reflects "the opinion of someone, either the trial court or the prosecuting party, that the action lacked merit or if pursued would result in a decision in favor of the Defendant"', in the case of Camerena.

168. In recognition of the wrong done to the victim of such a tort, settled law permits Plaintiff to recover the cost of defending the prior action including 1) reasonable attorney's fees, if applicable [citations], 2) compensation for injury to his reputation or impairment of his social and business standing in the community [citations], and 3) for mental or emotional distress [citation]," cited from Camerena.

169. "Damages in malicious prosecution actions are similar to those in defamation. Therefore, damage to one's reputation can be presumed from a charge of malicious prosecution. See Allard v. Church of Scientology (1976) 58 Cal.App.3d 439 [129 Cal.Rptr. 797].

PLAINTIFF'S EIGHT CAUSE OF ACTION AGAINST ALL DEFENDANTS FOR CONSPIRACY

170. Plaintiff incorporates herein the allegations of paragraphs 1 through 169, inclusive. Plaintiff is informed and believes and thereon alleges that at all times herein mentioned, Defendant LASD, Defendant DOES 1 to 10, and each of them, acted separately, in concert with, and/or in conspiracy with each of the remaining coDefendants, and in bad faith, actual fraud,

corruption, malice, intimidation and/or retaliation against Plaintiff.

171. Plaintiff believes and thereon alleges that at all times herein mentioned, Defendant LASD, and its agents, willfully and maliciously conspired, agreed and reached a mutual understanding among themselves to deny Plaintiff's State and U.S. Constitutional rights and privileges, to wit:

(a) Defendants agreed and acted to intentionally deny Plaintiff his exercising his constitutionally and statutorily protected rights to free and equal access to the metro public transit;

(b) Defendants agreed and acted to intentionally falsely arrest and handcuff Plaintiff as alleged above,

(c) Defendants agreed and acted to intentionally retaliate against and punish Plaintiff for exercising his constitutionally and statutorily protected rights to free and equal access to the public transit; and

(d) Defendants agreed and acted to intentionally deny Plaintiff prompt and any release from the jail upon Penal Code Section § 851.5 et seq.;

172. Defendants DOE 1 and DOE 2, and each of them, furthered the conspiracy by cooperation with coDefendants, lent aid and encouragement to coDefendants, and ratified and adopted the acts of coDefendants.

PLAINTIFF'S NINTH CAUSE OF ACTION AGAINST DEFENDANT FOR VIOLATION OF UNRUH CIVIL RIGHTS ACT SECTION 51 CAUSE OF ACTION FOR CONSIPIRACY

(Against all Defendants)

173. Plaintiff incorporates herein the allegations of paragraphs 1 through 172, inclusive. As a proximate result of the wrongful acts pursuant to the conspiracy, Plaintiff has suffered, continues to suffer and will suffer general and special damages and is entitled to exemplary and punitive damages as alleged in, and incorporated herein, paragraphs 1 through 172, inclusive.

PLAINTIFFS' DAMAGES BY ALL DEFENDANTS JOINTLY AND SEVERALLY

174. Plaintiff incorporates herein the allegations of paragraphs 1 through 173, inclusive. As a direct result of the Defendants Doe 1 and Doe 2 tight handcuffing and battery,

Plaintiff suffered severe pain and injury on his wrists, back and head.

175. By reason of the conduct of Defendants, including Plaintiff's unlawful arrest and false imprisonment and the injuries sustained as a result, Plaintiff was totally unable to attend to the duties of his profession as security guard for a period of five days, and sustained damages for loss of earnings during such period, in addition to ruining his reputation and job.

176. Defendants Doe 1 and Doe 2's acts were all intentional and malicious and done for the purpose of causing Plaintiff to suffer severe humiliation, intimidation, mental anguish, and emotional and physical distress.

177. Defendants' conduct in confirming and ratifying those acts was done with knowledge that Plaintiff's emotional and physical distress would thereby increase, and done with a wanton and reckless disregard of the consequences to Plaintiff.

178. As a proximate result of the aforementioned Defendants' acts, Plaintiff was hurt and injured in his reputation, subjected to humiliation, indignity, embarrassment and defamation of his character and reputation, shame and ridicule, and prevented from transacting his business, study and research, and sustained pains at wrists and back, discomfort, uncertainty, fear, anxiety, annoyance, shock and injury to his nervous system and person caused by fear for his life, safety, living in a jail for a long time, and loss of work and income, all of which have caused and will continue to cause for the rest of his lifetime, Plaintiff great mental, physical, and nervous pain and suffering, all to his general damages in the sum of $50,000.00 for pain, suffering and inconvenience, and in the additional sum of $50,000.00 for emotional distress and future medical treatment to for that distress caused and/or aggravated by Defendants.

178. The aforementioned conduct of Defendants, and each of them, i.e., arresting, handcuffing, detaining, searching, assaulting, battering, discriminating, and retaliating for 3 days without probable cause or fabricating a charge which Defendants knew were false, were willful and were intended to cause pain, suffering, and humiliation to Plaintiff.

179. In addition, Defendants knew that every citizen, including Plaintiff, had the rights to free and equal access to the metro transit service, and to be free from assault, battery, false arrest, false imprisonment, right to telephone services, right to an attorney; and right to bail and

right from unlawful search and seizure; humiliation and discrimination without probable cause.

180. Notwithstanding this knowledge, Defendants, in willful and conscious disregard of Plaintiff's such rights and safety, failed and refused to prevent or minimize the risk of false arrest and imprisonment and subjected Plaintiff to cruel and unjust hardship of pain, humiliation, intimidation, and being handcuffed.

181. Thus, Plaintiff is entitled to an award of exemplary and punitive damages against Defendants, under Civil Code Section § 3294 or any other applicable law. Defendants acts were in bad faith and without reasonable cause against the Plaintiff.

PRAYER FOR RELIEF:

Wherefore, Plaintiff prays for judgment against all Defendants and each, of them, as follows:

1. For special damages in the sum of $15,960.00;
2. For general damages in the sum of $100,000.00;
3. For statutory civil penalty of $40,000.00 under Civil Code section § 52(a) and $25,000 under Civil Code section § 52(b)(2);
4. For exemplary and punitive damages against individual Defendants;
5. For costs of suit herein incurred; and
6. For such other and further relief as the court deems proper and just.

DEMAND FOR JURY TRIAL

Plaintiff in the above-entitled action requests for a trial by jury.

Dated: 4/25/2016   By: _____

Luke E. Dumas, Plaintiff in pro per

Chapter 2
Case Management Statement

In an unlimited civil case in the California courts, the judge will require that each party submit, file, and serve a "case management statement" about 15 court days prior to the scheduled conference, see the California Rules of Court for exact procedures on the Case Management Statement and Conference.

Currently, with COVID-19 guidelines in effect, a good litigant, paralegal, and or attorney would check with the court's website for bulletins by the presiding judge, and also check with the court clerk in the judge's department for policies and rules regarding the case management conference.

Trial Court & Appeal: False Arrest, Imprisonment, and Civil Rights Violations By L.A. County

Dumas v. Los Angeles County Board of Supervisors et al. 45 Cal. App. 5th 348

CM-110

ATTORNEY OR PARTY WITHOUT ATTORNEY (Name, State Bar number, and address):
Luke Edward Dumas

TELEPHONE NO.: FAX NO. (Optional):
E-MAIL ADDRESS (Optional):
ATTORNEY FOR (Name): **Plaintiff in pro per**

SUPERIOR COURT OF CALIFORNIA, COUNTY OF LOS ANGELES
STREET ADDRESS: 111 N. HILL STREET
MAILING ADDRESS: DEPT. 61
CITY AND ZIP CODE: LOS ANGELES 90012
BRANCH NAME: STANLEY MOSK COURTHOUSE

PLAINTIFF/PETITIONER: **LUKE E. DUMAS**
DEFENDANT/RESPONDENT: Los Angeles County Board of Supervisors et al.

FOR COURT USE ONLY

CONFORMED COPY
ORIGINAL FILED
Superior Court of California
County of Los Angeles

JUN 23 2016

Sherri R. Carter, Executive Officer/Clerk
By Raul Sanchez, Deputy

CASE MANAGEMENT STATEMENT
(Check one): [✓] UNLIMITED CASE [ ] LIMITED CASE
(Amount demanded exceeds $25,000) (Amount demanded is $25,000 or less)

CASE NUMBER: BC618191

A CASE MANAGEMENT CONFERENCE is scheduled as follows:
Date: July 12, 2016   Time: 9:00 AM   Dept.: 61   Div.:   Room: 732
Address of court (if different from the address above):
SEE ABOVE

[ ] Notice of Intent to Appear by Telephone, by (name):

INSTRUCTIONS: All applicable boxes must be checked, and the specified information must be provided.

1. **Party or parties** (answer one):
   a. [✓] This statement is submitted by party (name): LUKE EDWARD DUMAS
   b. [ ] This statement is submitted jointly by parties (names):

2. **Complaint and cross-complaint** (to be answered by plaintiffs and cross-complainants only)
   a. The complaint was filed on (date): April 26, 2016
   b. [ ] The cross-complaint, if any, was filed on (date):

3. **Service** (to be answered by plaintiffs and cross-complainants only)
   a. [ ] All parties named in the complaint and cross-complaint have been served, have appeared, or have been dismissed.
   b. [✓] The following parties named in the complaint or cross-complaint
      (1) [ ] have not been served (specify names and explain why not):
      (2) [✓] have been served but have not appeared and have not been dismissed (specify names):
            Los Angeles Board of Supervisors, Los Angeles Sheriff's Department, Jim McDonnell
      (3) [ ] have had a default entered against them (specify names):
   c. [✓] The following additional parties may be added (specify names, nature of involvement in case, and date by which they may be served):
      James Murren

4. **Description of case**
   a. Type of case in [✓] complaint [ ] cross-complaint (Describe, including causes of action):
      Nine causes of action: 1. False arrest 2. Civil Rights/Discrimination 3. Violation of Cal. Const. 4. Gross Negligence 5. Failure to Discharge Duty 6. Delay 7. Malicious Prosec. 8. Conspiracy 9. Unruh Civil Rights Con.

Form Adopted for Mandatory Use
Judicial Council of California
CM-110 [Rev. July 1, 2011]

CASE MANAGEMENT STATEMENT

Cal. Rules of Court,
rules 3.720–3.730
www.courts.ca.gov

Copyright. © 2021. Paralegal Publishing Group.

Trial Court & Appeal: False Arrest, Imprisonment, and Civil Rights Violations By L.A. County

Dumas v. Los Angeles County Board of Supervisors et al. 45 Cal. App. 5th 348

CM-110

PLAINTIFF/PETITIONER: LUKE E. DUMAS	CASE NUMBER:
DEFENDANT/RESPONDENT: Los Angeles County Board of Supervisors et al.	BC618191

4. b. Provide a brief statement of the case, including any damages. *(If personal injury damages are sought, specify the injury and damages claimed, including medical expenses to date [indicate source and amount], estimated future medical expenses, lost earnings to date, and estimated future lost earnings. If equitable relief is sought, describe the nature of the relief.)*

   Plaintiff was falsely arrested and imprisoned by Defendants, was denied his civil rights and was discriminated against, delayed in processing, acted with gross negligence, maliciously prosecuted Plaintiff and conspired to do so. Defendant is liable for false imprisonment, stolen Plaintiff's property; statutory civil penalty, loss of earnings, and future medical expenses for emotional distress, punitive damages for $180, 960.00; removal of records.

   ☐ *(If more space is needed, check this box and attach a page designated as Attachment 4b.)*

5. **Jury or nonjury trial**
   The party or parties request ☑ a jury trial ☐ a nonjury trial. *(If more than one party, provide the name of each party requesting a jury trial):*

6. **Trial date**
   a. ☐ The trial has been set for *(date):*
   b. ☑ No trial date has been set. This case will be ready for trial within 12 months of the date of the filing of the complaint *(if not, explain):*
   c. Dates on which parties or attorneys will not be available for trial *(specify dates and explain reasons for unavailability):*
   N/A

7. **Estimated length of trial**
   The party or parties estimate that the trial will take *(check one):*
   a. ☑ days *(specify number):* 2
   b. ☐ hours (short causes) *(specify):*

8. **Trial representation** *(to be answered for each party)*
   The party or parties will be represented at trial ☑ by the attorney or party listed in the caption ☐ by the following:
   a. Attorney:
   b. Firm:
   c. Address:
   d. Telephone number:
   f. Fax number:
   e. E-mail address:
   g. Party represented:
   ☐ Additional representation is described in Attachment 8.

9. **Preference**
   ☐ This case is entitled to preference *(specify code section):*

10. **Alternative dispute resolution (ADR)**
    a. **ADR information package.** Please note that different ADR processes are available in different courts and communities; read the ADR information package provided by the court under rule 3.221 for information about the processes available through the court and community programs in this case.
       (1) For parties represented by counsel: Counsel ☐ has ☐ has not provided the ADR information package identified in rule 3.221 to the client and reviewed ADR options with the client.
       (2) For self-represented parties: Party ☑ has ☐ has not reviewed the ADR information package identified in rule 3.221.
    b. **Referral to judicial arbitration or civil action mediation** (if available).
       (1) ☐ This matter is subject to mandatory judicial arbitration under Code of Civil Procedure section 1141.11 or to civil action mediation under Code of Civil Procedure section 1775.3 because the amount in controversy does not exceed the statutory limit.
       (2) ☐ Plaintiff elects to refer this case to judicial arbitration and agrees to limit recovery to the amount specified in Code of Civil Procedure section 1141.11.
       (3) ☑ This case is exempt from judicial arbitration under rule 3.811 of the California Rules of Court or from civil action mediation under Code of Civil Procedure section 1775 et seq. *(specify exemption):*
       Cal. Rules of Court, rule 3.811 (b)(8); CCP 1775.5

CASE MANAGEMENT STATEMENT

Trial Court & Appeal: False Arrest, Imprisonment, and Civil Rights Violations By L.A. County

Dumas v. Los Angeles County Board of Supervisors et al. 45 Cal. App. 5th 348

CM-110

PLAINTIFF/PETITIONER: LUKE E. DUMAS	CASE NUMBER:
DEFENDANT/RESPONDENT: Los Angeles County Board of Supervisors et al.	BC618191

10. c. Indicate the ADR process or processes that the party or parties are willing to participate in, have agreed to participate in, or have already participated in *(check all that apply and provide the specified information)*:

	The party or parties completing this form **are willing** to participate in the following ADR processes *(check all that apply)*:	If the party or parties completing this form in the case **have agreed** to participate in or have already completed an ADR process or processes, indicate the status of the processes *(attach a copy of the parties' ADR stipulation)*:
(1) Mediation	✔	✔ Mediation session not yet scheduled ☐ Mediation session scheduled for *(date)*: ☐ Agreed to complete mediation by *(date)*: ☐ Mediation completed on *(date)*:
(2) Settlement conference	☐	☐ Settlement conference not yet scheduled ☐ Settlement conference scheduled for *(date)*: ☐ Agreed to complete settlement conference by *(date)*: ☐ Settlement conference completed on *(date)*:
(3) Neutral evaluation	☐	☐ Neutral evaluation not yet scheduled ☐ Neutral evaluation scheduled for *(date)*: ☐ Agreed to complete neutral evaluation by *(date)*: ☐ Neutral evaluation completed on *(date)*:
(4) Nonbinding judicial arbitration	☐	☐ Judicial arbitration not yet scheduled ☐ Judicial arbitration scheduled for *(date)*: ☐ Agreed to complete judicial arbitration by *(date)*: ☐ Judicial arbitration completed on *(date)*:
(5) Binding private arbitration	☐	☐ Private arbitration not yet scheduled ☐ Private arbitration scheduled for *(date)*: ☐ Agreed to complete private arbitration by *(date)*: ☐ Private arbitration completed on *(date)*:
(6) Other *(specify)*:	☐	☐ ADR session not yet scheduled ☐ ADR session scheduled for *(date)*: ☐ Agreed to complete ADR session by *(date)*: ☐ ADR completed on *(date)*:

CM-110 [Rev. July 1, 2011] **CASE MANAGEMENT STATEMENT**

Copyright. © 2021. Paralegal Publishing Group.

Trial Court & Appeal: False Arrest, Imprisonment, and Civil Rights Violations By L.A. County

Dumas v. Los Angeles County Board of Supervisors et al. 45 Cal. App. 5th 348

CM-110

PLAINTIFF/PETITIONER:	LUKE E. DUMAS	CASE NUMBER:
DEFENDANT/RESPONDENT:	Los Angeles County Board of Supervisors et al.	BC618191

11. Insurance
   a. ☐ Insurance carrier, if any, for party filing this statement *(name):*
   b. Reservation of rights: ☐ Yes ☐ No
   c. ☐ Coverage issues will significantly affect resolution of this case *(explain):*

12. Jurisdiction
Indicate any matters that may affect the court's jurisdiction or processing of this case and describe the status.
   ☐ Bankruptcy ☐ Other *(specify):*
Status:

13. Related cases, consolidation, and coordination
   a. ☐ There are companion, underlying, or related cases.
      (1) Name of case:
      (2) Name of court:
      (3) Case number:
      (4) Status:
      ☐ Additional cases are described in Attachment 13a.
   b. ☐ A motion to ☐ consolidate ☐ coordinate will be filed by *(name party):*

14. Bifurcation
   ☐ The party or parties intend to file a motion for an order bifurcating, severing, or coordinating the following issues or causes of action *(specify moving party, type of motion, and reasons):*

15. Other motions
   ☐ The party or parties expect to file the following motions before trial *(specify moving party, type of motion, and issues):*

16. Discovery
   a. ☐ The party or parties have completed all discovery.
   b. ☑ The following discovery will be completed by the date specified *(describe all anticipated discovery):*

Party	Description	Date
Defendants	Form Interrogatories	12/31/2016
Defendants	Request for Admissions	12/31/2016
Defendants	Special Interrogatories	12/31/2016
Defendants	Demand for Production of Documents	12/31/2016
Defendants	Depositions	3/31/2017

   c. ☐ The following discovery issues, including issues regarding the discovery of electronically stored information, are anticipated *(specify):*
Discovery of electronically stored information may be an issue and may be sought in this discovery process.

CASE MANAGEMENT STATEMENT

Copyright. © 2021. Paralegal Publishing Group.

Trial Court & Appeal: False Arrest, Imprisonment, and Civil Rights Violations By L.A. County

Dumas v. Los Angeles County Board of Supervisors et al. 45 Cal. App. 5th 348

PLAINTIFF/PETITIONER: LUKE E. DUMAS	CASE NUMBER: BC618191
DEFENDANT/RESPONDENT: Los Angeles County Board of Supervisors et al.	

CM-110

17. Economic litigation

a. ☐ This is a limited civil case (i.e., the amount demanded is $25,000 or less) and the economic litigation procedures in Code of Civil Procedure sections 90-98 will apply to this case.

b. ☐ This is a limited civil case and a motion to withdraw the case from the economic litigation procedures or for additional discovery will be filed *(if checked, explain specifically why economic litigation procedures relating to discovery or trial should not apply to this case)*:

18. Other issues

☑ The party or parties request that the following additional matters be considered or determined at the case management conference *(specify)*:

Plaintiff will seek to amend the complaint for damages to include injunctive, declaratory, and or equitable relief. Plaintiff will seek to amend the summons to add Deputy James Murren as an individual defendant and Sheriff Jim McDonnell as an individual, not in official capacity; Plaintiff will attempt to reserve Defendants by way of process server and or through notice and acknowledgment of summons' and complaint.

19. Meet and confer

a. ☐ The party or parties have met and conferred with all parties on all subjects required by rule 3.724 of the California Rules of Court *(if not, explain)*:

The parties have not met and conferred because although Plaintiff had them served with the initial summons and complaint, Defendants have not contacted Plaintiff. Plaintiff will need to amend summons'.

b. After meeting and conferring as required by rule 3.724 of the California Rules of Court, the parties agree on the following *(specify)*:

20. Total number of pages attached *(if any)*: _____

I am completely familiar with this case and will be fully prepared to discuss the status of discovery and alternative dispute resolution, as well as other issues raised by this statement, and will possess the authority to enter into stipulations on these issues at the time of the case management conference, including the written authority of the party where required.

Date: 6/23/2016

Luke Edward Dumas

(TYPE OR PRINT NAME) ▶ (SIGNATURE OF PARTY OR ATTORNEY)

_____ ▶ _____

(TYPE OR PRINT NAME) (SIGNATURE OF PARTY OR ATTORNEY)

☐ Additional signatures are attached.

CASE MANAGEMENT STATEMENT

Copyright. © 2021. Paralegal Publishing Group.

Chapter 3
Form Interrogatories

In the discovery phase of litigation there are judicial council forms for discovery available on the California court's website. Most of the blank forms are available for free in a PDF downloadable content. As a paralegal and self-represented litigant, I would have to read each number and subparagraph and made sure that I checked all of the applicable boxes very carefully.

In this legal case, the Plaintiff had sent "Judicial Council" Form Interrogatories, as provided below, and attached a Request for Admissions because the Form Interrogatories allowed for qualified admissions under oath. For example on page 7 of 8, in interrogatory question 17.0, allows for a specific response when serving Form Interrogatories along with Request for Admissions. Although the California courts had sabotaged and designed the Plaintiff's case for failure, it is best practice to always serve Interrogatories in any lawsuit.

Even after L.A. County's hired private attorney, Mr. John Coleman had violated the law and rules of civil procedure, privacy in medical records, and the code of ethics, the Plaintiff had to file a "Motion" to compel those answers and responses to the Interrogatories. Mr. Coleman replied with boilerplate objections, and under a fair trial judge, unlike Keosian, the court would have granted the Plaintiff in pro per's motion against the L.A. County Government. Although Mr. Dumas did not get a fair motion hearing, Interrogatories are an essential part of civil discovery.

Copyright. © 2021. Paralegal Publishing Group.

Trial Court & Appeal: False Arrest, Imprisonment, and Civil Rights Violations By L.A. County

<u>**Dumas v. Los Angeles County Board of Supervisors et al.**</u> 45 Cal. App. 5th 348

DISC-001

ATTORNEY OR PARTY WITHOUT ATTORNEY *(Name, State Bar number, and address)*:
Luke E Dumas
TELEPHONE NO.:
FAX NO. *(Optional)*:
E-MAIL ADDRESS *(Optional)*:
ATTORNEY FOR *(Name)*: Plaintiff in Pro Per

SUPERIOR COURT OF CALIFORNIA, COUNTY OF LOS ANGELES
111 N. HILL STREET, LOS ANGELES, CALIFORNIA, 90012
CENTRAL DISTRICT - Stanley Mosk Courthouse

SHORT TITLE OF CASE:
Dumas v. Los Angeles County Board of Supervisors

FORM INTERROGATORIES—GENERAL	CASE NUMBER:
Asking Party: Luke E Dumas	BC618191
Answering Party: Los Angeles County Board of Supervisors (County)	
Set No.: One	

Sec. 1. Instructions to All Parties

(a) Interrogatories are written questions prepared by a party to an action that are sent to any other party in the action to be answered under oath. The interrogatories below are form interrogatories approved for use in civil cases.

(b) For time limitations, requirements for service on other parties, and other details, see Code of Civil Procedure sections 2030.010–2030.410 and the cases construing those sections.

(c) These form interrogatories do not change existing law relating to interrogatories nor do they affect an answering party's right to assert any privilege or make any objection.

Sec. 2. Instructions to the Asking Party

(a) These interrogatories are designed for optional use by parties in unlimited civil cases where the amount demanded exceeds $25,000. Separate interrogatories, Form *Interrogatories—Limited Civil Cases (Economic Litigation)* (form DISC-004), which have no subparts, are designed for use in limited civil cases where the amount demanded is $25,000 or less; however, those interrogatories may also be used in unlimited civil cases.

(b) Check the box next to each interrogatory that you want the answering party to answer. Use care in choosing those interrogatories that are applicable to the case.

(c) You may insert your own definition of **INCIDENT** in Section 4, but only where the action arises from a course of conduct or a series of events occurring over a period of time.

(d) The interrogatories in section 16.0, Defendant's Contentions–Personal Injury, should not be used until the defendant has had a reasonable opportunity to conduct an investigation or discovery of plaintiff's injuries and damages.

(e) Additional interrogatories may be attached.

Sec. 3. Instructions to the Answering Party

(a) An answer or other appropriate response must be given to each interrogatory checked by the asking party.

(b) As a general rule, within 30 days after you are served with these interrogatories, you must serve your responses on the asking party and serve copies of your responses on all other parties to the action who have appeared. See Code of Civil Procedure sections 2030.260–2030.270 for details.

(c) Each answer must be as complete and straightforward as the information reasonably available to you, including the information possessed by your attorneys or agents, permits. If an interrogatory cannot be answered completely, answer it to the extent possible.

(d) If you do not have enough personal knowledge to fully answer an interrogatory, say so, but make a reasonable and good faith effort to get the information by asking other persons or organizations, unless the information is equally available to the asking party.

(e) Whenever an interrogatory may be answered by referring to a document, the document may be attached as an exhibit to the response and referred to in the response. If the document has more than one page, refer to the page and section where the answer to the interrogatory can be found.

(f) Whenever an address and telephone number for the same person are requested in more than one interrogatory, you are required to furnish them in answering only the first interrogatory asking for that information.

(g) If you are asserting a privilege or making an objection to an interrogatory, you must specifically assert the privilege or state the objection in your written response.

(h) Your answers to these interrogatories must be verified, dated, and signed. You may wish to use the following form at the end of your answers:

I declare under penalty of perjury under the laws of the State of California that the foregoing answers are true and correct.

_____   _____
(DATE)   (SIGNATURE)

Sec. 4. Definitions

Words in **BOLDFACE CAPITALS** in these interrogatories are defined as follows:

(a) *(Check one of the following):*

☑ (1) **INCIDENT** includes the circumstances and events surrounding the alleged accident, injury, or other occurrence or breach of contract giving rise to this action or proceeding.

Copyright. © 2021. Paralegal Publishing Group.

Trial Court & Appeal: False Arrest, Imprisonment, and Civil Rights Violations By L.A. County

Dumas v. Los Angeles County Board of Supervisors et al. 45 Cal. App. 5th 348

☐ (2) **INCIDENT** means *(insert your definition here or on a separate, attached sheet labeled "Sec. 4(a)(2)"):*
False arrest and imprisonment of Plaintiff from 4/25/2015 to 4/29/2015.

(b) **YOU OR ANYONE ACTING ON YOUR BEHALF** includes you, your agents, your employees, your insurance companies, their agents, their employees, your attorneys, your accountants, your investigators, and anyone else acting on your behalf.

(c) **PERSON** includes a natural person, firm, association, organization, partnership, business, trust, limited liability company, corporation, or public entity.

(d) **DOCUMENT** means a writing, as defined in Evidence Code section 250, and includes the original or a copy of handwriting, typewriting, printing, photostats, photographs, electronically stored information, and every other means of recording upon any tangible thing and form of communicating or representation, including letters, words, pictures, sounds, or symbols, or combinations of them.

(e) **HEALTH CARE PROVIDER** includes any **PERSON** referred to in Code of Civil Procedure section 667.7(e)(3).

(f) **ADDRESS** means the street address, including the city, state, and zip code.

Sec. 5. Interrogatories

The following interrogatories have been approved by the Judicial Council under Code of Civil Procedure section 2033.710:

CONTENTS

1.0 Identity of Persons Answering These Interrogatories
2.0 General Background Information—Individual
3.0 General Background Information—Business Entity
4.0 Insurance
5.0 *[Reserved]*
6.0 Physical, Mental, or Emotional Injuries
7.0 Property Damage
8.0 Loss of Income or Earning Capacity
9.0 Other Damages
10.0 Medical History
11.0 Other Claims and Previous Claims
12.0 Investigation—General
13.0 Investigation—Surveillance
14.0 Statutory or Regulatory Violations
15.0 Denials and Special or Affirmative Defenses
16.0 Defendant's Contentions Personal Injury
17.0 Responses to Request for Admissions
18.0 *[Reserved]*
19.0 *[Reserved]*
20.0 How the Incident Occurred—Motor Vehicle
25.0 *[Reserved]*
30.0 *[Reserved]*
40.0 *[Reserved]*
50.0 Contract
60.0 *[Reserved]*
70.0 Unlawful Detainer *[See separate form DISC-003]*
101.0 Economic Litigation *[See separate form DISC-004]*
200.0 Employment Law *[See separate form DISC-002]*
Family Law *[See separate form FL-145]*

DISC-001

1.0 Identity of Persons Answering These Interrogatories

☑ 1.1 State the name, **ADDRESS**, telephone number, and relationship to you of each **PERSON** who prepared or assisted in the preparation of the responses to these interrogatories. *(Do not identify anyone who simply typed or reproduced the responses.)*

2.0 General Background Information—Individual

☑ 2.1 State:
(a) your name;
(b) every name you have used in the past; and
(c) the dates you used each name.

☑ 2.2 State the date and place of your birth.

☑ 2.3 At the time of the **INCIDENT**, did you have a driver's license? If so state:
(a) the state or other issuing entity;
(b) the license number and type;
(c) the date of issuance; and
(d) all restrictions.

☑ 2.4 At the time of the **INCIDENT**, did you have any other permit or license for the operation of a motor vehicle? If so, state:
(a) the state or other issuing entity;
(b) the license number and type;
(c) the date of issuance; and
(d) all restrictions.

☑ 2.5 State:
(a) your present residence **ADDRESS**;
(b) your residence **ADDRESSES** for the past five years; and
(c) the dates you lived at each **ADDRESS**.

☑ 2.6 State:
(a) the name, **ADDRESS**, and telephone number of your present employer or place of self-employment; and
(b) the name, **ADDRESS**, dates of employment, job title, and nature of work for each employer or self-employment you have had from five years before the **INCIDENT** until today.

☐ 2.7 State:
(a) the name and **ADDRESS** of each school or other academic or vocational institution you have attended, beginning with high school;
(b) the dates you attended;
(c) the highest grade level you have completed; and
(d) the degrees received.

☑ 2.8 Have you ever been convicted of a felony? If so, for each conviction state:
(a) the city and state where you were convicted;
(b) the date of conviction;
(c) the offense; and
(d) the court and case number.

☐ 2.9 Can you speak English with ease? If not, what language and dialect do you normally use?

☐ 2.10 Can you read and write English with ease? If not, what language and dialect do you normally use?

FORM INTERROGATORIES—GENERAL

Copyright. © 2021. Paralegal Publishing Group.

Trial Court & Appeal: False Arrest, Imprisonment, and Civil Rights Violations By L.A. County

Dumas v. Los Angeles County Board of Supervisors et al. 45 Cal. App. 5th 348

DISC-001

[✓] 2.11 At the time of the INCIDENT were you acting as an agent or employee for any PERSON? If so, state:
(a) the name, ADDRESS, and telephone number of that PERSON; and
(b) a description of your duties.

[✓] 2.12 At the time of the INCIDENT did you or any other person have any physical, emotional, or mental disability or condition that may have contributed to the occurrence of the INCIDENT? If so, for each person state:
(a) the name, ADDRESS, and telephone number;
(b) the nature of the disability or condition; and
(c) the manner in which the disability or condition contributed to the occurrence of the INCIDENT.

[✓] 2.13 Within 24 hours before the INCIDENT did you or any person involved in the INCIDENT use or take any of the following substances: alcoholic beverage, marijuana, or other drug or medication of any kind (prescription or not)? If so, for each person state:
(a) the name, ADDRESS, and telephone number;
(b) the nature or description of each substance;
(c) the quantity of each substance used or taken;
(d) the date and time of day when each substance was used or taken;
(e) the ADDRESS where each substance was used or taken;
(f) the name, ADDRESS, and telephone number of each person who was present when each substance was used or taken; and
(g) the name, ADDRESS, and telephone number of any HEALTH CARE PROVIDER who prescribed or furnished the substance and the condition for which it was prescribed or furnished.

3.0 General Background Information—Business Entity

[ ] 3.1 Are you a corporation? If so, state:
(a) the name stated in the current articles of incorporation;
(b) all other names used by the corporation during the past 10 years and the dates each was used;
(c) the date and place of incorporation;
(d) the ADDRESS of the principal place of business; and
(e) whether you are qualified to do business in California.

[ ] 3.2 Are you a partnership? If so, state:
(a) the current partnership name;
(b) all other names used by the partnership during the past 10 years and the dates each was used;
(c) whether you are a limited partnership and, if so, under the laws of what jurisdiction;
(d) the name and ADDRESS of each general partner; and
(e) the ADDRESS of the principal place of business.

[ ] 3.3 Are you a limited liability company? If so, state:
(a) the name stated in the current articles of organization;
(b) all other names used by the company during the past 10 years and the date each was used;
(c) the date and place of filing of the articles of organization;
(d) the ADDRESS of the principal place of business; and
(e) whether you are qualified to do business in California.

[ ] 3.4 Are you a joint venture? If so, state:
(a) the current joint venture name;
(b) all other names used by the joint venture during the past 10 years and the dates each was used;
(c) the name and ADDRESS of each joint venturer; and
(d) the ADDRESS of the principal place of business.

[ ] 3.5 Are you an unincorporated association? If so, state:
(a) the current unincorporated association name;
(b) all other names used by the unincorporated association during the past 10 years and the dates each was used; and
(c) the ADDRESS of the principal place of business.

[ ] 3.6 Have you done business under a fictitious name during the past 10 years? If so, for each fictitious name state:
(a) the name;
(b) the dates each was used;
(c) the state and county of each fictitious name filing; and
(d) the ADDRESS of the principal place of business.

[ ] 3.7 Within the past five years has any public entity registered or licensed your business? If so, for each license or registration:
(a) identify the license or registration;
(b) state the name of the public entity; and
(c) state the dates of issuance and expiration.

4.0 Insurance

[✓] 4.1 At the time of the INCIDENT, was there in effect any policy of insurance through which you were or might be insured in any manner (for example, primary, pro-rata, or excess liability coverage or medical expense coverage) for the damages, claims, or actions that have arisen out of the INCIDENT? If so, for each policy state:
(a) the kind of coverage;
(b) the name and ADDRESS of the insurance company;
(c) the name, ADDRESS, and telephone number of each named insured;
(d) the policy number;
(e) the limits of coverage for each type of coverage contained in the policy;
(f) whether any reservation of rights or controversy or coverage dispute exists between you and the insurance company; and
(g) the name, ADDRESS, and telephone number of the custodian of the policy.

[✓] 4.2 Are you self-insured under any statute for the damages, claims, or actions that have arisen out of the INCIDENT? If so, specify the statute.

5.0 *[Reserved]*

6.0 Physical, Mental, or Emotional Injuries

[ ] 6.1 Do you attribute any physical, mental, or emotional injuries to the INCIDENT? *(If your answer is "no," do not answer interrogatories 6.2 through 6.7).*

[ ] 6.2 Identify each injury you attribute to the INCIDENT and the area of your body affected.

DISC-001 [Rev. January 1, 2008]   FORM INTERROGATORIES—GENERAL

Copyright. © 2021. Paralegal Publishing Group.

Trial Court & Appeal: False Arrest, Imprisonment, and Civil Rights Violations By L.A. County

Dumas v. Los Angeles County Board of Supervisors et al. 45 Cal. App. 5th 348

DISC-001

☐ 6.3 Do you still have any complaints that you attribute to the INCIDENT? If so, for each complaint state:
(a) a description;
(b) whether the complaint is subsiding, remaining the same, or becoming worse; and
(c) the frequency and duration.

☐ 6.4 Did you receive any consultation or examination (except from expert witnesses covered by Code of Civil Procedure sections 2034.210–2034.310) or treatment from a HEALTH CARE PROVIDER for any injury you attribute to the INCIDENT? If so, for each HEALTH CARE PROVIDER state:
(a) the name, ADDRESS, and telephone number;
(b) the type of consultation, examination, or treatment provided;
(c) the dates you received consultation, examination, or treatment; and
(d) the charges to date.

☐ 6.5 Have you taken any medication, prescribed or not, as a result of injuries that you attribute to the INCIDENT? If so, for each medication state:
(a) the name;
(b) the PERSON who prescribed or furnished it;
(c) the date it was prescribed or furnished;
(d) the dates you began and stopped taking it; and
(e) the cost to date.

☐ 6.6 Are there any other medical services necessitated by the injuries that you attribute to the INCIDENT that were not previously listed (for example, ambulance, nursing, prosthetics)? If so, for each service state:
(a) the nature;
(b) the date;
(c) the cost; and
(d) the name, ADDRESS, and telephone number of each provider.

☐ 6.7 Has any HEALTH CARE PROVIDER advised that you may require future or additional treatment for any injuries that you attribute to the INCIDENT? If so, for each injury state:
(a) the name and ADDRESS of each HEALTH CARE PROVIDER;
(b) the complaints for which the treatment was advised; and
(c) the nature, duration, and estimated cost of the treatment.

7.0 Property Damage

☐ 7.1 Do you attribute any loss of or damage to a vehicle or other property to the INCIDENT? If so, for each item of property:
(a) describe the property;
(b) describe the nature and location of the damage to the property;

(c) state the amount of damage you are claiming for each item of property and how the amount was calculated; and
(d) if the property was sold, state the name, ADDRESS, and telephone number of the seller, the date of sale, and the sale price.

☐ 7.2 Has a written estimate or evaluation been made for any item of property referred to in your answer to the preceding interrogatory? If so, for each estimate or evaluation state:
(a) the name, ADDRESS, and telephone number of the PERSON who prepared it and the date prepared;
(b) the name, ADDRESS, and telephone number of each PERSON who has a copy of it; and
(c) the amount of damage stated.

☐ 7.3 Has any item of property referred to in your answer to interrogatory 7.1 been repaired? If so, for each item state:
(a) the date repaired;
(b) a description of the repair;
(c) the repair cost;
(d) the name, ADDRESS, and telephone number of the PERSON who repaired it;
(e) the name, ADDRESS, and telephone number of the PERSON who paid for the repair.

8.0 Loss of Income or Earning Capacity

☐ 8.1 Do you attribute any loss of income or earning capacity to the INCIDENT? *(If your answer is "no," do not answer interrogatories 8.2 through 8.8).*

☐ 8.2 State:
(a) the nature of your work;
(b) your job title at the time of the INCIDENT; and
(c) the date your employment began.

☐ 8.3 State the last date before the INCIDENT that you worked for compensation.

☐ 8.4 State your monthly income at the time of the INCIDENT and how the amount was calculated.

☐ 8.5 State the date you returned to work at each place of employment following the INCIDENT.

☐ 8.6 State the dates you did not work and for which you lost income as a result of the INCIDENT.

☐ 8.7 State the total income you have lost to date as a result of the INCIDENT and how the amount was calculated.

☐ 8.8 Will you lose income in the future as a result of the INCIDENT? If so, state:
(a) the facts upon which you base this contention;
(b) an estimate of the amount;
(c) an estimate of how long you will be unable to work; and
(d) how the claim for future income is calculated.

FORM INTERROGATORIES—GENERAL

Copyright. © 2021. Paralegal Publishing Group.

9.0 Other Damages

☐ 9.1 Are there any other damages that you attribute to the INCIDENT? If so, for each item of damage state:
(a) the nature;
(b) the date it occurred;
(c) the amount; and
(d) the name, **ADDRESS**, and telephone number of each **PERSON** to whom an obligation was incurred.

☐ 9.2 Do any **DOCUMENTS** support the existence or amount of any item of damages claimed in interrogatory 9.1? If so, describe each document and state the name, **ADDRESS**, and telephone number of the **PERSON** who has each **DOCUMENT**.

10.0 Medical History

☐ 10.1 At any time before the INCIDENT did you have complaints or injuries that involved the same part of your body claimed to have been injured in the INCIDENT? If so, for each state:
(a) a description of the complaint or injury;
(b) the dates it began and ended; and
(c) the name, **ADDRESS**, and telephone number of each **HEALTH CARE PROVIDER** whom you consulted or who examined or treated you.

☐ 10.2 List all physical, mental, and emotional disabilities you had immediately before the INCIDENT. *(You may omit mental or emotional disabilities unless you attribute any mental or emotional injury to the INCIDENT.)*

☐ 10.3 At any time after the INCIDENT, did you sustain injuries of the kind for which you are now claiming damages? If so, for each incident giving rise to an injury state:
(a) the date and the place it occurred;
(b) the name, **ADDRESS**, and telephone number of any other **PERSON** involved;
(c) the nature of any injuries you sustained;
(d) the name, **ADDRESS**, and telephone number of each **HEALTH CARE PROVIDER** who you consulted or who examined or treated you; and
(e) the nature of the treatment and its duration.

11.0 Other Claims and Previous Claims

☐ 11.1 Except for this action, in the past 10 years have you filed an action or made a written claim or demand for compensation for your personal injuries? If so, for each action, claim, or demand state:
(a) the date, time, and place and location (closest street **ADDRESS** or intersection) of the INCIDENT giving rise to the action, claim, or demand;
(b) the name, **ADDRESS**, and telephone number of each **PERSON** against whom the claim or demand was made or the action filed;
(c) the court, names of the parties, and case number of any action filed;
(d) the name, **ADDRESS**, and telephone number of any attorney representing you;
(e) whether the claim or action has been resolved or is pending; and
(f) a description of the injury.

☐ 11.2 In the past 10 years have you made a written claim or demand for workers' compensation benefits? If so, for each claim or demand state:
(a) the date, time, and place of the INCIDENT giving rise to the claim;
(b) the name, **ADDRESS**, and telephone number of your employer at the time of the injury;
(c) the name, **ADDRESS**, and telephone number of the workers' compensation insurer and the claim number;
(d) the period of time during which you received workers' compensation benefits;
(e) a description of the injury;
(f) the name, **ADDRESS**, and telephone number of any **HEALTH CARE PROVIDER** who provided services; and
(g) the case number at the Workers' Compensation Appeals Board.

12.0 Investigation—General

☑ 12.1 State the name, **ADDRESS**, and telephone number of each individual:
(a) who witnessed the INCIDENT or the events occurring immediately before or after the INCIDENT;
(b) who made any statement at the scene of the INCIDENT;
(c) who heard any statements made about the INCIDENT by any individual at the scene; and
(d) who **YOU OR ANYONE ACTING ON YOUR BEHALF** claim has knowledge of the INCIDENT (except for expert witnesses covered by Code of Civil Procedure section 2034).

☑ 12.2 Have **YOU OR ANYONE ACTING ON YOUR BEHALF** interviewed any individual concerning the INCIDENT? If so, for each individual state:
(a) the name, **ADDRESS**, and telephone number of the individual interviewed;
(b) the date of the interview; and
(c) the name, **ADDRESS**, and telephone number of the **PERSON** who conducted the interview.

☑ 12.3 Have **YOU OR ANYONE ACTING ON YOUR BEHALF** obtained a written or recorded statement from any individual concerning the INCIDENT? If so, for each statement state:
(a) the name, **ADDRESS**, and telephone number of the individual from whom the statement was obtained;
(b) the name, **ADDRESS**, and telephone number of the individual who obtained the statement;
(c) the date the statement was obtained; and
(d) the name, **ADDRESS**, and telephone number of each **PERSON** who has the original statement or a copy.

12.4 Do **YOU OR ANYONE ACTING ON YOUR BEHALF** know of any photographs, films, or videotapes depicting any place, object, or individual concerning the **INCIDENT** or plaintiff's injuries? If so, state:

(a) the number of photographs or feet of film or videotape;
(b) the places, objects, or persons photographed, filmed, or videotaped;
(c) the date the photographs, films, or videotapes were taken;
(d) the name, **ADDRESS**, and telephone number of the individual taking the photographs, films, or videotapes; and
(e) the name, **ADDRESS**, and telephone number of each **PERSON** who has the original or a copy of the photographs, films, or videotapes.

12.5 Do **YOU OR ANYONE ACTING ON YOUR BEHALF** know of any diagram, reproduction, or model of any place or thing (except for items developed by expert witnesses covered by Code of Civil Procedure sections 2034.210–2034.310) concerning the **INCIDENT**? If so, for each item state:

(a) the type (i.e., diagram, reproduction, or model);
(b) the subject matter; and
(c) the name, **ADDRESS**, and telephone number of each **PERSON** who has it.

12.6 Was a report made by any **PERSON** concerning the **INCIDENT**? If so, state:

(a) the name, title, identification number, and employer of the **PERSON** who made the report;
(b) the date and type of report made;
(c) the name, **ADDRESS**, and telephone number of the **PERSON** for whom the report was made; and
(d) the name, **ADDRESS**, and telephone number of each **PERSON** who has the original or a copy of the report.

12.7 Have **YOU OR ANYONE ACTING ON YOUR BEHALF** inspected the scene of the **INCIDENT**? If so, for each inspection state:

(a) the name, **ADDRESS**, and telephone number of the individual making the inspection (except for expert witnesses covered by Code of Civil Procedure sections 2034.210–2034.310); and
(b) the date of the inspection.

13.0 Investigation—Surveillance

13.1 Have **YOU OR ANYONE ACTING ON YOUR BEHALF** conducted surveillance of any individual involved in the **INCIDENT** or any party to this action? If so, for each surveillance state:

(a) the name, **ADDRESS**, and telephone number of the individual or party;
(b) the time, date, and place of the surveillance;
(c) the name, **ADDRESS**, and telephone number of the individual who conducted the surveillance; and
(d) the name, **ADDRESS**, and telephone number of each **PERSON** who has the original or a copy of any surveillance photograph, film, or videotape.

13.2 Has a written report been prepared on the surveillance? If so, for each written report state:

(a) the title;
(b) the date;
(c) the name, **ADDRESS**, and telephone number of the individual who prepared the report; and
(d) the name, **ADDRESS**, and telephone number of each **PERSON** who has the original or a copy.

14.0 Statutory or Regulatory Violations

14.1 Do **YOU OR ANYONE ACTING ON YOUR BEHALF** contend that any **PERSON** involved in the **INCIDENT** violated any statute, ordinance, or regulation and that the violation was a legal (proximate) cause of the **INCIDENT**? If so, identify the name, **ADDRESS**, and telephone number of each **PERSON** and the statute, ordinance, or regulation that was violated.

14.2 Was any **PERSON** cited or charged with a violation of any statute, ordinance, or regulation as a result of this **INCIDENT**? If so, for each **PERSON** state:

(a) the name, **ADDRESS**, and telephone number of the **PERSON**;
(b) the statute, ordinance, or regulation allegedly violated;
(c) whether the **PERSON** entered a plea in response to the citation or charge and, if so, the plea entered; and
(d) the name and **ADDRESS** of the court or administrative agency, names of the parties, and case number.

15.0 Denials and Special or Affirmative Defenses

15.1 Identify each denial of a material allegation and each special or affirmative defense in your pleadings and for each:

(a) state all facts upon which you base the denial or special or affirmative defense;
(b) state the names, **ADDRESSES**, and telephone numbers of all **PERSONS** who have knowledge of those facts; and
(c) identify all **DOCUMENTS** and other tangible things that support your denial or special or affirmative defense, and state the name, **ADDRESS**, and telephone number of the **PERSON** who has each **DOCUMENT**.

16.0 Defendant's Contentions—Personal Injury

16.1 Do you contend that any **PERSON**, other than you or plaintiff, contributed to the occurrence of the **INCIDENT** or the injuries or damages claimed by plaintiff? If so, for each **PERSON**:

(a) state the name, **ADDRESS**, and telephone number of the **PERSON**;
(b) state all facts upon which you base your contention;
(c) state the names, **ADDRESSES**, and telephone numbers of all **PERSONS** who have knowledge of the facts; and
(d) identify all **DOCUMENTS** and other tangible things that support your contention and state the name, **ADDRESS**, and telephone number of the **PERSON** who has each **DOCUMENT** or thing.

16.2 Do you contend that plaintiff was not injured in the **INCIDENT**? If so:

(a) state all facts upon which you base your contention;
(b) state the names, **ADDRESSES**, and telephone numbers of all **PERSONS** who have knowledge of the facts; and
(c) identify all **DOCUMENTS** and other tangible things that support your contention and state the name, **ADDRESS**, and telephone number of the **PERSON** who has each **DOCUMENT** or thing.

Trial Court & Appeal: False Arrest, Imprisonment, and Civil Rights Violations By L.A. County
Dumas v. Los Angeles County Board of Supervisors et al. 45 Cal. App. 5th 348

DISC-001

[✓] 16.3 Do you contend that the injuries or the extent of the injuries claimed by plaintiff as disclosed in discovery proceedings thus far in this case were not caused by the INCIDENT? If so, for each injury:
(a) identify it;
(b) state all facts upon which you base your contention;
(c) state the names, ADDRESSES, and telephone numbers of all PERSONS who have knowledge of the facts; and
(d) identify all DOCUMENTS and other tangible things that support your contention and state the name, ADDRESS, and telephone number of the PERSON who has each DOCUMENT or thing.

[✓] 16.4 Do you contend that any of the services furnished by any HEALTH CARE PROVIDER claimed by plaintiff in discovery proceedings thus far in this case were not due to the INCIDENT? If so:
(a) identify each service;
(b) state all facts upon which you base your contention;
(c) state the names, ADDRESSES, and telephone numbers of all PERSONS who have knowledge of the facts; and
(d) identify all DOCUMENTS and other tangible things that support your contention and state the name, ADDRESS, and telephone number of the PERSON who has each DOCUMENT or thing.

[✓] 16.5 Do you contend that any of the costs of services furnished by any HEALTH CARE PROVIDER claimed as damages by plaintiff in discovery proceedings thus far in this case were not necessary or unreasonable? If so:
(a) identify each cost;
(b) state all facts upon which you base your contention;
(c) state the names, ADDRESSES, and telephone numbers of all PERSONS who have knowledge of the facts; and
(d) identify all DOCUMENTS and other tangible things that support your contention and state the name, ADDRESS, and telephone number of the PERSON who has each DOCUMENT or thing.

[✓] 16.6 Do you contend that any part of the loss of earnings or income claimed by plaintiff in discovery proceedings thus far in this case was unreasonable or was not caused by the INCIDENT? If so:
(a) identify each part of the loss;
(b) state all facts upon which you base your contention;
(c) state the names, ADDRESSES, and telephone numbers of all PERSONS who have knowledge of the facts; and
(d) identify all DOCUMENTS and other tangible things that support your contention and state the name, ADDRESS, and telephone number of the PERSON who has each DOCUMENT or thing.

[✓] 16.7 Do you contend that any of the property damage claimed by plaintiff in discovery Proceedings thus far in this case was not caused by the INCIDENT? If so:
(a) identify each item of property damage;
(b) state all facts upon which you base your contention;
(c) state the names, ADDRESSES, and telephone numbers of all PERSONS who have knowledge of the facts; and
(d) identify all DOCUMENTS and other tangible things that support your contention and state the name, ADDRESS, and telephone number of the PERSON who has each DOCUMENT or thing.

[✓] 16.8 Do you contend that any of the costs of repairing the property damage claimed by plaintiff in discovery proceedings thus far in this case were unreasonable? If so:
(a) identify each cost item;
(b) state all facts upon which you base your contention;
(c) state the names, ADDRESSES, and telephone numbers of all PERSONS who have knowledge of the facts; and
(d) identify all DOCUMENTS and other tangible things that support your contention and state the name, ADDRESS, and telephone number of the PERSON who has each DOCUMENT or thing.

[✓] 16.9 Do YOU OR ANYONE ACTING ON YOUR BEHALF have any DOCUMENT (for example, insurance bureau index reports) concerning claims for personal injuries made before or after the INCIDENT by a plaintiff in this case? If so, for each plaintiff state:
(a) the source of each DOCUMENT;
(b) the date each claim arose;
(c) the nature of each claim; and
(d) the name, ADDRESS, and telephone number of the PERSON who has each DOCUMENT.

[✓] 16.10 Do YOU OR ANYONE ACTING ON YOUR BEHALF have any DOCUMENT concerning the past or present physical, mental, or emotional condition of any plaintiff in this case from a HEALTH CARE PROVIDER not previously identified (except for expert witnesses covered by Code of Civil Procedure sections 2034.210–2034.310)? If so, for each plaintiff state:
(a) the name, ADDRESS, and telephone number of each HEALTH CARE PROVIDER;
(b) a description of each DOCUMENT; and
(c) the name, ADDRESS, and telephone number of the PERSON who has each DOCUMENT.

17.0 Responses to Request for Admissions

[✓] 17.1 Is your response to each request for admission served with these interrogatories an unqualified admission? If not, for each response that is not an unqualified admission:
(a) state the number of the request;
(b) state all facts upon which you base your response;
(c) state the names, ADDRESSES, and telephone numbers of all PERSONS who have knowledge of those facts; and
(d) identify all DOCUMENTS and other tangible things that support your response and state the name, ADDRESS, and telephone number of the PERSON who has each DOCUMENT or thing.

18.0 *[Reserved]*
19.0 *[Reserved]*

20.0 How the Incident Occurred—Motor Vehicle

[ ] 20.1 State the date, time, and place of the INCIDENT (closest street ADDRESS or intersection).

[ ] 20.2 For each vehicle involved in the INCIDENT, state:
(a) the year, make, model, and license number;
(b) the name, ADDRESS, and telephone number of the driver;

DISC-001 [Rev. January 1, 2008]   FORM INTERROGATORIES—GENERAL

Copyright. © 2021. Paralegal Publishing Group.

DISC-001

(c) the name, **ADDRESS**, and telephone number of each occupant other than the driver;
(d) the name, **ADDRESS**, and telephone number of each registered owner;
(e) the name, **ADDRESS**, and telephone number of each lessee;
(f) the name, **ADDRESS**, and telephone number of each owner other than the registered owner or lien holder; and
(g) the name of each owner who gave permission or consent to the driver to operate the vehicle.

☐ 20.3 State the **ADDRESS** and location where your trip began and the **ADDRESS** and location of your destination.

☐ 20.4 Describe the route that you followed from the beginning of your trip to the location of the **INCIDENT**, and state the location of each stop, other than routine traffic stops, during the trip leading up to the **INCIDENT**.

☐ 20.5 State the name of the street or roadway, the lane of travel, and the direction of travel of each vehicle involved in the **INCIDENT** for the 500 feet of travel before the **INCIDENT**.

☐ 20.6 Did the **INCIDENT** occur at an intersection? If so, describe all traffic control devices, signals, or signs at the intersection.

☐ 20.7 Was there a traffic signal facing you at the time of the **INCIDENT**? If so, state:
(a) your location when you first saw it;
(b) the color;
(c) the number of seconds it had been that color; and
(d) whether the color changed between the time you first saw it and the **INCIDENT**.

☐ 20.8 State how the **INCIDENT** occurred, giving the speed, direction, and location of each vehicle involved:
(a) just before the **INCIDENT**;
(b) at the time of the **INCIDENT**; and (c) just after the **INCIDENT**.

☐ 20.9 Do you have information that a malfunction or defect in a vehicle caused the **INCIDENT**? If so:
(a) identify the vehicle;
(b) identify each malfunction or defect;
(c) state the name, **ADDRESS**, and telephone number of each **PERSON** who is a witness to or has information about each malfunction or defect; and
(d) state the name, **ADDRESS**, and telephone number of each **PERSON** who has custody of each defective part.

☐ 20.10 Do you have information that any malfunction or defect in a vehicle contributed to the injuries sustained in the **INCIDENT**? If so:
(a) identify the vehicle;
(b) identify each malfunction or defect;
(c) state the name, **ADDRESS**, and telephone number of each **PERSON** who is a witness to or has information about each malfunction or defect; and

(d) state the name, **ADDRESS**, and telephone number of each **PERSON** who has custody of each defective part.

☐ 20.11 State the name, **ADDRESS**, and telephone number of each owner and each **PERSON** who has had possession since the **INCIDENT** of each vehicle involved in the **INCIDENT**.

25.0 *[Reserved]*
30.0 *[Reserved]*
40.0 *[Reserved]*

50.0 Contract

☐ 50.1 For each agreement alleged in the pleadings:
(a) identify each **DOCUMENT** that is part of the agreement and for each state the name, **ADDRESS**, and telephone number of each **PERSON** who has the **DOCUMENT**;
(b) state each part of the agreement not in writing, the name, **ADDRESS**, and telephone number of each **PERSON** agreeing to that provision, and the date that part of the agreement was made;
(c) identify all **DOCUMENTS** that evidence any part of the agreement not in writing and for each state the name, **ADDRESS**, and telephone number of each **PERSON** who has the **DOCUMENT**;
(d) identify all **DOCUMENTS** that are part of any modification to the agreement, and for each state the name, **ADDRESS**, and telephone number of each **PERSON** who has the **DOCUMENT**;
(e) state each modification not in writing, the date, and the name, **ADDRESS**, and telephone number of each **PERSON** agreeing to the modification, and the date the modification was made;
(f) identify all **DOCUMENTS** that evidence any modification of the agreement not in writing and for each state the name, **ADDRESS**, and telephone number of each **PERSON** who has the **DOCUMENT**.

☐ 50.2 Was there a breach of any agreement alleged in the pleadings? If so, for each breach describe and give the date of every act or omission that you claim is the breach of the agreement.

☐ 50.3 Was performance of any agreement alleged in the pleadings excused? If so, identify each agreement excused and state why performance was excused.

☐ 50.4 Was any agreement alleged in the pleadings terminated by mutual agreement, release, accord and satisfaction, or novation? If so, identify each agreement terminated, the date of termination, and the basis of the termination.

☐ 50.5 Is any agreement alleged in the pleadings unenforceable? If so, identify each unenforceable agreement and state why it is unenforceable.

☐ 50.6 Is any agreement alleged in the pleadings ambiguous? If so, identify each ambiguous agreement and state why it is ambiguous.

60.0 *[Reserved]*

DISC-001 [Rev. January 1, 2008]   **FORM INTERROGATORIES—GENERAL**

Trial Court & Appeal: False Arrest, Imprisonment, and Civil Rights Violations By L.A. County

<u>Dumas v. Los Angeles County Board of Supervisors et al.</u> 45 Cal. App. 5th 348

POS-030

ATTORNEY OR PARTY WITHOUT ATTORNEY (Name, State Bar number, and address):
Luke E Dumas

TELEPHONE NO.:
FAX NO. (Optional):
E-MAIL ADDRESS (Optional):
ATTORNEY FOR (Name): Plaintiff in pro per

SUPERIOR COURT OF CALIFORNIA, COUNTY OF LOS ANGELES
STREET ADDRESS: 111 N. Hill Street
MAILING ADDRESS:
CITY AND ZIP CODE: Los Angeles 90012
BRANCH NAME: Stanley Mosk Courthouse

PETITIONER/PLAINTIFF: Luke E Dumas

RESPONDENT/DEFENDANT: Los Angeles County Board of Supervisors (County of Los Angeles)

PROOF OF SERVICE BY FIRST-CLASS MAIL—CIVIL

CASE NUMBER: BC618191

(Do not use this Proof of Service to show service of a Summons and Complaint.)

1. I am over 18 years of age and not a party to this action. I am a resident of or employed in the county where the mailing took place.

2. My residence or business address is:

3. On (date): 8/21/2015 I mailed from (city and state): Signal Hill, CA
   the following documents (specify):

   Form Interrogatories - General, Set No. One; Requests for Admission (Set One)

   ☐ The documents are listed in the *Attachment to Proof of Service by First-Class Mail—Civil (Documents Served)* (form POS-030(D)).

4. I served the documents by enclosing them in an envelope and (check one):
   a. ☑ **depositing** the sealed envelope with the United States Postal Service with the postage fully prepaid.
   b. ☐ **placing** the envelope for collection and mailing following our ordinary business practices. I am readily familiar with this business's practice for collecting and processing correspondence for mailing. On the same day that correspondence is placed for collection and mailing, it is deposited in the ordinary course of business with the United States Postal Service in a sealed envelope with postage fully prepaid.

5. The envelope was addressed and mailed as follows:
   a. **Name** of person served: Los Angeles County Board of Supervisors (County of Los Angeles) c/o Mr. Coleman
   b. **Address** of person served:

      1111 South Arroyo Parkway, Suite 442, Pasadena, California, 91105

   ☐ The name and address of each person to whom I mailed the documents is listed in the *Attachment to Proof of Service by First-Class Mail—Civil (Persons Served)* (POS-030(P)).

I declare under penalty of perjury under the laws of the State of California that the foregoing is true and correct.

Date: 8/21/2016

(TYPE OR PRINT NAME OF PERSON COMPLETING THIS FORM) | (SIGNATURE OF PERSON COMPLETING THIS FORM)

Form Approved for Optional Use
Judicial Council of California
POS-030 [New January 1, 2005]

PROOF OF SERVICE BY FIRST-CLASS MAIL—CIVIL
(Proof of Service)

Code of Civil Procedure, §§ 1013, 1013a
www.courtinfo.ca.gov

Copyright. © 2021. Paralegal Publishing Group.

Trial Court & Appeal: False Arrest, Imprisonment, and Civil Rights Violations By L.A. County

Dumas v. Los Angeles County Board of Supervisors et al. 45 Cal. App. 5th 348

1 Luke E Dumas

SUPERIOR COURT OF THE STATE OF CALIFORNIA
COUNTY OF LOS ANGELES - CENTRAL DISTRICT
STANLEY MOSK COURTHOUSE

Luke E Dumas, an individual, Plaintiff, v. Los Angeles County Board of Supervisors, a public entity; the Los Angeles County Sherriff's Department, a public entity; Sheriff Jim McDonnell, a public official; and DOES 1-10, inclusive, Defendants	Case No.: BC618191 [Assigned for all purposes to the Hon. Judge Gregory Keosian in Dept. 61] **NOTICE OF MOTION AND MOTION TO COMPEL DEFENDANT'S FURTHER DISCOVERY RESPONSES AND FOR MONETARY SANCTIONS** **MEMORANDUM OF POINTS AND AUTHORITIES** **DECLARATION OF LUKE EDWARD DUMAS** Judge: Hon. Judge Gregory Keosian Hearing Date: February 15, 2017 Time: 9:00AM Dept: 61 Date: December 21, 2016 Date Action Filed: April 26, 2016 RES ID: 161208179573

TO THE HONORABLE JUDGE GREGORY KEOSIAN AND TO THE DEFENDANT COUNTY OF LOS ANGELES AND TO THIER ATTORNEY OF RECORD:

-1-
NOTICE OF MOTION AND MOTION TO COMPEL FURTHER DISCOVERY RESPONSES

Copyright. © 2021. Paralegal Publishing Group.

NOTICE IS HEREBY GIVEN that on February 15, 2017, at 9:00AM or as soon thereafter as the matter may be heard, on the 7th Floor, in Department 61 of this Court, located at 111 N. Hill Street, Los Angeles, California, 90012, that the Plaintiff Luke Edward Dumas ("Dumas") will and hereby does, move the Court for an Order to Compel Further Responses from the Defendant County of Los Angeles to the Plaintiff's "Judicial Council Unlimited Form Interrogatories, Set One" ("Official Form Interrogatories"), pursuant to the Code of Civil Procedure Section §2030.300(a) (1), (2), and (3).

1. Pursuant to the Plaintiff's propounded Official Form Interrogatories and the discovery and production of all specified documents demanded in each interrogatory as instructed and defined for each request specified in the Plaintiff's Separate Statement in Support of this Motion.

2. The Defendant County of Los Angeles has provided responses and or answers that are evasive and or incomplete, specifically to various subparts; and their response and production of the required specification of documents is inadequate; in addition to the objections to the interrogatories in dispute are without merit or are too general.

3. The Defendant County of Los Angeles must, and should be compelled to provide further discovery responses and complete answers to each Official Interrogatory such as [list]; and for monetary sanctions against Defendant County and or, jointly and severally, their Attorney of Record Mr. John Coleman, Esq. in the amount of $ 33.⁰⁰ USD pursuant to Code of Civil Procedure §2030.290(c); and §2030.240(a); and §2030.220(a), (b), and (c).

4. The Motion will be made on the grounds that the Defendant County of Los Angeles failed to provide complete and straightforward answers, made meritless and untimely objections to the Official Form Interrogatories that was propounded to the Defendant County of Los Angeles in this Unlimited Civil Case. The Motion will be based on this Notice of Motion and Motion, Memorandum of Points and Authorities, and on the Declaration of Plaintiff Dumas.

5. The Separate Statement set forth below contains all the information to be judicially reviewed without incorporating any other document by reference or otherwise; and on such evidence as may be presented at the hearing of the Motion.

Dated: 12/21/2016   By: _____

Luke E Dumas, Plaintiff in pro per

NOTICE OF MOTION AND MOTION TO COMPEL FURTHER DISCOVERY RESPONSES

DECLARATION OF LUKE EDWARD DUMAS

I, LUKE EDWARD DUMAS, declare:

1. I am the Plaintiff in pro per in this legal Action, and have capacity to represent myself in this legal matter. I have personal knowledge of the facts contained in this Declaration, and if called as a Witness, I could and would testify competently to those facts. I am a self-represented litigant that is currently responsible for the handling of this legal Action. As such, I am familiar with the files, records, and pleadings contained herein.

2. On August 21. 2016, I had a person over the age of 18 years of age and not a party to this Action serve on the Defendant County of Los Angeles the "Plaintiff's Judicial Council Unlimited Form Interrogatories, Set One" ("Official Interrogatories") via United States First Class Mail.

3. On September 26, 2016, the Defendant County of Los Angeles mailed me their "Responses" as all blanket objections to each Official Form Interrogatory with no Verification whatsoever.

4. On November 4, 2016, the Defendant has served "Further Responses" with no Verification with those Responses.

5. On November 9, 2016, the Defendant County sent an untimely Verification separately as an attachment and or supplemental response.

6. On November 28, 2016, at 8:10AM, after review of the Defendant County of Los Angeles' "Further Responses", I emailed Attorney of Record for Defendant County of Los Angeles a Mr. John Coleman Esq., requesting to meet and confer regarding the improper objections and incomplete responses to the Official Form Interrogatories. I informed Mr. Coleman that I would be willing to agree by way of stipulation to provide more time for the Defendant County of Los Angeles to provide further answers. Mr. Coleman replied back to me at 8:37AM, stating that "We will extend your time to file MTC further responses. Let's get this worked out." I replied back to Mr. Coleman that I expect us to have it "worked out" no later than November 30, 2016, in good faith under a duly signed Stipulation.

8. On December 2, 2016, I emailed Mr. Coleman, informing him of my final notice to meet and confer with him in good faith before filing this Motion to Compel Further Discovery Responses.

9. In my email on December 2, 2016, I informed Mr. Coleman that I have not heard from him

since November 28, 2016, and it would be unreasonable for me to be waiting for his reply and we should stipulate by December 5, 2016, in order to resolve this discovery matter informally.

10. On December 5, 2016 at 1:41PM, Mr. Coleman emailed me claiming that him and or his agents had made "numerous" attempts to contact me and that I was failing to "meet and confer" in "good faith" with him.

11. On December 6, 2016 at 4:57PM, I informed Mr. Coleman by email that I had double checked and verified that I received no such "numerous" calls from him nor his agents as he so claims in his email to me, except for his only reply on November 28, 2016, to me stating that "We will extend [me] time to file MTC further responses". I informed Mr. Coleman that his reply made no sense at all to me and I informed him of that fact. I informed Mr. Coleman that I have operated in good faith since November 28, 2016, in attempting to informally resolve this discovery dispute with him as the Attorney of Record for the Defendant County of Los Angeles.

12. On December 8, 2016 at 11:57AM, I informed Mr. Coleman via email again that I had verified for certain that I had not received any such "numerous" calls, voicemails, nor even emails from him, as he so claimed. I informed him of the specific interrogatory numbers and brief reasons why that are in dispute.

13. On December 8, 2016 at 12:27PM, I provided and drafted a 'separate statement' outlining each Interrogatory in dispute to Mr. Coleman by email. Mr. Coleman never replied back to me.

14. On December 14, 2016 at 11:40AM, I emailed Mr. Coleman again, requesting to resolve this discovery dispute informally and by way of Stipulation with my drafted separate statement. Mr. Coleman never replied back to me. I informed Mr. Coleman that I would have no other choice but to file this Motion to Compel the Defendant's Further Discovery Responses.

15. As a result of the direct failure of the Defendant County of Los Angeles to meet and confer in good faith and to properly Respond to the described discovery above, have incurred the following reasonable expenses $ 33.00 .

I declare under penalty of perjury under the laws of the State of California that the foregoing is true and correct, on December 21, 2016, in Long Beach, California.

Luke E Dumas, declarant

NOTICE OF MOTION AND MOTION TO COMPEL FURTHER DISCOVERY RESPONSES

MEMORANDUM OF POINTS AND AUTHORITIES

I.

CODE OF CIVIL PROCEDURE SECTION §2030.010 et seq. SETS FORTH THE DISCOVERY PROCEDURES & RIGHTS REGARDING OFFICAL FORM INTERROGATORIES

1. Pursuant to the Code of Civil Procedure Section §2030.020 subdivision (b), the Plaintiff propounded to the Defendant County "Judicial Council Unlimited Civil Form Interrogatories, Set One" ("Official Form Interrogatories").

2. Pursuant to the Code of Civil Procedure, Section § 2030.010(a) the Plaintiff may obtain discovery by propounding to the Defendant County written interrogatories to be answered under oath."

3. The Plaintiff propounded his first set of Official Form Interrogatories permitted by Code of Civil Procedure Section § 2030.030(a)(2); that are relevant to the subject matter in this pending action provided in the Plaintiff's Separate Statement in support of this Motion.

4. The Defendant County failed to timely answer under oath to the Plaintiff's Official Form Interrogatories; required under Code of Civil Procedure Section §2030.250 (a) and (b) by the Defendant County of Los Angeles failing to provide a proper Verification as is required for a party that is a governmental agency such as the Defendant County of Los Angeles under subdivision (b).

5. Pursuant to the Code of Civil Procedure Section §2030.250(b), the Defendant County as a governmental agency must have had one its agents or officers sign their "responses" under oath on behalf of the Defendant County. This specific statute must be interpreted to operate as a whole so that no part will be inoperative. Therefore, the Defendant County of Los Angeles must have complied with the whole provision set forth in Section §2030.250(b).

6. The court noted in Stephens v. Superior Court (2002) 96 Cal.App.4th 54, at page 59, that "a statute should be construed that so that effect is given to all its provisions, so that no part will be inoperative or superfluous, void or insignificant, and so that one section will not destroy another . . . "[Citations.]" (Rodriguez v. Superior Court (1993) 14 Cal.App.4th 1260, 1269 [18 Cal.Rptr.2d 120].)".

-5-

NOTICE OF MOTION AND MOTION TO COMPEL FURTHER DISCOVERY RESPONSES

7. Furthermore, California Code of Civil Procedure, Section §2030.010 subdivision (b) states:

"An interrogatory may relate to whether another party is making a certain contention, or to the facts, witnesses, and writings on which a contention is based. An interrogatory is not objectionable because an answer to it involves an opinion or contention that relates to fact or the application of law to fact, or would be based on information obtained or legal theories developed in anticipation of litigation or in preparation for trial".

8. Pursuant to California Code of Civil Procedure, Section §2023.010 states:
"Misuses of the discovery process include, but are not limited to, the following:
(d) Failing to respond or to submit to an authorized method of discovery.
(e) Making, without substantial justification, an unmeritorious objection to discovery.
(f) Making an evasive response to discovery.
(i) Failing to confer in person, by telephone, or by letter with an opposing party or attorney in a reasonable and good faith attempt to resolve informally any dispute concerning discovery, if the section governing a particular discovery motion requires the filing of a declaration stating facts showing that an attempt at informal resolution has been made."

9. Pursuant to Code of Civil Procedure Section §2030.260 herein states:
(a) "Within 30 days after service of interrogatories...the party to whom the interrogatories are propounded shall serve the original of the response to them on the propounding party..." Additionally, the court has determined that a party is entitled to demand answers to Official Interrogatories a matter of right unless his adversary has stated a valid objection under oath, see Petersen v. Vallejo (1968) 259 Cal 2d 757.

10. The court has also found that under the plain language of the Code of Civil Procedure Section §2030.030, provides for the recovery of costs incurred in obtaining an order to compel the Defendant County of Los Angeles' Further Responses, unless the trial court finds that the refusal to answer questions was with substantial justification, see Ember v. Superior Court (1967) 66 Cal.2d 601.

//

WHEREFORE, and based on the foregoing, moving party Plaintiff Dumas seeks an Order:

1. Compelling the Defendant County of Los Angeles to provide further respond properly and under oath to the Plaintiff's Official Interrogatories in dispute within twenty days of the hearing of this Motion.

2. Compelling the Defendant County of Los Angeles and or its Attorney of Record Mr. John Coleman Esq., jointly and severally, to pay the Plaintiff a monetary sanction in the amount of $ 33.00 for the total costs of printing and postage; and for the cost incurred for the motion fee directly paid to the Court clerk for the unnecessary burden and expense in having to bring forth this lawful Motion.

Dated: December 21, 2016

By:

Luke Edward Dumas, Plaintiff in pro per

Trial Court & Appeal: False Arrest, Imprisonment, and Civil Rights Violations By L.A. County

<u>Dumas v. Los Angeles County Board of Supervisors et al</u>. 45 Cal. App. 5th 348

POS-030

ATTORNEY OR PARTY WITHOUT ATTORNEY (Name, State Bar number, and address):	FOR COURT USE ONLY

TELEPHONE NO.: _____ FAX NO. (Optional):
E-MAIL ADDRESS (Optional):
ATTORNEY FOR (Name): Plaintiff in pro per

SUPERIOR COURT OF CALIFORNIA, COUNTY OF LOS ANGELES
STREET ADDRESS: 111 N. Hill Street
MAILING ADDRESS:
CITY AND ZIP CODE: Los Angeles 90012
BRANCH NAME: Stanley Mosk Courthouse

PETITIONER/PLAINTIFF: Luke E Dumas

RESPONDENT/DEFENDANT: Los Angeles County Board of Supervisors (County of Los Angeles)

PROOF OF SERVICE BY FIRST-CLASS MAIL—CIVIL

CASE NUMBER: BC618191

(Do not use this Proof of Service to show service of a Summons and Complaint.)

1. I am over 18 years of age and **not a party to this action.** I am a resident of or employed in the county where the mailing took place.

2. My residence or business address is:
   ███████████████

3. On (date): 12/21/2016   I mailed from (city and state): Los Angeles, CA
   the following documents (specify):
   Notice of Motion and Motion to Compel Defendant's Further Discovery Responses and for Monetary Sanctions; Memorandum of Points and Authorities; Declaration of Luke Edward Dumas; and Separate Statement in Support of Motion for Order Compelling Further Response to Plaintiff's Interrogatories, Set one
   ☐ The documents are listed in the *Attachment to Proof of Service by First-Class Mail—Civil (Documents Served)* (form POS-030(D)).

4. I served the documents by enclosing them in an envelope and (check one):
   a. ☑ **depositing** the sealed envelope with the United States Postal Service with the postage fully prepaid.
   b. ☐ **placing** the envelope for collection and mailing following our ordinary business practices. I am readily familiar with this business's practice for collecting and processing correspondence for mailing. On the same day that correspondence is placed for collection and mailing, it is deposited in the ordinary course of business with the United States Postal Service in a sealed envelope with postage fully prepaid.

5. The envelope was addressed and mailed as follows:
   a. **Name** of person served: Los Angeles County Board of Supervisors (County of Los Angeles) c/o Mr. Coleman
   b. **Address** of person served:

   1111 South Arroyo Parkway, Suite 442, Pasadena, California, 91105

   ☐ The name and address of each person to whom I mailed the documents is listed in the *Attachment to Proof of Service by First-Class Mail—Civil (Persons Served)* (POS-030(P)).

I declare under penalty of perjury under the laws of the State of California that the foregoing is true and correct.

Date: 12/21/2016

_____   /   _____
(TYPE OR PRINT NAME OF PERSON COMPLETING THIS FORM)   (SIGNATURE OF PERSON COMPLETING THIS FORM)

Form Approved for Optional Use
Judicial Council of California
POS-030 [New January 1, 2005]

PROOF OF SERVICE BY FIRST-CLASS MAIL—CIVIL
(Proof of Service)

Code of Civil Procedure, §§ 1013, 1013a
www.courtinfo.ca.gov

Copyright. © 2021. Paralegal Publishing Group.

Plaintiff in pro per

FILED
Superior Court of California
County of Los Angeles

DEC 21 2016

Sherri R. Carter, Executive Officer/Clerk
By_____, Deputy
Judi Lara

SUPERIOR COURT OF THE STATE OF CALIFORNIA

COUNTY OF LOS ANGELES - CENTRAL DISTRICT

STANLEY MOSK COURTHOUSE

Luke E Dumas, an individual, Plaintiff, v. Los Angeles County Board of Supervisors, a public entity; the Los Angeles County Sherriff's Department, a public entity; Sheriff Jim McDonnell, a public official; and DOES 1-10, inclusive, Defendants	Case No.: BC618191 [Assigned for all purposes to the Hon. Judge Gregory Keosian, Dept. 61] **SEPARATE STATEMENT IN SUPPORT OF MOTION FOR ORDER COMPELLING FURTHER RESPONSE TO PLAINTIFF'S INTERROGATORIES, SET ONE** Judge: Hon. Judge Gregory Keosian Hearing Date: February 15, 2017 Time: 9:00AM Dept: 61 Date: December 21, 2016 Date Action Filed: April 26, 2016 RES ID: 161208179573

TO THE HONORABLE JUDGE GREGORY KEOSIAN AND TO THE DEFENDANT COUNTY OF LOS ANGELES AND TO THIER ATTORNEY OF RECORD:

This Separate Statement is submitted in support of the Motion by Plaintiff Luke Edward Dumas ("Plaintiff") to Compel Further Discovery Responses from Defendant Los Angeles County Board of Supervisors ("County").

The Defendant County must provide adequate response to the Judicial Council Unlimited Form Interrogatories, Set One ("Official Form Interrogatory"), propounded by the Plaintiff.

As required under Cal. Rules of Court, rule 3.1345, this statement provides information relating to the interrogatories and response at issue in the motion, as follows:

    1. Official Form Interrogatory No. 2.3:

At the time of the INCIDENT, did you have a driver's license? If so state:

(a) the state or other issuing entity;

(b) the license number and type;

(c) the date of issuance; and

(d) all restrictions.

    2. Defendant County's Response to Official Form Interrogatory No. 2.3:

(a) n/a

(b) n/a

(c) n/a

(d) n/a

    3. Related Definitions and Instructions:

Sec. 3. Instructions to the Answering Party (a) An answer or other appropriate response must be given to each interrogatory checked by the asking party. (b) As a general rule, within 30 days after you are served with these interrogatories, you must serve your responses on the asking party and serve copies of your responses on the asking party and serve copies of your responses on all other parties to the action who have appeared. See Code of Civil Procedure sections 2030.260-230.270 for details. (c) Each answer must be complete and straightforward as the information reasonably available to you, including the information possessed by your attorneys or agents, permits. If an interrogatory cannot be answered completely, answer it to the extent possible. (d) If you do not have enough personal knowledge to fully answer an interrogatory, say so, but make a reasonable and good faith effort to get the information by asking the other persons or organizations, unless the information is equally available to the asking party. (f) Whenever an address and telephone number for the same person are requested in more than one interrogatory, you are required to furnish them in answering only the first interrogatory asking for that information. (g) If you are asserting a privilege or making an objection to an interrogatory, you must specifically assert the privilege or state the objection in your written response.

Sec. 4. Definitions (1) INCIDENT includes the circumstances and events surrounding the alleged accident, injury,, or other occurrence or breach of contract giving rise to this action or proceeding. (b) YOU OR ANYONE ACTING ON YOUR BEHALF includes you, your agents, your employees, your insurance companies, their agents, their employees, your attorneys, your accountants, your investigators, and anyone else acting on your behalf.

(c) PERSON includes a natural person, firm, association, organization, partnership, business, trust, limited liability company, corporation, or public entity.

(d) DOCUMENT means a writing, as defined in Evidence Code section 250, and includes the original or a copy of handwriting, typewriting, printing, photostats, photographs, electronically stored information, and every other means of recording upon any tangible thing and form of communication or representation, including letters, words, pictures, sounds, or symbols, or combinations of them.

(f) ADDRESS means the street address, including the city, state, and zip code.

Sec. 5. Interrogatories The following interrogatories have been approved by the Judicial Council under Code of Civil Procedure section 2033.710.

   4. Official Form Interrogatory No. 2.4:

At the time of the INCIDENT, did you have other permit or license for the operation of a motor vehicle? If so, state:

(a) the state or other issuing entity;

(b) the license number and type;

(c) the date of issuance; and

(d) all restrictions.

SEPARATE STATEMENT IN SUPPORT OF MOTION TO COMPEL FURTHER DISCOVERY RESPONSES

Copyright. © 2021. Paralegal Publishing Group.

5. Defendant County's Response to Official Form Interrogatory No. 2.4:

(a) n/a

(b) n/a

(c) n/a

(d) n/a

6. Related Definitions and Instructions:

(a) An answer or other appropriate response must be given to each interrogatory checked by the asking party. (c) Each answer must be complete and straightforward as the information reasonably available to you, including the information possessed by your attorneys or agents, permits. If an interrogatory canned be answered completely, answer it to the extent possible. (d) If you do not have enough personal knowledge to fully answer an interrogatory, say so, but make a reasonable and good faith effort to get the information by asking the other persons or organizations, unless the information is equally available to the asking party. (f) Whenever an address and telephone number for the same person are requested in more than one interrogatory, you are required to furnish them in answering only the first interrogatory asking for that information. (g) If you are asserting a privilege or making an objection to an interrogatory, you must specifically assert the privilege or state the objection in your written response.

7. Official Form Interrogatory 2.6:

(a) the name, ADDRESS, and telephone number of your present employer or place of self-employment; and (b) the name, ADDRESS, and dates of employment, job title, and nature of work for each employer or self-employment you have had from five years before the INCDENT until today.

9. Defendant County's Response to Official Form Interrogatory No. 2.6:

(a) n/a

(b) n/a

8. Related Definitions and Instructions:

(a) An answer or other appropriate response must be given to each interrogatory checked by the asking party. (c) Each answer must be complete and straightforward as the information reasonably available to you, including the information possessed by your attorneys or agents, permits. If an interrogatory canned be answered completely, answer it to the extent possible. (d) If you do not have enough personal knowledge to fully answer an interrogatory, say so, but make a reasonable and good faith effort to get the information by asking the other persons or organizations, unless the information is equally available to the asking party.

(f) Whenever an address and telephone number for the same person are requested in more than one interrogatory, you are required to furnish them in answering only the first interrogatory asking for that information. (g) If you are asserting a privilege or making an objection to an interrogatory, you must specifically assert the privilege or state the objection in your written response.

9. <u>Official Form Interrogatory No. 2.8:</u>

Have you ever been convicted of a felony? If so, for each conviction state:

(a) the city and state where you were convicted;

(b) the date of conviction;

(c) the offense; and

(d) the court and case number.

10. <u>Defendant County's Response to Official Form Interrogatory No. 2.8:</u>

(a) n/a

(b) n/a

(c) n/a

(d) n/a

11. <u>Related Definitions and Instructions:</u>

(a) An answer or other appropriate response must be given to each interrogatory checked by the asking party. (c) Each answer must be complete and straightforward as the information reasonably available to you, including the information possessed by your attorneys or agents, permits. If an interrogatory canned be answered completely, answer it to the extent possible. (d) If you do not have enough personal knowledge to fully answer an interrogatory, say so, but make a reasonable and good faith effort to get the information by asking the other persons or organizations, unless the information is equally available to the asking party.

(f) Whenever an address and telephone number for the same person are requested in more than one interrogatory, you are required to furnish them in answering only the first interrogatory asking for that information. (g) If you are asserting a privilege or making an objection to an interrogatory, you must specifically assert the privilege or state the objection in your written response.

12. Official Form Interrogatory No. 2.12:

At the time of the INCIDENT did you or any other person have any physical, emotional, or mental disability or condition that may have contributed to the occurrence of the INCIDENT? If so, state:

(a) the name, ADDRESS, and telephone number;

(b) the nature of the disability or condition; and

(c) the manner in which the disability or condition contributed to the occurrence of the INCIDENT.

13. Defendant County's Response to Official Form Interrogatory No. 2.12:

(a) n/a

(b) n/a

(c) n/a

14. Related Definitions and Instructions:

(a) An answer or other appropriate response must be given to each interrogatory checked by the asking party. (c) Each answer must be complete and straightforward as the information reasonably available to you, including the information possessed by your attorneys or agents, permits. If an interrogatory canned be answered completely, answer it to the extent possible.

(d) If you do not have enough personal knowledge to fully answer an interrogatory, say so, but make a reasonable and good faith effort to get the information by asking the other persons or organizations, unless the information is equally available to the asking party.

(f) Whenever an address and telephone number for the same person are requested in more than one interrogatory, you are required to furnish them in answering only the first interrogatory asking for that information.

(g) If you are asserting a privilege or making an objection to an interrogatory, you must specifically assert the privilege or state the objection in your written response.

15. <u>Official Form Interrogatory No. 2.13</u>:

Within 24 hours before the INCIDENT did you or any person involved in the INCIDENT use or take any of the following substances: alcoholic beverage, marijuana, or other drug or medication of any kind (prescription or not)? If so, for each person state:

(a) the name, ADDRESS, and telephone number;

(b) the nature or description of each substance;

(c) the quantity of each substance used or taken;

(d) the date and time of day when each substance was used or taken;

(e) the ADDRESS where each substance was used or taken;

(f) the name, ADDRESS, and telephone number of each person who was present when each substance was used or taken; and

(g) the name, ADDRESS, and telephone number of any HEALTH CARE PROVIDER who prescribed or furnished the substance and the condition for which it was prescribed or furnished.

16. <u>Defendant County's Response to Official Form Interrogatory No. 2.13</u>:

(a) n/a

(b) n/a

(c) n/a

17. <u>Related Definitions and Instructions</u>:

(a) An answer or other appropriate response must be given to each interrogatory checked by the asking party. (c) Each answer must be complete and straightforward as the information reasonably available to you, including the information possessed by your attorneys or agents, permits. If an interrogatory canned be answered completely, answer it to the extent possible. (d) If you do not have enough personal knowledge to fully answer an interrogatory, say so, but make a reasonable and good faith effort to get the information by asking the other persons or organizations, unless the information is equally available to the asking party. (f) Whenever an address and telephone number for the same person are requested in more than one interrogatory, you are required to furnish them in answering only the first interrogatory asking for that information. (g) If you are asserting a privilege or making an objection to an interrogatory, you must specifically assert the privilege or state the objection in your written response.

18. <u>Official Form Interrogatory No. 12.1:</u>

State the name, ADDRESS, and telephone number of each individual:

(a) who witnessed the INCIDENT or the events occurring immediately before or after the INCIDENT;

(b) who made any statements at the scene of the INCIDENT;

(c) who heard any statements made about the INCIDENT by any individual at the scene; and

(d) who YOU OR ANYONE ACTING ON YOUR BEHALF claims has knowledge of the INCIDENT (except for expert witnesses covered by Code of Civil Procedure section 2034).

19. <u>Defendant's Further Response to Official Form Interrogatory No. 12.1:</u>

COUNTY objects to this interrogatory on the grounds the terms used herein are vague, ambiguous, and overly broad, and seek discovery of information that is irrelevant to the subject matter of this litigation and not calculated, nor likely, to lead to discovery of admissible evidence. COUNTY objects to this interrogatory on grounds and to the extent it may seek discovery of information prepared in anticipation of litigating which is protect from disclosure by the Attorney-Client Privilege and work Product Doctrine.

COUNTY also objects to this Interrogatory on the grounds it may seek discovery of private information (i.e., address and telephone number) which is protected from disclosure by the Right to Privacy under the United States Constitution and California State Constitution.

COUNTY further objects on grounds this Request is premature at this time. Investigation and Discovery are at their earliest stages and Responding Party is in the process of conducting such Investigation and Discovery. Therefore, Responding Party may lack sufficient information upon which to base a response to this Request at this time.

Without waiving these objection, COUNTY responds as follows:

a) Plaintiff, Luke Dumas; Deputy James Murren; Deputy Brian Bostick; Pamela Marshall.

b) Plaintiff, Luke Dumas; Deputy James Murren; Deputy Brian Bostick; Pamela Marshall.

c) Plaintiff, Luke Dumas; Deputy James Murren; Deputy Brian Bostick; Pamela Marshall.

d) Plaintiff, Luke Dumas; Deputy James Murren; Deputy Brian Bostick; Pamela Marshall. Discovery and investigation are ongoing. Depositions of witnesses have yet to be taken in this matter. Responding Party reserves its right to amend this response as information becomes available, and specifically reserves it right to induce additional information and evidence at time of Arbitration, Mediation, and/or Trial.

20. Related Definitions and Instructions:

(a) An answer or other appropriate response must be given to each interrogatory checked by the asking party. (c) Each answer must be complete and straightforward as the information reasonably available to you, including the information possessed by your attorneys or agents, permits. If an interrogatory canned be answered completely, answer it to the extent possible. (d) If you do not have enough personal knowledge to fully answer an interrogatory, say so, but make a reasonable and good faith effort to get the information by asking the other persons or organizations, unless the information is equally available to the asking party. (f) Whenever an address and telephone number for the same person are requested in more than one interrogatory, you are required to furnish them in answering only the first interrogatory asking for that information. (g) If you are asserting a privilege or making an objection to an interrogatory, you must specifically assert the privilege or state the objection in your written response.

21. Official Form Interrogatory No. 12.2:

Have YOU OR ANYONE ACTING ON YOUR BEHALF interviewed any individual concerning the INCIDENT? if so, for each statement state:

(a) the name, ADDRESS, and telephone number of the individual interviewed;

(b) the date of the interview; and

(c) the name, ADDRESS, and telephone number of the PERSON who conducted the interview.

22. Defendant's Further Response to Official Form Interrogatory No. 12.2:

COUNTY objects to this interrogatory on the grounds the terms used herein are vague, ambiguous, and overly broad, and seek discovery of information that is irrelevant to the subject matter of this litigation and not calculated, nor likely, to lead to discovery of admissible evidence. Objection. Responding Party objects to this Interrogatory as it calls for information protected by the Right of Privacy guaranteed by both the Constitution of the United States as well as State of California. This information is privileged and protected from disclosure by Government Code §§6254, 6254.1, and 6254.8. The information sought is also protected from disclosure by Evidence Code §§ 1040 through 1047 and Penal Code 832.7. See Kerr v. U.S. District Court, 511 F.2d 192 (1975) and Davis v. City of Sacramento, 24 Cal.4th 393 (1994)This interrogatory may also call for disclosure of information protected by both the Attorney-Client Privilege and the Work Product Doctrine.

In addition, Responding Party objects to this Interrogatory as any Reports prepared would have been done in anticipation of litigation and/or at the request of counsel.

COUNTY further objects on grounds this Request is premature at this time. Investigation and Discovery are at their earliest stages and Responding Party is in the process of conducting such Investigation and Discovery. Therefore, Responding Party may lack sufficient information upon which to base a response to this Request at this time.

23. **Related Definitions and Instructions:**

(a) An answer or other appropriate response must be given to each interrogatory checked by the asking party. (c) Each answer must be complete and straightforward as the information reasonably available to you, including the information possessed by your attorneys or agents, permits. If an interrogatory canned be answered completely, answer it to the extent possible.

(d) If you do not have enough personal knowledge to fully answer an interrogatory, say so, but make a reasonable and good faith effort to get the information by asking the other persons or organizations, unless the information is equally available to the asking party.

(f) Whenever an address and telephone number for the same person are requested in more than one interrogatory, you are required to furnish them in answering only the first interrogatory asking for that information. (g) If you are asserting a privilege or making an objection to an interrogatory, you must specifically assert the privilege or state the objection in your written response.

24. **Official Form Interrogatory No. 12.3:**

Have YOU OR ANYONE ACTING ON YOUR BEHALF obtained a written or recorded statement from any individual concerning the INCIDENT? If so, for each statement state:

(a) the name, ADDRESS, and telephone number of the individual from whom the statement was obtained;

(b) the name, ADDRESS, and telephone number often individual who obtained the statement;

(c) the date the statement was obtained; and

(d) the name, ADDRESS, and telephone number of each PERSON who has the original statement or a copy.

25. **Defendant County's Response to Official Form Interrogatory No. 12.3:**

COUNTY objects to this interrogatory on the grounds the terms used herein are vague, ambiguous, and overly broad, and seek discovery of information that is irrelevant to the subject matter of this litigation and not calculated, nor likely, to lead to discovery of admissible evidence. Objection. Responding Party objects to this Interrogatory as it calls for information protected by the Right of Privacy guaranteed by both the Constitution of the United States as well as State of California. This information is privileged and protected from disclosure by Government Code §§ 6254, 6254.1, and 6254.8. The information sought is also protected from disclosure by Evidence Code §§ 1040 through 1047 and Penal Code 832.7. See Kerr v. U.S. District Court, 511 F.2d 192 (1975) and Davis v. City of Sacramento, 24 Cal.4th 393 (1994)This interrogatory may also call for disclosure of information protected by both the Attorney-Client Privilege and the Work Product Doctrine.

In addition, Responding Party objects to this Interrogatory as any Reports prepared would have been done in anticipation of litigation and/or at the request of counsel.

COUNTY further objects on grounds this Request is premature at this time. Investigation and Discovery are at their earliest stages and Responding Party is in the process of conducting such Investigation and Discovery. Therefore, Responding Party may lack sufficient information upon which to base a response to this Request at this time.

26. **Related Definitions and Instructions:**

(a) An answer or other appropriate response must be given to each interrogatory checked by the asking party. (c) Each answer must be complete and straightforward as the information reasonably available to you, including the information possessed by your attorneys or agents, permits. If an interrogatory canned be answered completely, answer it to the extent possible.

(d) If you do not have enough personal knowledge to fully answer an interrogatory, say so, but make a reasonable and good faith effort to get the information by asking the other persons or organizations, unless the information is equally available to the asking party.

(f) Whenever an address and telephone number for the same person are requested in more than one interrogatory, you are required to furnish them in answering only the first interrogatory asking for that information. (g) If you are asserting a privilege or making an objection to an interrogatory, you must specifically assert the privilege or state the objection in your written response.

27. <u>Official Form Interrogatory No. 12.4:</u>

Do YOU OR ANYONE ACTING ON YOUR BEHALF know of any photographs, films, or videotapes depicting any place, object, or individual concerning the INCIDENT or plaintiff's injuries? If so, state:

(a) the number of photographs or feet of film or videotape;

(b) the places, objects, or persons photographed, filmed, or videotaped;

(c) the date the photographs, films, or videotapes were taken;

(d) the name, ADDRESS, and telephone number of the individual taking the photographs, films, or videotapes; and

(e) the name, ADDRESS, and telephone number of each PERSON who has the original or a copy of the photographs, films, or videotapes.

28. <u>Defendant County's Response to Official Form Interrogatory No. 12.4:</u>

COUNTY objects to this interrogatory on the grounds the terms used herein are vague, ambiguous, and overly broad, and seek discovery of information that is irrelevant to the subject matter of this litigation and not calculated, nor likely, to lead to discovery of admissible evidence. Objection. Responding Party objects to this Interrogatory as it calls for information protected by the Right of Privacy guaranteed by both the Constitution of the United States as well as State of California. This information is privileged and protected from disclosure by Government Code §§ 6254, 6254.1, and 6254.8. The information sought is also protected from disclosure by Evidence Code §§ 1040 through 1047 and Penal Code 832.7. See Kerr v. U.S. District Court, 511 F.2d 192 (1975) and Davis v. City of Sacramento, 24 Cal.4th 393 (1994)This

-12-

SEPARATE STATEMENT IN SUPPORT OF MOTION TO COMPEL FURTHER DISCOVERY RESPONSES interrogatory may also call for disclosure of information protected by both the Attorney-Client Privilege and the Work Product Doctrine.

In addition, Responding Party objects to this Interrogatory as any Reports prepared would have been done in anticipation of litigation and/or at the request of counsel.

COUNTY further objects on grounds this Request is premature at this time. Investigation and Discovery are at their earliest stages and Responding Party is in the process of conducting such Investigation and Discovery. Therefore, Responding Party may lack sufficient information upon which to base a response to this Request at this time.

29. **Related Definitions and Instructions:**

(a) An answer or other appropriate response must be given to each interrogatory checked by the asking party. (c) Each answer must be complete and straightforward as the information reasonably available to you, including the information possessed by your attorneys or agents, permits. If an interrogatory canned be answered completely, answer it to the extent possible.

(d) If you do not have enough personal knowledge to fully answer an interrogatory, say so, but make a reasonable and good faith effort to get the information by asking the other persons or organizations, unless the information is equally available to the asking party.

(f) Whenever an address and telephone number for the same person are requested in more than one interrogatory, you are required to furnish them in answering only the first interrogatory asking for that information. (g) If you are asserting a privilege or making an objection to an interrogatory, you must specifically assert the privilege or state the objection in your written response.

30. **Official Form Interrogatory No. 12.6:**

Was a report made by any PERSON concerning the INCIDENT? If so, state:

(a) the name, title, identification number, and employer of the PERSON who made in the report;

(b) the date and type of report made;

(c) the name, ADDRESS, and telephone number of each PERSON who has the original or a copy of the report.

//

31. Defendant County's Response to Official Form Interrogatory No. 12.6:

COUNTY objects to this interrogatory on the grounds the terms used herein are vague, ambiguous, and overly broad, and seek discovery of information that is irrelevant to the subject matter of this litigation and not calculated, nor likely, to lead to discovery of admissible evidence. Objection. Responding Party objects to this Interrogatory as it calls for information protected by the Right of Privacy guaranteed by both the Constitution of the United States as well as State of California. This information is privileged and protected from disclosure by Government Code §§ 6254, 6254.1, and 6254.8. The information sought is also protected from disclosure by Evidence Code §§ 1040 through 1047 and Penal Code 832.7. See Kerr v. U.S. District Court, 511 F.2d 192 (1975) and Davis v. City of Sacramento, 24 Cal.4th 393 (1994)This interrogatory may also call for disclosure of information protected by both the Attorney-Client Privilege and the Work Product Doctrine.

In addition, Responding Party objects to this Interrogatory as any Reports prepared would have been done in anticipation of litigation and/or at the request of counsel.

32. Related Definitions and Instructions:

(a) An answer or other appropriate response must be given to each interrogatory checked by the asking party. (c) Each answer must be complete and straightforward as the information reasonably available to you, including the information possessed by your attorneys or agents, permits. If an interrogatory canned be answered completely, answer it to the extent possible.

(d) If you do not have enough personal knowledge to fully answer an interrogatory, say so, but make a reasonable and good faith effort to get the information by asking the other persons or organizations, unless the information is equally available to the asking party.

(f) Whenever an address and telephone number for the same person are requested in more than one interrogatory, you are required to furnish them in answering only the first interrogatory asking for that information. (g) If you are asserting a privilege or making an objection to an interrogatory, you must specifically assert the privilege or state the objection in your written response.

//

33. **Statement of Reasons for Compelling Defendant's Further Response(s):**

Defendant County's agents and or their attorneys had proceeded ex parte without any advanced notification and disclosed that they had distributed to a third party (judicial officer) a "secret report", thus waiving any attorney client privilege asserted in their response.

34. **Official Form Interrogatory No 14.2:**

Was any PERSON cited or charged with a violation of any statute, ordinance, or regulation as a result of this INCIDENT? If so, for each PERSON state:

(a) the name, ADDRESS, and telephone number of the PERSON;

(b) the statute, ordinance, or regulation allegedly violated;

(c) whether the PERSON entered a pleas in response to the citation or charge and, if so, the plea entered; and (d) the name and ADDRESS of the court or administrative agency, names o the parties, and case number.

35. **Defendant's Response to Official Form Interrogatory No. 14.2:**

COUNTY objects to this interrogatory on the grounds the terms used herein are vague, ambiguous, and overly broad, and seek discovery of information that is irrelevant to the subject matter of this litigation and not calculated, nor likely, to lead to discovery of admissible evidence. Objection. Responding Party objects to this Interrogatory as it calls for information protected by the Right of Privacy guaranteed by both the Constitution of the United States as well as State of California. This information is privileged and protected from disclosure by Government Code §§6254, 6254.1, and 6254.8. The information sought is also protected from disclosure by Evidence Code §§1040 through 1047 and Penal Code 832.7. See Kerr v. U.S. District Court, 511 F.2d 192 (1975) and Davis v. City of Sacramento, 24 Cal.4th 393 (1994)This interrogatory may also call for disclosure of information protected by both the Attorney-Client Privilege and the Work Product Doctrine.

In addition, Responding Party objects to this Interrogatory as any Reports prepared would have been done in anticipation of litigation and/or at the request of counsel.

COUNTY further objects on grounds this Request is premature at this time. Investigation and Discovery are at their earliest stages and Responding Party is in the process of conducting such

1 Investigation and Discovery. Therefore, Responding Party may lack sufficient information upon
2 which to base a response to this Request at this time.
3 Without waiving these objections, COUNTY responds as follows:
4 Yes. Plaintiff, Luke Dumas. Penal Code § 21310-Posession of a Dirk or Dagger.
5 Discovery and investigation are in the early stages. Responding Party reserves its right to amend
6 this response as information and/or documents become available, and specifically reserves its
7 right to introduce additional evidence at time of Medication and/or Trial.
8   36. Related Definitions and Instructions:
9 (a) An answer or other appropriate response must be given to each interrogatory checked by the
10 asking party. (c) Each answer must be complete and straightforward as the information
11 reasonably available to you, including the information possessed by your attorneys or agents,
12 permits. If an interrogatory canned be answered completely, answer it to the extent possible.
13 (d) If you do not have enough personal knowledge to fully answer an interrogatory, say so, but
14 make a reasonable and good faith effort to get the information by asking the other persons or
15 organizations, unless the information is equally available to the asking party.
16 (f) Whenever an address and telephone number for the same person are requested in more than
17 one interrogatory, you are required to furnish them in answering only the first interrogatory
18 asking for that information. (g) If you are asserting a privilege or making an objection to an
19 interrogatory, you must specifically assert the privilege or state the objection in your written
20 response.
21   37. Statement of Reasons for Compelling Further Response(s):
22 Defendant County failed to answer completely subparts (a), (b), (c), and (d).
23   38. Official Form Interrogatory No 15.1:
24 Identify each denial of a material allegation and each special or affirmative defense in your
25 pleadings and for each:
26 (a) state all facts upon which you base the denial or special or affirmative defense;
27 (b) state the names, ADDRESSES, and telephone numbers of all PERSONS who have
28 knowledge of those facts; and (c) identify all DOCUMENTS and other tangible things that

SEPARATE STATEMENT IN SUPPORT OF MOTION TO COMPEL FURTHER DISCOVERY RESPONSES

Copyright. © 2021. Paralegal Publishing Group.

support your denial or special or affirmative defense, and state the name, ADDRESS, and telephone number of the PERSON who has each DOCUMENT.

39. Defendant's Further Response to Official Form Interrogatory No. 15.1:
OBJECTION. Responding Party objects to this Interrogatory as its calls for information protected by the Right of Privacy guaranteed by both the Constitution of the United States as well as State of California. This information is privileged and protected from disclosure by Government Code §§6254, 62544.8. The information sough is also protected from disclosure by Evidence Code §§1040 through 1047 and Penal Code 832.7. See Kerr v. U.S. District Court, 511, F.2d 192 (1975) and Davis v. City of Sacramento, 24 Cal.4th 393 (1994). This interrogatory also calls for information not reasonably calculated to lead to the discovery of admissible evidence. this interrogatory may also call for disclosure of information protected by both the attorney-client privilege and the work product doctrine.

Additionally, this interrogatory asks Responding Party to identify/speculate as to allegations important enough to be considered "material" in violation of the attorney-client privilege and work product doctrine.

Responding Party filed a general denial to an unverified complaint, and in compliance with the California Code of Civil Procedure, which provides that affirmative defenses must be plead at the time of answering the complaint. Responding Party asserted affirmative defenses in good faith. Responding Party's affirmative defenses are on file and need not be repeated herein. Investigation and discovery are in their earliest stages and Responding Party is in the process of conducting further investigation and discovery.

Therefore, Responding Party lacks sufficient information upon which to base a response to this interrogatory at this time.

Discovery and invitation are continuing

Responding Party reserves their right to amend this response as information becomes available and specifically reserves their right to introduce additional evidence at the time of arbitration mediation, or trial.

//

40. Related Definitions and Instructions:

(a) An answer or other appropriate response must be given to each interrogatory checked by the asking party. (c) Each answer must be complete and straightforward as the information reasonably available to you, including the information possessed by your attorneys or agents, permits. If an interrogatory canned be answered completely, answer it to the extent possible.

(d) If you do not have enough personal knowledge to fully answer an interrogatory, say so, but make a reasonable and good faith effort to get the information by asking the other persons or organizations, unless the information is equally available to the asking party.

(f) Whenever an address and telephone number for the same person are requested in more than one interrogatory, you are required to furnish them in answering only the first interrogatory asking for that information. (g) If you are asserting a privilege or making an objection to an interrogatory, you must specifically assert the privilege or state the objection in your written response.

41. Statement of Reasons for Compelling Further Response(s):

Defendant County has documents in its possession that it is failing to provide to the plaintiff; Defendant County has failed to completely answer the subparts of ...as is required in the Official Interrogatory instructions.

42. Official Form Interrogatory No 16.1:

Do you contend that any PERSON, other than you or plaintiff, contributed to the occurrence of the INCIDENT or the injuries or damages claimed by plaintiff? If so, for each PERSON:

(a) state the name, ADDRESS, and telephone number of the PERSON;

(b) state all facts upon which you base your contention;

(c) state the names, ADDRESSES, and telephone number of all PERSONS who have knowledge of the facts; and (d) identify all DOCUMENTS and other tangible things that support your contention and state the name, ADDRESS, and telephone number of the PERSON who has each DOCUMENT or thing.

43. Defendant County's Further Response to Official Form Interrogatory No. 16.1:

Responding Party objects to this interrogatory on the grounds it is premature at this time. Section 2 of the Judicial Council Interrogatories, Instructions to the Asking Party, subsection

-18-
SEPARATE STATEMENT IN SUPPORT OF MOTION TO COMPEL FURTHER DISCOVERY RESPONSES

(d), indicates contention interrogatories should not be used until responding party has a had a reasonable opportunity to conduct an investigation or discovery of a plaintiff's damages. Responding Party further objects to this interrogatory to the extent the requested information calls for or requires the opinion of an Expert Witness, which this Responding Party is not qualified to give. Without waiving these objection, Responding Party responds as Follows:

At this time, Responding Patty cannot verify that any INCIDENT occurred that could cause the personal injuries claimed by Plaintiff.

Discovery and investigation are continuing.

Responding Party reserves their right to amend this response as information becomes available and specifically reserves their right to amend this respond as information becomes available and specifically reserves their right to introduce additional evidence at the time of arbitration, mediation, or trial.

44. Related Definitions and Instructions:

(a) An answer or other appropriate response must be given to each interrogatory checked by the asking party. (c) Each answer must be complete and straightforward as the information reasonably available to you, including the information possessed by your attorneys or agents, permits. If an interrogatory canned be answered completely, answer it to the extent possible. (d) If you do not have enough personal knowledge to fully answer an interrogatory, say so, but make a reasonable and good faith effort to get the information by asking the other persons or organizations, unless the information is equally available to the asking party.

(f) Whenever an address and telephone number for the same person are requested in more than one interrogatory, you are required to furnish them in answering only the first interrogatory asking for that information. (g) If you are asserting a privilege or making an objection to an interrogatory, you must specifically assert the privilege or state the objection in your written response.

45. Official Form Interrogatory No 16.2:

Do you contend that plaintiff was not injured in the INCIDENT? If so:

(a) state all facts upon which you base your contention;

(b) state the names, ADDRESSES, and telephone numbers of all PERSONS who have knowledge of the facts; and

(c) identify all DOCUMENTS and other tangible things that support your contention and state the name, ADDRESS, and telephone number of the PERSON who has each DOCUMENT or thing.

46. **Defendant County's Further Response to Official Form Interrogatory No. 16.2:**
Responding Party objects to this interrogatory on the grounds it is premature at this time. Section 2 of the Judicial Council Interrogatories, Instructions to the Asking Party, subsection (d), indicates contention interrogatories should not be used until responding party has a had a reasonable opportunity to conduct an investigation or discovery of a plaintiff's damages. Responding Party further objects to this interrogatory to the extent the requested information calls for/requires the opinion of an Expert Witness, which this Responding Party is not qualified to give. Without waiving these objection, Responding Party responds as Follows:

At this time, Responding Patty cannot verify that any INCIDENT occurred that could cause the personal injuries claimed by Plaintiff.

Discovery and investigation are continuing.

Responding Party reserves their right to amend this response as information becomes available and specifically reserves their right to amend this respond as information becomes available and specifically reserves their right to introduce additional evidence at the time of arbitration, mediation, or trial.

47. **Related Definitions and Instructions:**
(a) An answer or other appropriate response must be given to each interrogatory checked by the asking party.

(c) Each answer must be complete and straightforward as the information reasonably available to you, including the information possessed by your attorneys or agents, permits. If an interrogatory canned be answered completely, answer it to the extent possible.

(d) If you do not have enough personal knowledge to fully answer an interrogatory, say so, but make a reasonable and good faith effort to get the information by asking the other persons or organizations, unless the information is equally available to the asking party.

(f) Whenever an address and telephone number for the same person are requested in more than one interrogatory, you are required to furnish them in answering only the first interrogatory asking for that information.

(g) If you are asserting a privilege or making an objection to an interrogatory, you must specifically assert the privilege or state the objection in your written response.

48. <u>Official Form Interrogatory No 16.3:</u>

Do you contend that the injuries or the extent of the injuries claimed by plaintiff as disclosed in discovery proceedings *thus far* in this case were not caused by the INCIDENT? If so, for each injury:

(a) indentify it;

(b) state all facts upon which you base your contention;

(c) state the names, ADDRESS, and telephone numbers of all PERSONS who have knowledge of the facts; and

(d) identify all DOCUMENTS and other tangible things that support your contention and state the name, ADDRESS, and telephone number of the PERSON who has beach DOCUMENT or thing.

49. <u>Defendant County's Further Response to Official Form Interrogatory No. 16.3:</u>

Responding Party objects to this interrogatory on the grounds it is premature at this time. Section 2 of the Judicial Council Interrogatories, Instructions to the Asking Party, subsection (d), indicates contention interrogatories should not be used until responding party has a had a reasonable opportunity to conduct an investigation or discovery of a plaintiff's damages. Responding Party further objects to this interrogatory to the extent the requested information calls for/requires the opinion of an Expert Witness, which this Responding Party is not qualified to give. Without waiving these objection, Responding Party responds as Follows:

At this time, Responding Patty cannot verify that any INCIDENT occurred that could cause the personal injuries claimed by Plaintiff.

Discovery and investigation are continuing.

Responding Party reserves their right to amend this response as information becomes available and specifically reserves their right to amend this respond as information becomes available and specifically reserves their right to introduce additional evidence at the time of arbitration, mediation, or trial.

50. Related Definitions and Instructions:

(a) An answer or other appropriate response must be given to each interrogatory checked by the asking party.

(c) Each answer must be complete and straightforward as the information reasonably available to you, including the information possessed by your attorneys or agents, permits. If an interrogatory canned be answered completely, answer it to the extent possible.

(d) If you do not have enough personal knowledge to fully answer an interrogatory, say so, but make a reasonable and good faith effort to get the information by asking the other persons or organizations, unless the information is equally available to the asking party.

(f) Whenever an address and telephone number for the same person are requested in more than one interrogatory, you are required to furnish them in answering only the first interrogatory asking for that information.

(g) If you are asserting a privilege or making an objection to an interrogatory, you must specifically assert the privilege or state the objection in your written response.

51. Official Form Interrogatory No. 16.6:

Do you contend that any part of the loss of earnings or income claimed by plaintiff in discovery proceedings thus far in this case was unreasonable or was not caused by the INCIDENT? if so:

(a) identify each part of the loss;

(b) state all facts upon which you base your contention;

(c) state the names, ADDRESSES, and telephone number of all PERSON who have knowledge of the facts; and

(d) identify all DOCUMENTS and other tangible things that support your contention and state the name, ADDRESS, and telephone number of the PERSQN who has each DOCUMENT or thing.

52. Defendant's Response to Official Form Interrogatory No. 16.6:

Responding Party objects to this interrogatory on the grounds it is premature at this time. Section 2 of the Judicial Council Interrogatories, Instructions to the Asking Party, subsection (d), indicates contention interrogatories should not be used until responding party has a had a reasonable opportunity to conduct an investigation or discovery of a plaintiff's damages. Responding Party further objects to this interrogatory to the extent the requested information calls for/requires the opinion of an Expert Witness, which this Responding Party is not qualified to give. Without waiving these objection, Responding Party responds as Follows:

At this time, Responding Patty cannot verify that any INCIDENT occurred that could cause the personal injuries claimed by Plaintiff.

Discovery and investigation are continuing.

Responding Party reserves their right to amend this response as information becomes available and specifically reserves their right to amend this respond as information becomes available and specifically reserves their right to introduce additional evidence at the time of arbitration, mediation, or trial.

53. Related Definitions and Instructions:

(a) An answer or other appropriate response must be given to each interrogatory checked by the asking party. (c) Each answer must be complete and straightforward as the information reasonably available to you, including the information possessed by your attorneys or agents, permits. If an interrogatory canned be answered completely, answer it to the extent possible. (d) If you do not have enough personal knowledge to fully answer an interrogatory, say so, but make a reasonable and good faith effort to get the information by asking the other persons or organizations, unless the information is equally available to the asking party. (f) Whenever an address and telephone number for the same person are requested in more than one interrogatory, you are required to furnish them in answering only the first interrogatory asking for that information. (g) If you are asserting a privilege or making an objection to an interrogatory, you must specifically assert the privilege or state the objection in your written response.

54. Official Form Interrogatory No. 16.7:

Do you contend that any of the property damage claimed by plaintiff in discovery Proceedings thus far in this case was not caused by the INCIDENT? If so:

(a) identify each item of property damage;

(b) state all facts upon which you base your contention;

(c) state the names, ADDRESSES, and telephone numbers of all PERSONS who have knowledge of the facts; and

(d) identify all DOCUMENTS and other tangible things that support your contention and state the name, ADDRESS, and telephone number of the person who has each DOCUMENT or thing.

55. <u>Defendant County's Further Response to Official Form Interrogatory No.16.7:</u>

Responding Party objects to this interrogatory on the grounds it is premature at this time. Section 2 of the Judicial Council Interrogatories, Instructions to the Asking Party, subsection (d), indicates contention interrogatories should not be used until responding party has a had a reasonable opportunity to conduct an investigation or discovery of a plaintiff's damages. Responding Party further objects to this interrogatory to the extent the requested information calls for/requires the opinion of an Expert Witness, which this Responding Party is not qualified to give. Without waiving these objection, Responding Party responds as Follows:

At this time, Responding Patty cannot verify that any INCIDENT occurred that could cause the personal injuries claimed by Plaintiff.

Discovery and investigation are continuing.

Responding Party reserves their right to amend this response as information becomes available and specifically reserves their right to amend this respond as information becomes available and specifically reserves their right to introduce additional evidence at the time of arbitration, mediation, or trial.

56. <u>Related Definitions and Instructions:</u>

(a) An answer or other appropriate response must be given to each interrogatory checked by the asking party. (c) Each answer must be complete and straightforward as the information reasonably available to you, including the information possessed by your attorneys or agents, permits. If an interrogatory canned be answered completely, answer it to the extent possible.

(d) If you do not have enough personal knowledge to fully answer an interrogatory, say so, but make a reasonable and good faith effort to get the information by asking the other persons or organizations, unless the information is equally available to the asking party.

(f) Whenever an address and telephone number for the same person are requested in more than one interrogatory, you are required to furnish them in answering only the first interrogatory asking for that information. (g) If you are asserting a privilege or making an objection to an interrogatory, you must specifically assert the privilege or state the objection in your written response.

57. Official Form Interrogatory No. 16.8:

Do you contend that any of the cost of repairing the property damage claimed by plaintiff in discovery proceedings thus far in this case were unreasonable? If so:

(a) identify each costs item:

(b) state all facts upon which you base your contention;

(c) state the names, ADDRESSES, and telephone numbers of all PERSONS who have knowledge of the facts; and

(d) identify all DOCUMENTS and other tangible things that support your contention and state the name, ADDRESS, and telephone number of the PERSON who has each DOCUMENT or thing.

58. Defendant County's Further Response to Official Interrogatory No. 16.8:

Responding Party objects to this interrogatory on the grounds it is premature at this time. Section 2 of the Judicial Council Interrogatories, Instructions to the Asking Party, subsection (d), indicates contention interrogatories should not be used until responding party has a had a reasonable opportunity to conduct an investigation or discovery of a plaintiff's damages. Responding Party further objects to this interrogatory to the extent the requested information calls for/requires the opinion of an Expert Witness, which this Responding Party is not qualified to give. Without waiving these objection, Responding Party responds as Follows: At this time, Responding Patty cannot verify that any INCIDENT occurred that could cause the personal injuries claimed by Plaintiff.

Discovery and investigation are continuing.

Responding Party reserves their right to amend this response as information becomes available and specifically reserves their right to amend this respond as information becomes available and specifically reserves their right to introduce additional evidence at the time of arbitration, mediation, or trial.

    59. Related Definitions and Instructions:

(a) An answer or other appropriate response must be given to each interrogatory checked by the asking party. (c) Each answer must be complete and straightforward as the information reasonably available to you, including the information possessed by your attorneys or agents, permits. If an interrogatory canned be answered completely, answer it to the extent possible.

(d) If you do not have enough personal knowledge to fully answer an interrogatory, say so, but make a reasonable and good faith effort to get the information by asking the other persons or organizations, unless the information is equally available to the asking party.

(f) Whenever an address and telephone number for the same person are requested in more than one interrogatory, you are required to furnish them in answering only the first interrogatory asking for that information. (g) If you are asserting a privilege or making an objection to an interrogatory, you must specifically assert the privilege or state the objection in your written response.

Dated: December 21, 2016

By:

Luke E Dumas, Plaintiff in pro per

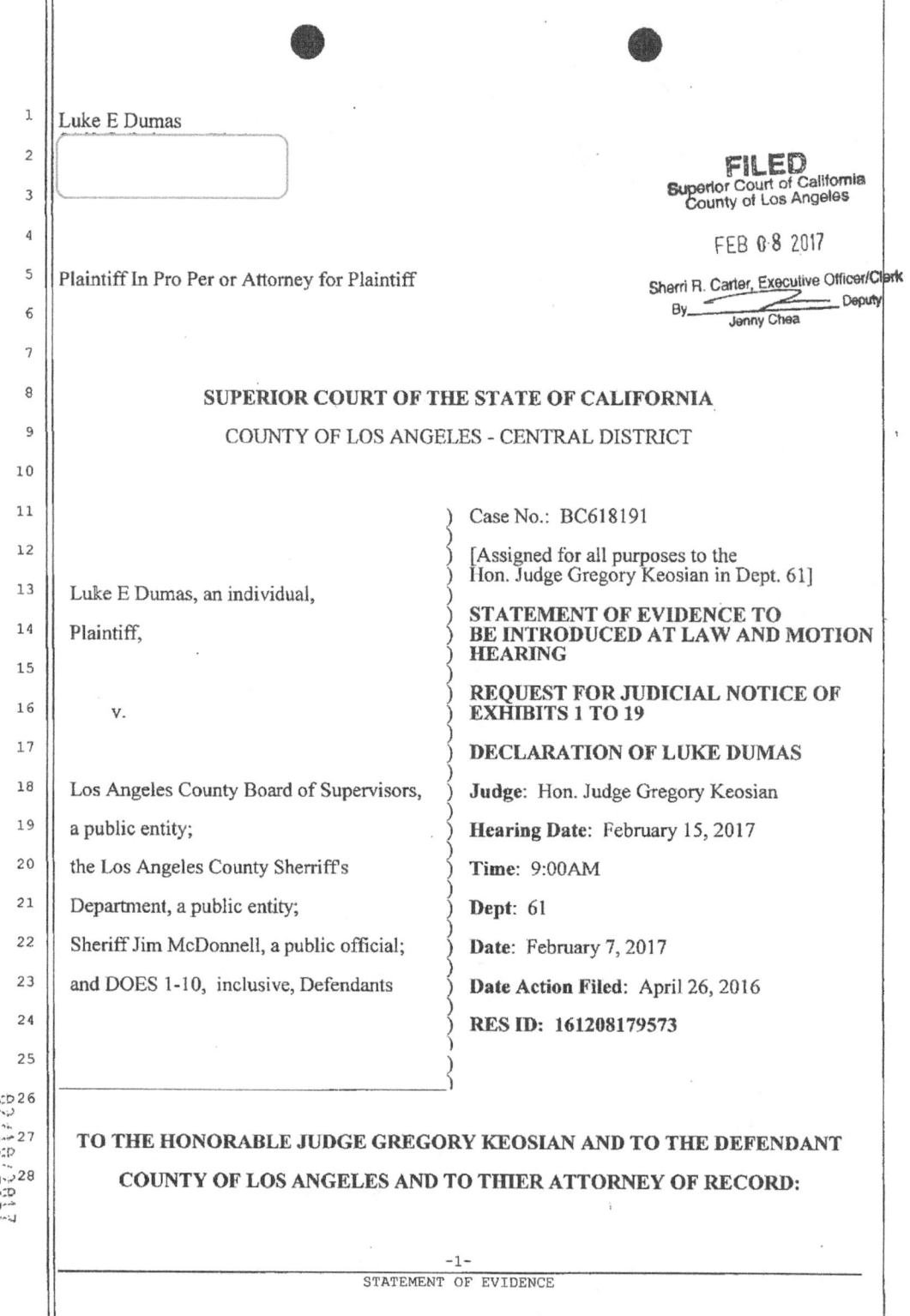

Luke E Dumas

Plaintiff In Pro Per or Attorney for Plaintiff

FILED
Superior Court of California
County of Los Angeles

FEB 08 2017

Sherri R. Carter, Executive Officer/Clerk
By_____ Deputy
Jenny Chea

SUPERIOR COURT OF THE STATE OF CALIFORNIA

COUNTY OF LOS ANGELES - CENTRAL DISTRICT

Luke E Dumas, an individual,

Plaintiff,

v.

Los Angeles County Board of Supervisors, a public entity;

the Los Angeles County Sherriff's Department, a public entity;

Sheriff Jim McDonnell, a public official;

and DOES 1-10, inclusive, Defendants

Case No.: BC618191

[Assigned for all purposes to the Hon. Judge Gregory Keosian in Dept. 61]

STATEMENT OF EVIDENCE TO BE INTRODUCED AT LAW AND MOTION HEARING

REQUEST FOR JUDICIAL NOTICE OF EXHIBITS 1 TO 19

DECLARATION OF LUKE DUMAS

Judge: Hon. Judge Gregory Keosian

Hearing Date: February 15, 2017

Time: 9:00AM

Dept: 61

Date: February 7, 2017

Date Action Filed: April 26, 2016

RES ID: 161208179573

TO THE HONORABLE JUDGE GREGORY KEOSIAN AND TO THE DEFENDANT COUNTY OF LOS ANGELES AND TO THIER ATTORNEY OF RECORD:

-1-
STATEMENT OF EVIDENCE

NOTICE IS HEREBY GIVEN that on February 15, 2017, at 9:00AM or as soon thereafter as the matter may be heard, on the 7th Floor, in Department 61 of this Court, located at 111 N. Hill Street, Los Angeles, California, 90012, that the Plaintiff Luke Edward Dumas ("Dumas") will and hereby does, move the Court for an Order to Compel Further Responses from the Defendant County of Los Angeles to the Plaintiff's "Judicial Council Unlimited Form Interrogatories, Set One" ("Official Form Interrogatories"), pursuant to the Code of Civil Procedure Section §2030.300(a) (1), (2), and (3).

Pursuant to Rule 3.1306 of the California Rules of Court, the Plaintiff hereby introduces the following Evidence to be received at the law and motion hearing described herein by Declaration and Request for Judicial Notice pursuant to Rule 3.1306 (a) and (c), to introduce the following material evidence, under Evidence Code Section 452 (d) and (h) to be admitted in support of Plaintiff's Motion to Compel Further Discovery.

NATURE OF EVIDENCE

Exhibit 1:

Judicial Council Unlimited Civil Form Interrogatories - General, Set One ("Official Interrogatories"), propounded by the Plaintiff on, and served to Defendant County on August 21, 2016, with a true and correct copy of the proof of service attached.

Exhibit 2:

Defendant County's "Response" to Plaintiff's Official Interrogatories, returned to the Plaintiff on September 26, 2016; all blanket objections with no verification.

Exhibit 3:

Defendant County's Counsel of Record Mr. John M. Coleman Esq.'s letter to the Plaintiff in pro per, dated September 26, 2016, stating that he has enclosed "Responses" to Plaintiff's Interrogatories and will provide "further responses".

Exhibit 4:

Plaintiff's email correspondence to Defendant County's Counsel of Record Mr. Coleman, dated October 18, 2016, to meet and confer regarding the Discovery Requests; noting the blanket objections as improper and untimely; and the Plaintiff informed Mr. Coleman that he may

-2-
STATEMENT OF EVIDENCE

compel discovery, not further discovery.

Exhibit 5:

Plaintiff's email correspondence to Defendant County's Counsel of Record Mr. Coleman, requesting full and complete straightforward answers to Plaintiff's Official Interrogatories dated on October 26, 2016.

Exhibit 6:

Email chain of the Defendant County's Counsel of Record Mr. Scott McIntosh Esq.'s offer and demand that the Plaintiff wait two weeks for Defendant County to provide further responses and or answers to the Plaintiff's Official Interrogatories, dated October 27, 2016. The Plaintiff asked Mr. McIntosh to draft a stipulation to that proposal.

Exhibit 7:

Plaintiff's email-chain correspondence to Defendant County's Counsel of Record Mr. Coleman and Mr. McIntosh, to provide proper responses to the Plaintiff's Official Interrogatories, agree by stipulation for more time to properly respond, or a motion to compel discovery, not further discovery may filed with regard to this discovery dispute.

Exhibit 8:

Plaintiff's email-chain correspondence between Defendant County's Counsel of Record Mr. McIntosh regarding responding to the Official Interrogatories, dated October 26-28, 2016. Mr. McIntosh informed the Plaintiff that they will have by November 9, 2016, to respond; and did not draft any stipulation to provide their discovery responses, not further discovery responses.

Exhibit 9:

Plaintiff's email-chain correspondence to Defendant County's Counsel of Record Mr. Coleman and Mr. McIntosh, dated October 29, 2016, that the Defendant County should respond to the discovery request, not further discovery, by November 4, 2016, absent a written stipulation between the parties.

//
//

STATEMENT OF EVIDENCE

Exhibit 10:

The Defendant County's Counsel of Record Mr. Coleman's letter dated November 4, 2016, enclosing the Defendant County's "Further Responses to Plaintiff's Interrogatories, Set One", with no Verification.

Exhibit 11:

The Defendant County's "Further Response to Plaintiff's Interrogatories (Set One)", returned to the Plaintiff on about November 4, 2016, with no Verification.

Exhibit 12:

Plaintiff's email to Defendant County's Counsel of Record Mr. Coleman and to Mr. McIntosh, summarizing the dates of the communications and responses to the Official Interrogatories, dated November 5, 2016.

Exhibit 13:

Plaintiff's email to Defendant County's Counsel of Record Mr. Coleman regarding their communications regarding their client, Defendant County's responses, lack of stipulation, and intention to compel discovery, not further discovery.

Exhibit 14:

Defendant County's Counsel of Record Mr. Coleman's letter dated November 9, 2016, enclosing the Defendant County's "Verification" to be attached to their "Further Responses" to the Plaintiff's Official Interrogatories, as a supplemental response.

Exhibit 15:

Plaintiff's email correspondence to the Defendant County's Counsel of Record Mr. Coleman, dated November 28, 2016, requesting and demanding that further responses be provided because the further responses were incomplete and evasive, and the Plaintiff's intent to compel further discovery responses to the Official Interrogatories.

Exhibit 16:

Plaintiff's emailed "Final Notice" to meet and confer regarding the Official Interrogatories and with resolving their client's "further responses"; Plaintiff's attempt to resolve the discovery matter informally and to extend more time to Defendant by written stipulation.

-4-
STATEMENT OF EVIDENCE

Exhibit 17:

Plaintiff's email-chain of his response, dated December 6, 2016, and Mr. Coleman's claims to have called numerous times and unfounded allegations, dated December 5, 2016, in which Mr. Coleman's claims were not true and unverified, and evidence of bad faith acted on by Mr. Coleman via email's unfounded allegations as addressed in Plaintiff response.

Exhibit 18:

Plaintiff's email, dated December 8, 2016, noting Defendant County's supplemental response by Verification, and demanded further responses to answered in full and completely to the Official Interrogatories; and provided a Separate Statement in which indentified each interrogatory by number at issue.

Exhibit 19:

Plaintiff's email to Defendant County's Counsel of Record Mr. Coleman, notifying him of his repeated attempts to stipulate in writing to extend for more time to his client, Defendant County, and provided another Separate Statement identifying the interrogatories by number at issue.

DATED: 2/7/2017   Respectfully submitted,

By: _____

Luke E Dumas, Plaintiff in pro per

//
//
//
//
//
//

DECLARATION OF LUKE EDWARD DUMAS

I, LUKE EDWARD DUMAS, declare:

1. I am the Plaintiff in pro per in this legal Action, and have capacity to represent myself in this legal matter. I have personal knowledge of the facts contained in this Declaration, and if called as a Witness, I could and would testify competently to those facts. I am a self-represented litigant that is currently responsible for the handling of this legal Action. As such, I am familiar with the files, records, and pleadings contained herein.

2. On August 21. 2016, I had a person over the age of 18 years of age and not a party to this Action serve on the Defendant County of Los Angeles the "Plaintiff's Judicial Council Unlimited Form Interrogatories, Set One" ("Official Interrogatories") via United States First Class Mail. Please see Plaintiff's "Exhibit 1".

3. On September 26, 2016, the Defendant County of Los Angeles mailed me their "Responses" as all blanket objections to each Official Form Interrogatory with no Verification whatsoever. Please see Plaintiff's "Exhibit 2".

4. On November 4, 2016, the Defendant has served "Further Responses" with no Verification with those Responses. Please see Plaintiff's "Exhibit 11".

5. On November 9, 2016, the Defendant County sent an untimely Verification separately as an attachment and or supplemental response. Please see Plaintiff's "Exhibit 14".

6. On November 28, 2016, at 8:10AM, after review of the Defendant County of Los Angeles' "Further Responses", I emailed Attorney of Record for Defendant County of Los Angeles a Mr. John Coleman Esq., requesting to meet and confer regarding the improper objections and incomplete responses to the Official Form Interrogatories. I informed Mr. Coleman that I would be willing to agree by way of stipulation to provide more time for the Defendant County of Los Angeles to provide further answers. Mr. Coleman replied back to me at 8:37AM, stating that "We will extend your time to file MTC further responses. Let's get this worked out." I replied back to Mr. Coleman that I expect us to have it "worked out" no later than November 30, 2016, in good faith under a duly signed Stipulation. Please see Plaintiff's "Exhibit 15".

STATEMENT OF EVIDENCE

8. On December 2, 2016, I emailed Mr. Coleman, informing him of my final notice to meet and confer with him in good faith before filing this Motion to Compel Further Discovery Responses. Please see Plaintiff's "Exhibit 16".

9. In my email on December 2, 2016, I informed Mr. Coleman that I have not heard from him since November 28, 2016, and it would be unreasonable for me to be waiting for his reply and we should stipulate by December 5, 2016, in order to resolve this discovery matter informally. Please see Plaintiff's "Exhibit 16".

10. On December 5, 2016 at 1:41PM, Mr. Coleman emailed me claiming that him and or his agents had made "numerous" attempts to contact me and that I was failing to "meet and confer" in "good faith" with him. Please see Plaintiff's "Exhibit 17".

11. On December 6, 2016 at 4:57PM, I informed Mr. Coleman by email that I had double checked and verified that I received no such "numerous" calls from him nor his agents as he so claims in his email to me, except for his only reply on November 28, 2016, to me stating that "We will extend [me] time to file MTC further responses". I informed Mr. Coleman that his reply made no sense at all to me and I informed him of that fact. I informed Mr. Coleman that I have operated in good faith since November 28, 2016, in attempting to informally resolve this discovery dispute with him as the Attorney of Record for the Defendant County of Los Angeles. Please see Plaintiff's "Exhibit 17".

12. On December 8, 2016 at 11:57AM, I informed Mr. Coleman via email again that I had verified for certain that I had not received any such "numerous" calls, voicemails, nor even emails from him, as he so claimed. I informed him of the specific interrogatory numbers and brief reasons why that are in dispute.
Please see Plaintiff's "Exhibit 18".

13. On December 8, 2016 at 12:27PM, I provided and drafted a 'separate statement' outlining each Interrogatory in dispute to Mr. Coleman by email. Mr. Coleman never replied back to me. Please see Plaintiff's "Exhibit 18".

14. On December 14, 2016 at 11:40AM, I emailed Mr. Coleman again, requesting to resolve this discovery dispute informally and by way of Stipulation with my drafted separate statement. Please see Plaintiff's "Exhibit 19".

Mr. Coleman never replied back to me. I informed Mr. Coleman that I would have no other choice but to file this Motion to Compel the Defendant's Further Discovery Responses.

15. As a result of the direct failure of the Defendant County of Los Angeles to meet and confer in good faith and to properly Respond to the described discovery above, have incurred ADDITIONAL EXPENSES, the following reasonable expenses $ 24.⁰⁰.

I declare under penalty of perjury under the laws of the State of California that the foregoing is true and correct, on December February 7, 2017, in Long Beach, California.

Luke E Dumas, declarant

STATEMENT OF EVIDENCE

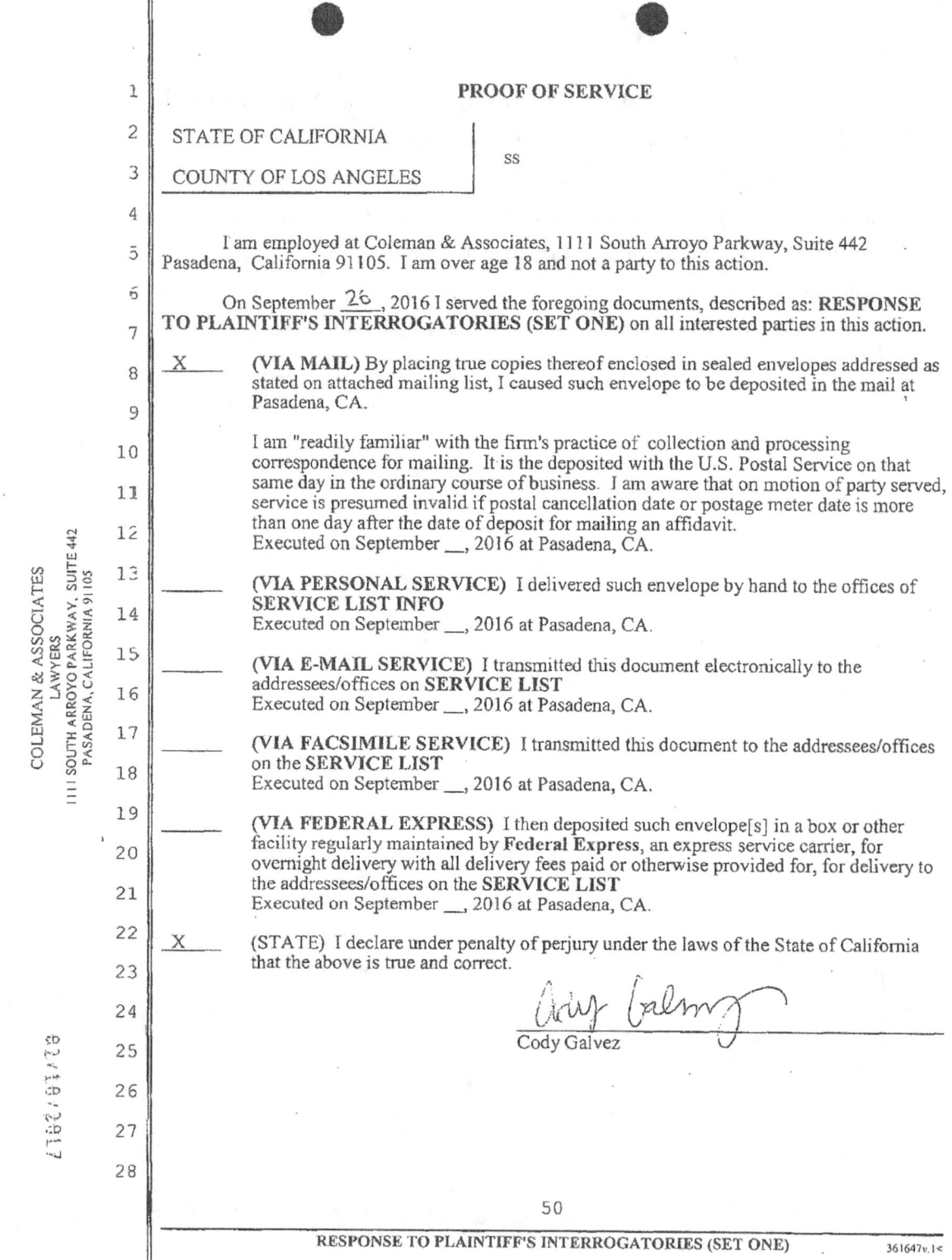

PROOF OF SERVICE

STATE OF CALIFORNIA ss
COUNTY OF LOS ANGELES

I am employed at Coleman & Associates, 1111 South Arroyo Parkway, Suite 442 Pasadena, California 91105. I am over age 18 and not a party to this action.

On September 26, 2016 I served the foregoing documents, described as: **RESPONSE TO PLAINTIFF'S INTERROGATORIES (SET ONE)** on all interested parties in this action.

__X__ **(VIA MAIL)** By placing true copies thereof enclosed in sealed envelopes addressed as stated on attached mailing list, I caused such envelope to be deposited in the mail at Pasadena, CA.

I am "readily familiar" with the firm's practice of collection and processing correspondence for mailing. It is the deposited with the U.S. Postal Service on that same day in the ordinary course of business. I am aware that on motion of party served, service is presumed invalid if postal cancellation date or postage meter date is more than one day after the date of deposit for mailing an affidavit.
Executed on September __, 2016 at Pasadena, CA.

_____ **(VIA PERSONAL SERVICE)** I delivered such envelope by hand to the offices of **SERVICE LIST INFO**
Executed on September __, 2016 at Pasadena, CA.

_____ **(VIA E-MAIL SERVICE)** I transmitted this document electronically to the addressees/offices on **SERVICE LIST**
Executed on September __, 2016 at Pasadena, CA.

_____ **(VIA FACSIMILE SERVICE)** I transmitted this document to the addressees/offices on the **SERVICE LIST**
Executed on September __, 2016 at Pasadena, CA.

_____ **(VIA FEDERAL EXPRESS)** I then deposited such envelope[s] in a box or other facility regularly maintained by **Federal Express**, an express service carrier, for overnight delivery with all delivery fees paid or otherwise provided for, for delivery to the addressees/offices on the **SERVICE LIST**
Executed on September __, 2016 at Pasadena, CA.

__X__ **(STATE)** I declare under penalty of perjury under the laws of the State of California that the above is true and correct.

_____
Cody Galvez

RESPONSE TO PLAINTIFF'S INTERROGATORIES (SET ONE)

Copyright. © 2021. Paralegal Publishing Group.

SERVICE LIST

LUKE E DUMAS v. LOS ANGELES COUNTY BOARD OF SUPERVISORS; THE LOS ANGELES COUNTY SHERIFF'S DEPARTMENT; SHERIFF JIM MCDONNELL

Plaintiff in Pro Per:
Luke E Dumas
5462 E. Del Amo Blvd.
Long Beach, CA, 90808
Tel: (562)356-0492

51

RESPONSE TO PLAINTIFF'S INTERROGATORIES (SET ONE)

Trial Court & Appeal: False Arrest, Imprisonment, and Civil Rights Violations By L.A. County

Dumas v. Los Angeles County Board of Supervisors et al. 45 Cal. App. 5th 348

Subject:	Discovery Requests - Meet and Confer for Case No. BC618191
From:	L Dumas
To:	jmc@coleman-law.com;
Cc:	main@coleman-law.com;
Date:	Wednesday, October 26, 2016 4:25 PM

Dear Mr. Coleman,

I am writing to further inquire as to how much time you are going to need to be able to submit the Defendant County of Los Angeles' answers and responses in full, truthfully, and completely by? Does your client, Los Angeles County, have any intention of answering the Form Interrogatories and Requests for Admissions at all?

This herein serves as evidence of Plaintiff Dumas' efforts to meet and confer with the Defendant Los Angeles County with regards to his discovery requests on around August 21, 2016, that included the Judicial Council's Unlimited Form Interrogatories and Plaintiff's non-form Request for Admission, Set One, before reserving a motion date and filing a motion to compel the discovery responses forthwith.

Please reply back to me via email, thank you.

Regards,

L. Edward Dumas

Copyright. © 2021. Paralegal Publishing Group.

Trial Court & Appeal: False Arrest, Imprisonment, and Civil Rights Violations By L.A. County

Dumas v. Los Angeles County Board of Supervisors et al. 45 Cal. App. 5th 348

Subject:	Notice of Intent to File a Motion to Compel Plaintiff's Discovery Responses
From:	L Dumas
To:	jmc@coleman-law.com;
Cc:	smcintosh@coleman-law.com;
Date:	Saturday, November 5, 2016 4:30 PM

This email correspondence herein memorializes that on August 21, 2016, the Plaintiff Luke Edward Dumas had a person over the age of 18, not a party to this Action, serve the Defendant County of Los Angeles, the Judicial Council Unlimited Civil Form Interrogatories and Request for Admissions to Mr. Coleman, Esq., the County of Los Angeles' Attorney of Record in this legal matter.

On September 26, 2016, the Defendant County of Los Angeles returned their responses to Plaintiff's discovery requests referenced above as all blanket objections to all of the Judicial Council's Unlimited Civil Form Interrogatories, even the Interrogatories that are 'objection proof', and Plaintiff's non-form Request for Admissions as well were not answered at all.

On October 17, 2016, the Plaintiff called Mr. Coleman Esq. to discuss resolving the propounded discovery requests and left a message with his receptionist.

On October 18, 2016, at 11:55AM PST, the Plaintiff, directly emailed Mr. Coleman Esq., Attorney of Record for Defendant Los Angeles County, in order to meet and confer with regard to resolving the incomplete and evasive responses by the Defendant Los Angeles County to the Plaintiff's lawful and valid discovery requests.

On October 26, 2016, at 4:25PM PST, the Plaintiff directly emailed Mr. Coleman Esq. to his email and to his staff at their email at "main@coleman-law.com", further inquiring as to if Defendant County of Los Angeles will properly and truthfully respond before having to file a motion to compel those responses set forth herein.

On October 26, 2016, at 5:31PM PST, Mr. Scott McIntosh acting on behalf of Mr. Coleman Esq., emailed the Plaintiff demanding that the Plaintiff wait until November 9th, 2016 to be served with their "responses", absent a duly executed written Stipulation signed and agreed by all parties; November the 9th of 2016 is the last day to file a motion to compel the sought after Discovery Responses, to file a motion to compel the discovery requests under California law.

On October 27, 2016, at 11:04AM PST, the Plaintiff in pro per emailed Mr. McIntosh requesting that he draft a written Stipulation to that proposal for the parties to agree in writing, in order not to confer nor to waive the Plaintiff's right to compel the Defendant to answer truthfully, completely, and properly in this legal matter.

On October 28, 2016, at 2:26PM PST, Plaintiff Dumas directly emailed Mr. Coleman Esq. and Mr. McIntosh, informing them that it would be unreasonable to make the Plaintiff wait to see if they deliver the Defendant's proper responses until the last day to file a motion to compel the discovery responses in dispute, unless the Defendant County, their Attorney of Record, and the

Copyright. © 2021. Paralegal Publishing Group.

Plaintiff can agree in writing under an executed stipulation signed by both parties, Mr. McIntosh's unilateral demand for the Plaintiff to wait until the last day to file a Civil Procedure is unreasonable, made in bad faith, and is a litigation tactic in order to suppress the Truth.

On October 28, 2016, at 4:05PM PST, Mr. McIntosh, directly emailed the Plaintiff, and acting in bad faith and under false pretenses stated that the Defendant County of Los Angeles and the Plaintiff L. Edward Dumas have a "stipulation/agreement" between them, in which they do not have a "stipulation/agreement" properly executed in writing signed and dated by both parties in blue or black ink.

On October 29, 2016, the Plaintiff emailed the Defendants' Attorneys of Record, Mr. Coleman and Mr. McIntosh, and informed them that the Plaintiff and the Defendant have NO current agreement and NO current Stipulation in writing and signed by both parties, therefore the Plaintiff has not agreed to wait to November the 9th of 2016, in which is the same date as the Case Management Conference in Department 61 in Central District - LASC. Plaintiff informed the Defendant's attorney of record that he would wait until November 4, 2016 by 5:00PM PST to receive the responses and or answers from the Defendant County before filing a motion to compel those responses.

Truthfully,

L. Edward Dumas
Plaintiff in pro per

Trial Court & Appeal: False Arrest, Imprisonment, and Civil Rights Violations By L.A. County

Dumas v. Los Angeles County Board of Supervisors et al. 45 Cal. App. 5th 348

Print

Subject: Dumas v. County of Los Angeles
From: L Dumas
To: jmc@coleman-law.com;
Date: Monday, November 7, 2016 9:27 PM

Dear Mr. Coleman Esq.,

I am writing just to be clear to you and your client, my County Government, that in your letter dated on September 26, 2016, as you were acting on the County's behalf; you stated that "County will provide further responses to these Discovery Requests as provided by the Code of Civil Procedure".

However, you only contacted me once through **one** letter, then on October 26, 2016, you had a Mr. Scott McIntosh email me directly to tell me to wait until November the 9th of 2016, in which I did not agree with, absent a duly executed written stipulation made in good faith by all parties as provided by the "Code of Civil Procedure".
So I replied directly to him to ask if he would be willing to draft a Stipulation to what exactly he was proposing to me and demanding me to take as his Offer. My question was evaded, misrepresented, and disregarded in bad faith by Mr. McIntosh in his reply to me.

On October 28, 2016, I emailed you and your agent, Mr. McIntosh, that it would be unreasonable to keep me waiting until November the 9th of 2016, as he says on your behalf; and without a duly executed agreement as provided by the "Code of Civil Procedure".

Later that day, at 4:05PM PST, Mr. McIntosh directly emailed me and stated that you and I already have a "stipulation/agreement" between us, in which is not true, we do not have a duly executed written stipulation or agreement in writing as provided by the "Code of Civil Procedure".

You have only contacted me once by letter dated September 26, 2016, and then you sent Mr. McIntosh to inform me that "we have a "stipulation/agreement", and Mr. McIntosh claims, acting on your behalf, that your law firm is "requesting an Extension to respond to [my] discovery. . ." but you have failed in good faith to put it forth in writing as a duly executed and lawful written agreement provided by the Code of Civil Procedure.

As you stated so vaguely in your letter dated "September 26, 2016, "County will provide further responses to these Discovery Requests as provided by the Code of Civil Procedure". However, as you should know that the "Code of Civil Procedure" make mandatory that the responses you answered on behalf of the County in part was not properly verified as provided by the "Code of Civil Procedure".

So if we have a duly executed "stipulation/agreement" in writing signed by us, as Mr. McIntosh claims then where exactly is it? And why did I not get a copy sir? Because I do not recall signing a "stipulation/agreement" to provide me with truthful, complete, and full answers as provided by the "Code of Civil Procedure", in which you allege my County government will provide me with, which has actually very misleading by your firm.

Copyright. © 2021. Paralegal Publishing Group.

I look forward to resolving the Discovery Dispute in regards to this legal matter, and as you know I made numerous good faith attempts in order to put it forth in a real legal duly executed written Stipulation to resolve the non-compliant and evasive responses I have been served with. Furthermore, as to what your staff has put forth on behalf of the County of Los Angeles, it is like you never served me with any responses on their behalf at all.

Now Mr. McIntosh takes the road-less traveled and decides to lie about us having a "stipulation/agreement", therefore if I am misunderstanding you sir, then please explain why you did not want to resolve this Discovery dispute in a timely fashion, now I have no choice but to put forth a Motion to Compel the Discovery Responses I served you with on August 21, 2016. I am simply writing you sir as a courtesy in good faith pursuant to the truth, and to see if you really mean what you say in your letter dated September 26, 2016, in which was actually about 42 days ago since we last touched base.

Furthermore, please be advised that I have not received anything in the mail as of today, with regard to your statement in your letter to me that the "County will provide further responses..", so please sir, if so when?

Please note, the way your law firm returned the Judicial Council Form Interrogatories and to my non-form pleading Requests for Admissions, served concurrently forthwith; it was actually like if you never responded to any of the Discovery Requests at all, as provided by the Code of Civil Procedure.

Therefore, a Motion to Compel Discovery Responses are in order and must be filed to preserve my right to obtain lawful discovery with regards to this legal matter.

Truthfully,

L. Edward Dumas

Trial Court & Appeal: False Arrest, Imprisonment, and Civil Rights Violations By L.A. County

Dumas v. Los Angeles County Board of Supervisors et al. 45 Cal. App. 5th 348

Subject:	Final Notice for Meet & Confer Further Responses to Form Interrogatories, Set One
From:	L Dumas
To:	jmc@coleman-law.com;
Cc:	main@coleman-law.com;
Date:	Friday, December 2, 2016 11:50 AM

Dear Mr. Coleman Esq.,

I am corresponding to you as final notice with regards to the meet and confer requirements regarding resolving the Further Responses to the Judicial Council's Unlimited Form Interrogatories, Set One, for case number BC618191 in the matter of Dumas v. County of Los Angeles in Department 61, at the Stanley Mosk Courthouse, assigned for all purposes to the Honorable Judge Gregory Keosian.

I have not heard from you as of to date, further with regard to Stipulating in writing so your client, Los Angeles County, can have an additional 30 days to submit those Further Responses to me as part of the Discovery Process in this legal matter; nevertheless in good faith this is my final and last attempt before having to file a Motion to Compel Further Discovery Responses to the Judicial Council's Unlimited Form Interrogatories, Set One since I have not heard from you since November 28, 2016, in my good faith attempts to resolve this specific dispute.

No further notices shall be provided to you before filing this Motion because it would not be reasonable to keep me waiting until the statutory time expires unless we can agree by Stipulation before Monday, December 5, 2016, no later than 4:30PM. I look forward to hearing from you and setting forth a proper agreement to provide complete, non-evasive, and truthful Answers and Responses to the Judicial Council's Unlimited Form Interrogatories, Set One.

Thank you for your prompt attention to this matter, please have a great day.

Regards,

L. Edward Dumas

Copyright. © 2021. Paralegal Publishing Group.

Trial Court & Appeal: False Arrest, Imprisonment, and Civil Rights Violations By L.A. County

Dumas v. Los Angeles County Board of Supervisors et al. 45 Cal. App. 5th 348

Title Three Rules

http://www.courts.ca.gov/cms/rules/index.cfm?title=three&linkid=rule...

2017 California Rules of Court

Rule 3.1306. Evidence at hearing

(a) Restrictions on oral testimony

Evidence received at a law and motion hearing must be by declaration or request for judicial notice without testimony or cross-examination, unless the court orders otherwise for good cause shown.

(Subd (a) amended effective January 1, 2007; previously amended effective January 1, 2003.)

(b) Request to present oral testimony

A party seeking permission to introduce oral evidence, except for oral evidence in rebuttal to oral evidence presented by the other party, must file, no later than three court days before the hearing, a written statement stating the nature and extent of the evidence proposed to be introduced and a reasonable time estimate for the hearing. When the statement is filed less than five court days before the hearing, the filing party must serve a copy on the other parties in a manner to assure delivery to the other parties no later than two days before the hearing.

(Subd (b) amended and relettered effective January 1, 2003; adopted as part of subd (a).)

(c) Judicial notice

A party requesting judicial notice of material under Evidence Code sections 452 or 453 must provide the court and each party with a copy of the material. If the material is part of a file in the court in which the matter is being heard, the party must:

(1) Specify in writing the part of the court file sought to be judicially noticed; and

(2) Either make arrangements with the clerk to have the file in the courtroom at the time of the hearing or confirm with the clerk that the file is electronically accessible to the court.

(Subd (c) amended effective January 1, 2017; adopted as subd (b); previously amended and relettered effective January 1, 2003; previously amended effective January 1, 2007.)

Rule 3.1306 amended effective January 1, 2017; adopted as rule 323 effective January 1, 1984; previously amended effective January 1, 2003; previously amended and renumbered as rule 3.1306 effective January 1, 2007.

Copyright. © 2021. Paralegal Publishing Group.

PROOF OF SERVICE

STATE OF CALIFORNIA
} ss
COUNTY OF LOS ANGELES

I am employed at Coleman & Associates, 1111 South Arroyo Parkway, Suite 442 Pasadena, California 91105. I am over age 18 and not a party to this action.

On ~~January~~ February 1st, 2017 I served the foregoing documents, described as: **RESPONSE AND OPPOSITION TO PLAINTIFF'S SEPARATE STATEMENT RE: MOTION TO COMPEL FURTHER RESPONSES TO FORM INTERROGATORIES, SET ONE** on all interested parties in this action.

____ **(VIA MAIL)** By placing true copies thereof enclosed in sealed envelopes addressed as stated on attached mailing list, I caused such envelope to be deposited in the mail at Pasadena, CA.

I am "readily familiar" with the firm's practice of collection and processing correspondence for mailing. It is the deposited with the U.S. Postal Service on that same day in the ordinary course of business. I am aware that on motion of party served, service is presumed invalid if postal cancellation date or postage meter date is more than one day after the date of deposit for mailing an affidavit.
Executed on January __, 2017 at Pasadena, CA.

____ **(VIA PERSONAL SERVICE)** I delivered such envelope by hand to the offices of **SERVICE LIST INFO**
Executed on January __, 2017 at Pasadena, CA.

____ **(VIA E-MAIL SERVICE)** I transmitted this document electronically to the addressees/offices on **SERVICE LIST**
Executed on January __, 2017 at Pasadena, CA.

____ **(VIA FACSIMILE SERVICE)** I transmitted this document to the addressees/offices on the **SERVICE LIST**
Executed on January __, 2017 at Pasadena, CA.

 X   **(VIA FEDERAL EXPRESS)** I then deposited such envelope[s] in a box or other facility regularly maintained by **Federal Express**, an express service carrier, for overnight delivery with all delivery fees paid or otherwise provided for, for delivery to the addressees/offices on the **SERVICE LIST**
Executed on ~~January~~ February 1, 2017 at Pasadena, CA.

 X   **(STATE)** I declare under penalty of perjury under the laws of the State of California that the above is true and correct.

Oliva Robles

RESPONSE AND OPPOSITION TO PLAINTIFF'S SEPARATE STATEMENT RE: MOTION TO COMPEL FURTHER RESPONSES TO FORM INTERROGATORIES, SET ONE

PROOF OF SERVICE

STATE OF CALIFORNIA) ss
COUNTY OF LOS ANGELES)

I am employed at Coleman & Associates, 1111 South Arroyo Parkway, Suite 442 Pasadena, California 91105. I am over age 18 and not a party to this action.

On ~~January~~ February 1st, 2017 I served the foregoing documents, described as: **OPPOSITION TO PLAINTIFF'S MOTION TO COMPEL FURTHER RESPONSES TO INTERROGATORIES, SET ONE** on all interested parties in this action.

____ **(VIA MAIL)** By placing true copies thereof enclosed in sealed envelopes addressed as stated on attached mailing list, I caused such envelope to be deposited in the mail at Pasadena, CA.

I am "readily familiar" with the firm's practice of collection and processing correspondence for mailing. It is the deposited with the U.S. Postal Service on that same day in the ordinary course of business. I am aware that on motion of party served, service is presumed invalid if postal cancellation date or postage meter date is more than one day after the date of deposit for mailing an affidavit.
Executed on January __, 2017 at Pasadena, CA.

____ **(VIA PERSONAL SERVICE)** I delivered such envelope by hand to the offices of **SERVICE LIST INFO**
Executed on January __, 2017 at Pasadena, CA.

____ **(VIA E-MAIL SERVICE)** I transmitted this document electronically to the addressees/offices on **SERVICE LIST**
Executed on January __, 2017 at Pasadena, CA.

____ **(VIA FACSIMILE SERVICE)** I transmitted this document to the addressees/offices on the **SERVICE LIST**
Executed on January __, 2017 at Pasadena, CA.

__X__ **(VIA FEDERAL EXPRESS)** I then deposited such envelope[s] in a box or other facility regularly maintained by **Federal Express**, an express service carrier, for overnight delivery with all delivery fees paid or otherwise provided for, for delivery to the addressees/offices on the **SERVICE LIST**
Executed on ~~January~~ February 1, 2017 at Pasadena, CA.

__X__ **(STATE)** I declare under penalty of perjury under the laws of the State of California that the above is true and correct.

_____
Oliva Robles

OPPOSITION TO PLAINTIFF'S MOTION TO COMPEL FURTHER RESPONSES TO INTERROGATORIES, SET ONE   366900

SUPERIOR COURT OF CALIFORNIA, COUNTY OF LOS ANGELES

DATE: 02/15/17	DEPT. 61
HONORABLE GREGORY KEOSIAN, JUDGE	L. WOODS, DEPUTY CLERK
HONORABLE #9, JUDGE PRO TEM	ELECTRONIC RECORDING MONITOR
N. ALVARADO, C.A., Deputy Sheriff	NONE, Reporter

9:01 am BC618191

LUKE E DUMAS ET AL
VS
LOS ANGELES COUNTY BOARD OF SUPERVISORS ET AL

Plaintiff Counsel: LUKE E DUMAS (PP)
Defendant Counsel: W. SCOTT MCINTOSH (X)

NATURE OF PROCEEDINGS:

MOTION BY PLAINTIFF IN PRO PER LUKE E. DUMAS, TO COMPEL DEFENDANT'S FURTHER DISCOVERY RESPONSES AND FOR MONETARY SANCTIONS;

The Court issues a tentative ruling and the matter is called for hearing.

Defendants submit to the Court's tentative ruling.

Argument is heard from the parties.

The Court adopts the tentative ruling as its Order. Order is signed and filed this date and incorporated herein by reference.

Plaintiff's Motion to Compel Further Responses to Form Interrogatories is denied. Plaintiff's request for sanctions is denied.

Notice is deemed waived.

MINUTES ENTERED
02/15/17
COUNTY CLERK

[Court clerk certification stamp, APR 21 2017, D. WILDE]

CHAPTER 4
Statement of Disqualification of Judicial Officer

There are two ways to disqualify a Judicial Officer, Judge, or Commissioner in the California Courts. One way is by a "Peremptory Challenge to a Judicial Officer by using the California's judicial council form found on its website. The other way is under Code of Civil Procedure Section §170.3, by drafting a non-form pleading under oath. I have included an example and actual real document in this legal case that was filed by the Plaintiff. If you look at the entire Code of Civil Procedure governing judicial disqualifications, you will find that the judicial officer and clerk is supposed to schedule a hearing before the presiding judge of the court on the merits of the disqualification. In this case, no one from the Los Angeles Superior Court – Stanley Mosk Courthouse had followed the rule of law. The Court of Appeal ignored the legal procedure for error and the rest of the facts regarding the sabotage, bribery, and or racism institutionalized by the California Courts. The California courts are against Mexican-American males and often target us for incarceration, oppression, and treat us as second-class citizens. Read the filed Disqualification and format it to fit your own case in pro per, or your client's case.

Luke E Dumas

Plaintiff in pro per

RECEIVED JAN 19 2018 DEPT. 61

CONFORMED COPY ORIGINAL FILED
Superior Court of California
County of Los Angeles
JAN 23 2018
Sherri R. Carter, Executive Officer/Clerk
By LaTrina Woods, Deputy

SUPERIOR COURT OF THE STATE OF CALIFORNIA
COUNTY OF LOS ANGELES - CENTRAL DISTRICT
STANLEY MOSK COURTHOUSE

Luke E Dumas, an individual, Plaintiff, v. Los Angeles County Board of Supervisors, a public entity; the Los Angeles County Sherriff's Department, a public entity; Sheriff Jim McDonnell, a public official; and DOES 1-10, inclusive, Defendants.	Case No.: BC618191 [*Objection* to the Assigned for all purposes to the Honorable Judge Gregory Keosian, Dept. 61] **PLAINTIFF IN PRO PER'S VERIFIED STATEMENT OF DISQUALIFICATION OF ASSIGNED JUDGE GREGORY KEOSIAN** **Judge:** Hon. Judge Gregory Keosian **Trial Date:** February 13, 2018 **Time:** 8:30AM **Place:** Department 61 **Location:** Stanley Mosk Courthouse **Date Action Filed:** April 26, 2016 **JURY TRIAL DEMANDED** **UNLIMITED CIVIL CASE**

//

Luke E Dumas

Plaintiff in pro per

SUPERIOR COURT OF THE STATE OF CALIFORNIA

COUNTY OF LOS ANGELES - CENTRAL DISTRICT

STANLEY MOSK COURTHOUSE

Luke E Dumas, an individual, Plaintiff, v. Los Angeles County Board of Supervisors, a public entity; the Los Angeles County Sherriff's Department, a public entity; Sheriff Jim McDonnell, a public official;	Case No.: BC618191 [*Objection* to the Assigned for all purposes to the Honorable Judge Gregory Keosian, Dept. 61] **PLAINTIFF IN PRO PER'S VERIFIED STATEMENT OF DISQUALIFICATION OF ASSIGNED JUDGE GREGORY KEOSIAN** Judge: Hon. Judge Gregory Keosian Trial Date: February 13, 2018 Time: 8:30AM Place: Department 61 Location: Stanley Mosk Courthouse Date Action Filed: April 26, 2016

Copyright. © 2021. Paralegal Publishing Group.

and DOES 1-10, inclusive,

Defendants.

**JURY TRIAL DEMANDED
UNLIMITED CIVIL CASE**

_____

TO THE LOS ANGELES SUPERIOR COURT, JUDGE GREGORY KEOSIAN, AND TO ALL PARTIES AND TO THEIR ATTORNEYS OF RECORD:

I, Luke Edward Dumas, hereby declare:

1. I am the Plaintiff in propria persona, Luke Edward Dumas, (hereinafter "Plaintiff"); and in good faith Opposition to the Assignment of the Hon. Judge Gregory Keosian (herein "Judge Keosian").

2. I now state and allege in this Verified Statement of Disqualification that Judge Gregory Keosian of the Los Angeles Superior Court for the County of Los Angeles in and for the State of California, is in fact prejudiced against the Plaintiff.

3. Judge Keosian has acted with unjust unlawful oppression and suppression of the Plaintiff's legal rights in favor of the Defendant Los Angeles County Board of Supervisors ("County Government").

4. Judge Keosian is hereby disqualified from presiding further in this case under California **Code of Civil Procedure Section §170.3**.

5. Judge Keosian has acted with abuse of power, disregard for the rule of California law; Judge Keosian has acted with unlawful prejudice and bias against the Plaintiff because he is in propria persona; and Judge Keosian harbors anti-civil rights sentiments, unjustly denies due process of law; and Judge Keosian unjustly favors the Defendant County Government over civil rights and aids the Defendant County Government in suppressing civil rights and under the rules of fair litigation.

6. Judge Keosian has suppressed the Plaintiff in pro per's right to due process of law simply because he is not a lawyer and has acted with prejudice against the Plaintiff in pro per. The Judge Keosian has abused his power and misused his authority specifically against the Plaintiff in pro per.

7. The Judge Keosian denies the Plaintiff his right to due process, right to lawful discovery, right to be free from continued and continuous unreasonable search and seizure by the Defendant County Government in violation of the rule of law. Judge Keosian abuses his power and own governmental authority and has acted with common design and or directly conspired with the Defendant County Government's attorney of record to rubberstamp a sham declaration in order to deny the Plaintiff in pro per his right to due process and civil discovery in violation of California law.

8. The Judge Keosian, a former lawyer now an "elected-judge' knew or should have known that the Defendant County Government's attorney of record was lying under oath in his declaration because the Plaintiff in pro per had verbally informed Judge Keosian in person at the law and motion hearing on about February 15, 2017, at about 9:00AM.

9. The Defendant County Government's attorney Mr. Scott McIntosh lied and the Judge Keosian had knew about it and lend him a helping hand.

10. So Judge Keosian still denied the Plaintiff in pro per his legal right to lawful discovery in this case in order to help the County Government further suppress the evidence of their civil rights violations.

11. The Judge Keosian, as a practice, grants and approves California licensed lawyers' motions to compel judicial council civil discovery forms as a matter of right but has denied the Plaintiff in pro per his legal right.

12. The Judge Keosian has acted in conspiracy with the Defendant County Government in order to set up the Plaintiff's case for failure. The Judge Keosian has with common design or directly ensured that the Plaintiff in pro per is denied his legal rights during the course of this litigation against the County Government. Judge Keosian has no interest in justice nor has any interest in the truth and supports the County Government's attorneys lying under oath in order to get away with false arrest and for false imprisonment of the Plaintiff in pro per.

13. The Judge Keosian, acting as an official judicial officer as a "Judge of the Los Angeles Superior Court for the County of Los Angeles" has acted with impropriety, an abuse of discretion, an abuse of power, misuse of official governmental state power as the judicial branch of government.

CONFLICT OF INTERESTS, JUDICIAL CORRUPTION, AND UNLAWFUL COMPENSATION

14. The Judge Gregory Keosian may have a conflict of interest by receiving or have received unlawful supplemental benefit payments from the County Government, which has tantamount to bribery[1].

---

[1] See https://www.judicialwatch.org/press-room/press-releases/judicial-watch files-taxpayer-suit-against-los-angeles-county-to-end-illegal-supplemental-judicial-benefits-to-superior-court-judges/; See https://www.dailykos.com/stories/2017/2/9/1631775/-The-Dirty-Truth-Behind-California-s-400-Million-of-Supplemental-Judicial-Benefits; See https://medicalkidnap.com/2016/06/13/la-county-bribing-judges-declared-illegal-but-who-will-uphold-justice-in-la/

15. If Judge Keosian had accepted the declared unlawful payments from the Defendant County Government then he had violated the California Constitution and the public trust. But make no mistake, the California Legislature changed the law and gave their own rubberstamp on misprisoning felonies committed by Los Angeles County Superior Court Judges, which gave them special immunity from prosecution under California law, see **Senate Bill No. 11 Chapter 9; Government Code Section 68220, 68221, 68222**. As duly noted without public debate or awareness the California "Judicial Council" conspired with the California Legislature to enact a provision to grant Los Angeles Superior Court judges like Gregory Keosian and County Government officials retroactive immunity from criminal prosecution[2].

16. Judge Keosian is no fair and impartial judge when it comes to litigating against the Defendant County Government for their civil rights violations.

17. Judge Keosian believes in superiority and inferiority complexes, which help fuel the Los Angeles County Board of Supervisors' civil rights violations. Judge Keosian reduces the State of California to liken a third world dictator inwhere no citizen can get fair and impartial trial against their Government, and completely disregards to the U.S. Constitutional provision for an individual citizen to "Petition Their Government for Grievances".

18. Because under Judge Gregory Keosian, he denies the right to petition the County Government for grievances.

19. Judge Gregory Keosian has only allowed the Plaintiff's Complaint to partially stand and stay active in order for the Defendant County Government's counsel of record, the "Coleman & Associates" law firm, to make $150.00 dollars an hour off of County of Los Angeles taxpayer money. Because it is very suspicious and

---

[2] http://www.tulanelink.com/tulanelink/sturgeon_box.htm

Copyright. © 2021. Paralegal Publishing Group.

prejudicial for a Judge of the Superior Court, with all of their law school training and ten year requirement as a law practitioner by governmental standards to be ignoring fundamental rules of law, substantial rights of parties, and due process of law.

20. Judge Gregory Keosian is oppressive, covers up lies, ignores the truth, and permits the Defendant County Government to violate rules of law. Judge Gregory Keosian makes it a policy to rule against the impoverished self-represented Mexican-American litigants such as the Plaintiff in favor of the Defendant County Government.

21. Judge Keosian today represents the history of oppression of ethnic minorities in the United States of America and in the State of California and has failed in his duty to be upholding the legal rights and civil liberties of the impoverished self-represented Mexican-American male with Native North American descent in favor of fascism, racism, and civil rights violations.

22. The Honorable Stanley Mosk who stood up for legal civil rights of the Plaintiff is turning in his grave because of corrupt Judges like Gregory Keosian.

23. Judge Keosian helps the County Government suppress civil rights, evidence, and violates the public trust. For example, it is common knowledge among law professors and law practitioners that a party is entitled to civil discovery but Judge Keosian has only allowed the Defendant County Government, aided by their attorney in their own personal capacities to conduct whatever kind of so-called "discovery" they want, even as far as going into the Plaintiff in pro per's private life and medical records from about 20 years ago, something totally unrelated to this civil case for damages for civil rights violations.

24. So Judge Keosian has authorized unlawful discovery in this case. Therefore, Judge Gregory Keosian is acting corruptly and cannot afford the Plaintiff a fair and impartial trial.

25. The Plaintiff as a Mexican-American legal citizen of the State of California and of the United States of America has been afforded no legal rights under the governmental authority of Judge Gregory Keosian in Department 61, 7th Floor, at the Stanley Mosk Courthouse, Los Angeles Superior Court - Central District. Stanley Mosk Courthouse is misrepresented by Judge Gregory Keosian.

26. The judicial branch of Government is poorly represented by the crooked, prejudicial, and oppressive Judge Gregory Keosian. Judge Keosian is only concerned with advancing his own political agenda[3].

27. This is a public policy and original concern.

28. The Plaintiff as a Mexican American citizen is being unjustly denied his legal rights because the agenda of Judge Gregory Keosian is to oppress him in his very own native land and country. Judge Gregory Keosian's corrupt performance in this legal case is now exposed and the Plaintiff has a right to an immediate assignment to a judicial officer with no racist, oppressive, or non-American agenda.

29. Since Judge Gregory Keosian is a racist and oppresses Mexican American males in their own Homeland, it is no wonder why he allows the racist Los Angeles County Sherriff's Department to get away with civil rights violations[4].

30. It is no wonder why Judge Gregory Keosian allows the Plaintiff's medical records and medical privacy to be violated in violation of California and Federal law.

---

[3] https://anca.org/judges-zaven-sinanian-and-greg-keosian-to-receive-top-honors-at-armenian-bars-judges-night/
[4] http://beta.latimes.com/local/california/la-me-sheriff-burbank-emails-20160427-story.html

31. When a Judge of the Superior Court acts corruptly, abuses power, misprisons felonies, in the form of a legal and or illegal bribe from the County Government and or their agents, then the California taxpayers have a right to know and there needs to be a change.

32. The simple change is for the legal disqualification of the Judge Gregory Keosian in this case and to simply assign a judicial officer with high ethics, high morals, and the utmost interest in the rules of law.

33. If Judge Gregory Keosian wants to play politics and disregard rules of law then the public needs to know; if the supervising judges of the superior court and judicial branch of government do nothing in order and aid the cover-up of all the County Government corruption then the judicial branch of Government is broken.

34. The overall problem, if corrupt and oppressive Gregory Keosian is permitted to preside on this case; then the question begs: Is the judicial branch of government as a self-regulated industry, devoid of distributing any kind of authentic justice for the natural born citizens of the State?

35. In this instant case, Judge Keosian continues to violate the Constitution, rule of law, and further divides the trust of the public from the judicial branch of government because he cannot afford the Plaintiff a fair trial.

36. Under Judge Keosian, the Los Angeles Superior Court is acting under the color of law, furthering negating civil rights abuses by the County of Los Angeles, enabling the County Government to act with corruption, and Judge Gregory Keosian is getting paid $181,292 of taxpayer dollars or more for it.

37. This is why the County Government is granted their requests for unlawful orders from Judge Keosian and why the Plaintiff in pro per is denied his requests for lawful orders from Judge Keosian in this instant case.

38. In fact this is why the County Government consistently gets away with false arrest, false imprisonment, discrimination, civil rights abuses, and privacy violations because of corrupt judicial officers such as Judge Gregory Keosian.

39. In fact, statistics have shown that the Los Angeles Superior Court for the County of Los Angeles is in fact corrupt and favors the County Government over individual civil liberties and civil rights[5].

40. Judge Keosian proves the point in this case that the Los Angeles Superior Court allows the County Government to violate the rule of law, due process of law, and to violates the State and Federal Constitutions.

41. Judge Keosian is a barrier and obstacle to ensuring that natural born Californian and Mexican-American citizens such as the Plaintiff in pro per are provided a fair and impartial trial; are provided their right to lawful and relevant discovery, and to due process of law under the rule of law in favor of civil rights litigation.

42. Judge Keosian, whom earns $181,292 a year for Office 87 of the Los Angeles County Superior Court does not care about California citizens or Mexican-Americans' legal rights and right to due process of law but takes tax money for himself and denies Mexican-Americans their legal rights.[6]

43. The Judge Keosian has intentionally failed to personify the embodiment of California law by making sure that the Government suppresses all of the available and potentially admissible evidence in this case.

44. The Judge Keosian has made it his official policy in this legal case for false arrest, false imprisonment, unlawful discrimination, and violations of California

---

[5] https://healthimpactnews.com/2016/la-county-bribing-judges-declared-illegal-but-who-will-uphold-justice-in-la/

[6] https://ballotpedia.org/Gregory_Keosian

law. Judge Keosian has helped the Defendant County Government to deny the Plaintiff his right to due process of law and admissible evidence in order to tip the scales of justice in favor of the Defendant County Government.

45. The Judge Keosian has ensured that this instant case for civil rights is a loser for the Plaintiff in pro per.

46. The Judge Keosian has ensured that the Defendant County Government can violate the Plaintiff in pro per's constitutional rights by unlawfully obtaining medical information from about 20 years ago that was never related to this instant case! How corrupt is that? What law professor teaches their students to violate a person's privacy? Only a corrupt one, someone like Judge Gregory Keosian.

47. The Judge Keosian, acting with evil intent and malice, has given the County Government a greenlight to violate his personal medical data from last century and the Plaintiff's medical information is a privacy violation and totally unrelated to this case.

48. The Judge Keosian is misprisoning another felony and his Orders are void and unlawful under California law.

49. The Judge Keosian is in cohorts with John Coleman and his associates, have allowed the Plaintiff in pro per's right to privacy to be violated in favor of the Defendant County Government.

50. Judge Keosian has an official unwritten policy of giving the Government whatever it wants regardless of California law and under the State and Federal Constitution.

51. Judge Keosian has taken the lesser road, conspires to deny right to fair and impartial litigation because of the Plaintiff in pro per's self representation, in forma

paupris, Mexican-American male with Native North American descent, and because he is disabled.

52. Judge Keosian has taken advantage of the Plaintiff as an ethnic minority attempting to exercise his legal civil rights under California law and under the Constitutions of the State of California and of the United States of America.

53. Under appointed and elected official for District 87 for the Superior Court for the County of Los Angeles, no justice can be properly, fairly, and impartially delivered by Judge Gregory Keosian.

54. Under the judicial watch of Gregory Keosian, the Defendant County Government is allowed to violate civil rights, violate due process of law, violate the right to privacy of the Plaintiff, and grant "orders" based on sham declaration(s).

55. Judge Keosian allows the Government to violate the Constitution's and laws of the State of California and the United States of America.

56. Judge Keosian has acted with bias with respect to the Plaintiff's legal rights in the State of California and under the color of law.

57. Therefore the Judge Keosian cannot afford a fair and impartial trial to the Plaintiff at all and has ensured that the Plaintiff is disadvantaged and has tipped the scales of justice in favor of the Defendant County of Los Angeles for no lawful reason at all.

58. In fact the Judge Keosian has not provided the Plaintiff access to due process of law, and in his judicial capacity will in no way afford the Plaintiff a fair and impartial trial under the laws of and for the State of California and under the Federal Constitution of the United States of America.

59. The Judge Keosian has dishonored the judicial branch of government by allowing "officers of the court" to falsify their declaration(s) in order to obtain the Judge Keosian granting unlawful orders; and has acted with bias in order to violate the Plaintiff's right to due process.

60. The Judge Keosian is disqualified from hearing the above-entitled matter as a rule of law because he has allowed, aided, and abetted the Defendant County Government and their attorney of record Mr. Scott McIntosh Esq. to set forth false information under penalty of perjury in order to deny the Plaintiff his right to due process and fair litigation under the rule of law in the State of California and under the **U.S. Constitution**.

61. The Judge Keosian has no interest in justice in this case for civil rights; Judge Keosian has no interest in enforcing the rule of law on false imprisonment and false arrest in the State of California but accepts the taxpayer's money.

62. The Judge Keosian has not been a fair and impartial Judge for the State of California with respect to this instant case because he has intentionally, with bias and prejudice, omitted the Plaintiff's pleading in the Motion to Strike on August 10, 2016 at 9:00AM.

63. The Judge Keosian has intentionally acted with bias by disregarding the fact that the Plaintiff did submit timely Opposition to the Defendant's Motion to Strike on July 28, 2016.

64. The Judge Keosian's actions were not simply erroneous but conspired by common design or by direct knowledge that he, Judge Keosian, knew that he had omitted the Plaintiff Opposition pleading.

65. The Judge Keosian is against the Plaintiff's interest in this case and is against private citizens exercising their legal rights against the Defendant County Government.

66. Judge Keosian adds to the corruption and racist institutional policies set forth by the Defendant County Government and by their attorney of record. Judge Keosian has acted with bias and prejudice against the Plaintiff because the Plaintiff is in propria persona and in forma paupris.

67. Judge Keosian uses his court as bully pulpit in favor of the Defendant County Government so he can help cover-up the Defendant County Government's civil rights abuses and legal violations.

68. Judge Keosian is not interested in the truth at all and has acted with prejudice and bias against the Plaintiff in pro per in order to suppress his civil rights and right to fair and impartial litigation practices in this instant case.

69. For example, in the law and motion on August 10, 2016, the Plaintiff specifically brought the fact to Judge Keosian's attention that he omitted the Plaintiff pleading Opposition. The Plaintiff brought the direct fact to Judge Keosian's immediate attention.

70. The Judge Keosian stated directly to the Plaintiff that he would look at it, and then picked up the Plaintiff's Opposition pleading for less than one minute, quickly flipped through the pages, and then threw it back down onto the table and looked up at the Plaintiff and carelessly stated "Anything else?".

72. The Judge Keosian has acted unlawfully against the Plaintiff as a self-represented litigant in forma paupris and has intentionally suppressed the Plaintiff's right to due process under California law and under the color of law.

Copyright. © 2021. Paralegal Publishing Group.

73. Judge Keosian affords Mexican-American males who are in propria persona and in forma paupris no legal rights whatsoever in the California court system.

74. For example, on 2/15/2017, Defendant County Government's attorney of record has perjured himself in a Declaration submitted on February 1, 2017, for the law and motion hearing held on February 15, 2017.

75. The Judge Keosian has allowed the Defendant County of Los Angeles to operate above the rule of law, to commit perjury in their Declaration to the Superior Court in order to obtain a court order from the Judge Keosian on about February 15, 2017.

76. The Judge Keosian's actions of prejudicial conduct and abuse of discretion is good cause for disqualification under California **Code of Civil Procedure Section 170.3**.

77. The Judge Keosian has aided the Defendant's attorney of record Mr. Scott McIntosh Esq. to commit perjury and lie under oath in a Declaration on February 15, 2017.

78. The Judge Keosian Gregory Keosian has disqualified himself by intentionally oppressing the legal rights of the Plaintiff; the Judge Keosian has acted with malice, aiding lawyers in committing felonies like John Coleman and Scott McIntosh, and single-handedly has unlawfully denied the Plaintiff's rights to due process of law, and has rights guaranteed under the in their Declaration to obtain an Order against the Plaintiff; the Judge Keosian has misprisoned a felony by allowing and permitting the Defendant's attorney to commit perjury in his courtroom and in this case; the Judge Keosian will not nor has not provided the Plaintiff with the opportunity to be heard and the Judge Keosian has denied the Plaintiff due process under the law. The Judge Keosian consistently ignores the Plaintiff's pleadings and under California law.

79. Gregory Keosian was first a private attorney of California law, then became a Judge Keosian by virtue of appointment by California's 37th Governor Grey Davis (D) in 2002. In 2003 Gov. Grey Davis was recalled and removed from office. Gov. Davis was also another private attorney before he was removed from the California's Governor Office.

80. Judge Gregory Keosian has 15 years in position with an annual salary of about $181, 292 paid by the taxpayers of the State of California such as the Plaintiff.

Judge Keosian ran unopposed in the election for 'Office 87' of the Los Angeles County Superior Court. Judge Keosian's name did not appear on the ballot and Judge Keosian was "automatically elected" following the general election, see California Courts, "Trial Courts Roster", April 9, 2014; see https://Ballotpedia.org/Gregory_Keosian.

81. Judge Keosian may have taken unlawful payments from the Defendant

County of Los Angeles in violation of California law, see **Sturgeon**; and this type of scandal has been referred to in the public domain as a form of "bribery" or "bribes".

STATEMENT OF FACTS PERTINENT TO THIS VERIFIED STATEMENT OF DISQUALIFICATION

82. The County of Los Angeles is a public entity also known as county local government (herein "County Government") that comprises of five supervising locally elected officials and a duly elected sheriff for the county as the chief law enforcement officer for the County Government. The Sherriff Jim McDonnell

hires racist persons against Mexican-Americans in high level positions for the Los Angeles County Sherriff's Department[7].

83. Sheriff Jim McDonnell institutionalizes racism against Mexican-Americans in the State of California by hiring for his "chief of staff" to ensure institutional racism to thrive at the Los Angeles County Sherriff's Department without consequence.

84. The Plaintiff filed a Complaint for Damages against the County government for false arrest and imprisonment on April 26, 2016 pursuant to a lawful claim for damages.

85. The Defendants demurred to the Plaintiff's Complaint against the Defendant County of Los Angeles and moved to strike the Plaintiff's Complaint against them. The matter was called for a law and motion hearing on the Defendant's demurrer on August 10, 2016.

86. In the Judge Keosian's tentative ruling on the demurrer in page 5 dated February 15, 2017, the court stated the following:

"As an initial matter, Dumas failed to meet and confer before filing this motion.

Dumas' meet and confer emails to COLA fail to specify at all the substantive issues he has with COLA's responses. (McIntosh Decl. Ex. B, C)". Nothing could be further from the truth. And the above paragraph is a lie straight from the Judge Gregory Keosian himself. This is more than example of drawing a false legal conclusion. This is an example of the Judge Gregory Keosian suppressing the rule of law in the Los Angeles Superior Court - Central District, Stanley Mosk Courthouse.

---

[7] http://www.latimes.com/local/california/la-me-sheriff-burbank-emails-20160427-story.html

87. The Judge Keosian wrote a false statement that the Plaintiff did not submit an Opposition to the Defendant County of Los Angeles' motion to strike, but in fact the Plaintiff did submit a timely Opposition to the Defendant's motion to strike his Complaint.

88. On August 10, 2016, in the law and motion hearing, the Plaintiff did in fact bring to the attention to the Judge Keosian of the false statement regarding his Opposition to the motion to strike that was written by Judge Keosian in his tentative ruling.

THE JUDGE KEOSIAN ALLOWS OFFICERS OF THE COURT TO LIE IN THEIR DECLARATIONS IN ORDER TO PROVIDE THEM WITH UNLAWFUL COURT ORDERS

89. The Defendant's attorney of record Mr. John Coleman Esq. of the law firm "Coleman and Associates, Lawyers", has been hired at $150.00 an hour to represent the Defendant County of Los Angeles in this legal matter for civil rights violations and damages against the Plaintiff according to their request for sanctions against the Plaintiff in pro per.

90. On January 31, 2017, Mr. Scott McIntosh for "Coleman and Associates, Lawyers" signed a sham Declaration that contained false statements under penalty of perjury.

91. For example, Mr. McIntosh states and alleges that he called the Plaintiff in pro per and left him a voicemail message.

92. But as a matter of fact he did not such thing and it was lie under oath. But Judge Keosian approved of it and helped cover up the fact. Scott McIntosh never produced any direct evidence supporting his claim and never even named the

person who he claimed called the Plaintiff because no such servant for his law firm ever did what he claimed in his sham declaration.

93. Judge Keosian knew or should have known that there was no offer of proof for such other than the lie that Mr. McIntosh wrote in his declaration.

94. Judge Keosian looked the other way despite the controverted evidence as the Plaintiff in pro per in fact noted in his declaration that he did in fact contact the "Coleman and Associates" law firm for the meet and confer requirement.

95. The Plaintiff fulfilled his duty but the Government's lawyers intentionally evaded him and never responded to repeated emails before filing the motion to compel judicial council forms.

96. The Plaintiff was denied the legal right to judicial council forms by Judge Keosian because he is self-represented, Mexican-American with Native North American descent, in forma paupris, male with disability, and over the age of 40 years of age.

97. The Judge, Gregory Keosian, whom was first a lawyer before becoming a judge of the superior court has acts with judicial corruption, and the California taxpayers have a right to know and have a right to fair and an impartial judge because the Plaintiff is paying for it in his taxes.

98. Mr. McIntosh has failed to proffer any direct evidence such as a telephone record, for proof of his allegation because he had no proof and declared a lie but the Judge Keosian looked the other way, just like a corrupt government official, from the County Government to the Judicial Branch, is there any end to this glass-wall of oppression instituted by the Los Angeles County Board of Supervisors and Judge Gregory Keosian?

99. The Plaintiff declared and informed the Judge Keosian on February 15, 2017 at 9:00AM in the law and motion hearing that Mr. McIntosh never called him at his telephone number and Mr. McIntosh never left the Plaintiff a voicemail message. The Plaintiff knew from directly handling his own telephone calls and voicemail messages if Mr. McIntosh would have called.

100. The Plaintiff further declared and controverted the fact that he fulfilled his duty to meet and confer but the Judge Keosian failed to acknowledge that fact, like so many others, and thus denied the Plaintiff in pro per due process of law in favor of the Defendant County Government.

101. The Judge Keosian allowed and permitted the Defendant's attorney of record to fail and follow the rule of California law. Therefore, the Judge Keosian is throwing the pitches and not calling the balls and strikes'.

THE JUDGE KEOSIAN ALLOWS OFFICERS OF THE COURT TO OBSTRUCT LAW BECAUSE HE IS PREJUDICED AGAINST MEXICAN-AMERICAN MALES IN PRO PER AND IN FORMA PAUPRIS

102. The attorney of record Mr. John M. Coleman Esq. had declared that he had "meet and conferred" with the Plaintiff by letter. Does Judge Gregory Keosian forget how to rule on the law?

103. Under California law pursuant to Code of Civil Procedure Section 430.41 this course of action precursor to a demurrer is in fact unlawful.

104. The Defendant County acting through their attorney John M. Coleman Esq. had in fact failed to properly met and confer in person or by telephone under California law and Judge Keosian knew it and helped John M. Coleman side-step the rule of law. The Judge did this action with prejudicial intent and it was not

innocent; the Judge Keosian with common design or direct contact aided the Defendant County Government and their attorney John M. Coleman in instituting "slime ball litigation tactics" by covert and overt racists.

105. It was obvious on the face of the pleadings and the Judge Keosian knew or should have known on the face of the Defendant County's attorney of record's declaration.

106. Mr. Coleman stated as a matter of fact that they only attempted to meet by way of letter via US Mail, but not by the statutory legal requirement as is stated under California law, see Code of Civil Procedure Section 430.41.

107. The Judge Keosian knew or should have known that this is a violation of California law. Judge Gregory Keosian is not blind to the facts but in fact blind when it comes to fair and impartial litigation, so taxpayers like the Plaintiff in pro per are getting ripped off and oppressed in their own natural country and county. California law makes it unlawful for a party or an attorney for a party to only attempt to meet and confer by writing the Plaintiff a letter.

108. As this was not a lawful and legal procedure, the Judge Keosian ignored the law and failed to follow California law. As Judge Gregory Keosian does consistently in this case against the County Government for civil rights violations.

109. The Judge Keosian has conspired by common design, to deny the Plaintiff his legal right to due process of law in the State of California and in serving as a Judge Keosian in California courts.

110. The Plaintiff brought the fact of the Defendants failure to lawfully act in accordance with California law, the Plaintiff in the law and motion hearing directed the fact to the attention to the Judge Keosian but he failed to acknowledge the fact with prejudice.

111. The Judge Keosian intentionally disregarded that fact because he has prejudice against the Plaintiff in pro per and has no interest in providing the Plaintiff due process of law.

112. For example, the Defendant's attorney John M. Coleman Esq. failed to follow the statutory procedure, and this was in fact brought to the attention to the Judge Keosian but the ignored the fact and law in the hearing on the Demurrer.

113. This judicial action was prejudiced, an abuse of discretion, and made by the Judge Keosian in collusion with the Defendant and their attorney of record in order to deny the Plaintiff his right to due process.

114. The Plaintiff submitted an Opposition to the Defendant's attorney's motion to strike his complaint, but the Judge Keosian completely ignored it and falsely wrote that the Plaintiff did not submit any Opposition in his tentative decision August 10, 2016.

115. The Judge Keosian intentionally wrote to omit the Opposition because he is prejudiced and does not want to provide the Plaintiff, a California taxpayer and injured person by the Defendants, to be able to have a fair and impartial trial at the Stanley Mosk Courthouse.

116. During the hearing, the Plaintiff pointed out that he did in fact submit an Opposition to the Defendant's motion to strike.

117. The Judge Keosian very quickly flipped through it and then threw back down at his Honor's desk, in less than one minute in fact.

118. Therefore, by physical observation the Judge Keosian did not even read one sentence of the Opposition and intentionally ignored the Plaintiff's pleadings in this hearing.

119. The Judge Keosian granted partial dismissal to the Defendants' attorney's demurrer to Plaintiff's complaint. The Judge Keosian never changed nor corrected his tentative decision for the fact that the Plaintiff did file an Opposition to the Motion to Strike.

120. The Judge Keosian is biased and against the Plaintiff's interests in this case and his pleadings must have been considered but the Judge Keosian has refused to consider the opposition because he is prejudiced, and the Plaintiff cannot have a fair and impartial trial before the Judge Keosian.

THE DECLARATION OF W. SCOTT MCINTOSH WAS A SHAM DECLARATION AND NOT TRUTHFUL, BUT THE JUDGE KEOSIAN SUPERIOR COURT PERMITTED MR. MCINTOSH TO PLAY FAST AND LOOSE WITH THE DISCOVERY PROCESS AND SHOWING PREJUDICE AGAINST THE PLAINTIFF IN PRO PER

121. Mr. W. Scott McIntosh Esq., State Bar. No. 304124 ("Mr. McIntosh Esq."), an associate attorney at law working on behalf of Mr. Coleman Esq.

122. The Defendant County Government in Interest the County of Los Angeles had hired "Coleman & Associates" to represent them in this legal matter. Judge Keosian is allowing, conspiring, and helping Mr. McIntosh Esq. to play fast and loose with the rules of discovery.

123. Judge Keosian has permitted and or conspired with Mr. McIntosh to set forth a sham declaration in support of the Defendant County Government's Opposition to their civil rights violations.

124. Mr. McIntosh Esq. had declared under penalty of perjury that some mysterious "Office Staff[er]" contacted the Plaintiff in pro per via telephone:

"On Thursday, September 22, 2016, I directed Coleman & Associates' Office Staff to contact Plaintiff via telephone at the number Mr. Dumas has on file with the Court ((562)-356-0492) and request an extension in order to respond to Plaintiff's Discovery, as COUNTY's investigation was still ongoing. Mr. Dumas did not answer or respond to our telephone call and did not contact anyone at Coleman & Associates in response to that telephone call".

125. Mr. McIntosh has set forth a complete lie and fabrication in his declaration under penalty of perjury. Judge Keosian has allowed it and officially approved of it in order to deny the Plaintiff in pro per his legal rights further in this case. As a matter of fact, no one from "Coleman & Associates' Office Staff" contacted the Plaintiff in pro per at his telephone number as Mr. McIntosh Esq. so vaguely claims.

126. No one from the Coleman and Associates law firm ever wrote a supporting declaration to Mr. McIntosh's false claim. Mr. McIntosh's claim was a complete lie under oath and Judge Gregory Keosian approved of it, misprisoned a felony, aided and abetted a felony, and further aided the County Government to act under the color of state law in violation of the Constitutions and civil rights.

127. The Plaintiff in pro per informed the Judge Gregory Keosian of this fact but the Judge Keosian completely disregarded the truth with prejudice and injustice.

128. The Plaintiff in pro per never submitted to the Judge Keosian's corrupt tentative decision.

129. Mr. McIntosh Esq. does not specifically identify by name exactly who in from the 'Coleman & Associates' Office Staff" contacted the Plaintiff in pro per.

But this fact does not matter to Judge Keosian because he is not concerned with the truth, the rule of law, or civil rights.

130. Why did not Mr. McIntosh Esq. attach a supporting declaration of that mysterious Office Staff person? It simply was not truthful, a lie, and Judge Keosian knew or should have known of it but intentionally failed to acknowledge the truth and fact.

131. On November 4, 2016, the County Government provided "Further Responses", therefore, Mr. McIntosh Esq. was misrepresenting the fact that this was satisfying a "meet and confer" pursuant to the supplemental response.

132. The Judge Keosian should have known of its irrelevancy and misrepresentation as fraudulent.

133. The Plaintiff in pro per did in fact inform the Judge Keosian at the law and motion hearing that <u>no one</u> from the "law offices of John M. Coleman" had called him and the Plaintiff in pro per verified that fact in his lawful Declaration. The Judge Keosian completely ignored this fact and abused its discretion by favoring Mr. McIntosh's fraudulent declaration in opposition over the Plaintiff in pro per's truthful declaration.

134. Judge Keosian has no interest in the truth nor justice and is allowing the County Government to get away with civil rights violations. Mr. McIntosh Esq. further claims under penalty of perjury that "On Friday, September 23, 2016, one day later, I called Mr. Dumas. . .". "No one answered or responded to my September 23, 2016 phone call . . . and I left a voicemail detailing County's request for an extension of time to responds to Plaintiff's Discovery and required Mr.

Dumas contact Coleman & Associates to discuss. Plaintiff failed to respond to my September 23, 2016 voicemail".

135. The fact of this legal matter is that no such voicemail was left by Mr. McIntosh Esq. on the Plaintiff in pro per's voicemail and the Judge Keosian was made aware of this specific fact in the law and motion hearing.

136. The Judge Keosian intentionally abused his judicial discretion by ignoring the facts and simply failed by not asking Mr. McIntosh Esq. to simply prove it and or to provide rebuttable evidence to the Plaintiff in pro per's. Judge Keosian knew or should have known that no such evidence of a voicemail existed and helped the County Government cover up the fact.

137. Mr. McIntosh Esq. claims in his declaration, which should be found as a sham:

> "On November 28, 2016, and December 2, 2016, Plaintiff sent emails purporting to 'Meet and Confer' re COUNTY's responses to Plaintiff's Form Interrogatories, Set One." "14. The November 28, 2016 emails failed to identify any discrete reason(s) why COUNTY"s Responses were allegedly deficient, and instead generally concluded the Responses were "incomplete" and /or 'evasive," without identifying which Interrogatory Response(s) Plaintiff was referring to". . . Plaintiff's purported 'Meet and Confer' efforts . . . contained any substantive discussion of any of COUNTY'S Responses to Interrogatories, Set One, but instead vaguely concluded COUNTY's Responses were 'incomplete' or 'evasive'. Plaintiff offered no basis for his positions as to any specific Form Interrogatory Response to Meet and Confer. As such, COUNTY was and is unable to address Plaintiff's suggestions that the Interrogatory Response is deficient".

138. The County Government, Scott McIntosh, and Judge Gregory Keosian intentionally distort the truth. Mr. McIntosh Esq. for the County Government allowed and aided by Judge Gregory Keosian in fact violated **California Code of Civil Procedure Section §128.7(b)**, by presenting to the Los Angeles Superior

Court false information by signing, filing, submitting, and later advocating their sham pleadings and papers. The County Government acting through their Attorney of Record did in fact certify to the best of their knowledge, information, and belief, allegedly formed after "an inquiry reasonable under the circumstance", that all of the following conditions have been met: (1) It is not being presented primarily for an improper purpose, such as to harass or to cause unnecessary delay or needles increase in the cost of litigation. (2) The claims, defense, other legal contentions therein are warranted by existing . . ., or reversal of exiting law or the establishment of new law".; see **Bockrath v. Aldrich Chem. Co**. (1999) 21 Cal.4th 71.

139. Mr. McIntosh Esq. not only violated California's rules of ethics for state licensed lawyers but violated California law by perjuring himself. Judge Gregory Keosian after rubber-stamping lies, misprisons another felony. The County Government gets away with breaking the law again. The Plaintiff in pro per informed the Judge Keosian that Mr. McIntosh Esq. was in fact lying and misleading Judge Keosian in his declaration and it was disturbing that "his Honor" would rubberstamp it; **Business and Professions Code Section §6068(d)**; **Business and Professions Code Section §6106**; and **Business and Professions Code Section §6128**. Under **Business and Professions Code Section §6067**, the requirement for a lawyer is to "faithfully to discharge the duties of any attorney at law to the best of [their] knowledge and ability". The Defendant County Government has acted above the rule of law without consequence in regard to this legal matter and is an institutional problem.

THE JUDGE KEOSIAN TENTATIVE RULING WAS A CLEAR ABUSE OF DISCRETION AND NOT ONE SINGLE WORD FROM THE PLAINTIFF IN PRO PER'S PLEADINGS WERE CITED; THE JUDGE KEOSIAN ABUSED ITS DISCRETION IN FAVOR OF THE LOS ANGELES COUNTY BOARD OF SUPERVISORS

139. How can a trial judge completely disregard a pro per's pleadings, not even cite the moving party in a tentative decision, and not be an abuse of discretion?

140. The Judge Keosian is allowing the Defendant County Government to evade lawful discovery by making all blanket objections. However, at **footnote 14** in **Sinaiko**, in which the Judge Keosian cited in the tentative ruling, to the effect that even absence a separate statement, a trial court can still rule to continue the law and motion hearing.

141. The Judge Keosian abused its discretion in giving a discovery exemption to the Defendant County Government, and this type of impropriety is cause for disqualification, and raises serious doubt as to if the Judge Keosian is in fact impartial to the Plaintiff in pro per's claims against the County of Los Angeles.

THE DEFENDANT COUNTY GOVERNMENT'S OPPOSITION TO PLAINTIFF'S GOOD FAITH MEET AND CONFER REQUESTS TO MR. JOHN M. COLEMAN ESQ. WAS BASED ON A SHAM DECLARATION BY HIS ASSOCIATE COUNSEL OF RECORD MR. WILLIAM SCOTT MCINTOSH ESQ.

142. A number of factors identified in the Plaintiff's "Statement of Evidence to be Introduced" was completely disregarded by the Judge Keosian, thus leading to its prejudicial abuse of discretion. The Plaintiff has presented this to the Judge Keosian as direct evidence, but they have neglected to include it into the record,

thus showing substantial prejudice. The Defendant County Government is allowed to declare that "someone" made a phone call not even related to the Motion.

The Defendant County Government, acting through their attorney Mr. Coleman Esq., contend that in their reason for not compelling further responses to Judicial Council Form Interrogatories are because: "Plaintiff failed to properly 'Meet and Confer' as required by case law, statute, and Local Court Rules, as set forth in the "Declaration of W. Scott McIntosh". The purpose of the 'Meet and Confer' requirement contained California **Code of Civil Procedure §2016.040** is to force the parties to reexamine their positions and narrow discovery disputes, see **Stewart v. Colonial Western Agency, Inc**. 87 CA4th 1006, 1016-1017 (2001).

As Plaintiff's 'Meet and Confer' letters did not identify any specific issue(s) with County's Response, Plaintiff's 'Meet and Confer' efforts were therefore not a good faith attempt to resolve this discovery issue".

143. The Defendant County Government only purports that the Plaintiff in pro per ". . . failed to properly 'Meet and Confer' as required . . ." but does not establish any factual or legal basis for this conclusion. The Judge Keosian ignores the Declaration of Luke Edward Dumas set forth in the Motion.

144. The Judge Keosian in its tentative ruling abusively re-asserted the Defendant County Government's statement as a conclusion but not as a matter of fact thus abusing its discretion. The Defendant County Government, in citing **Stewart v. Colonial Western Agency, Inc**. (2001) 87 Cal.App.4th 1006, misapplies the case and the Judge Keosian abuses its discretion in disregarding the caselaw presented before it.

145. The Plaintiff in pro per did exactly what the Court said to do in **Stewart**, "**The Discovery Act**" requires that, prior to the initiation of a motion to compel, the moving party declare that he or she has made a serious attempt to obtain 'an informal resolution of each issue.' (**§ 2025, subd. (o)**). This rule is designed 'to encourage the parties to work out their differences informally so as to avoid the necessity for a formal order . . .' (**McElhaney v. Cessna Aircraft Co**. (1982) 134 Cal.App.3d 285, 289. . .". Further in **Stewart**, the Court noted that:

> "A determination of whether an attempt at informal resolution is adequate . . . involves the exercise of discretion. The level of effort at informal resolution which satisfied the 'reasonable and good faith attempt' standard depends upon the circumstances. in a larger, more complex discovery context, a greater effort at informal resolution may be warranted. In a simpler, or more narrowly focused case, a more modest effort may suffice. The history of the litigation, the nature of the interaction between counsel, the nature other issues, the type and scope of discovery requested, the prospects for success and other similar factors can be relevant. A judge has broad powers and responsibility to determine what measure and procedures are appropriate in varying circumstances." (**Obregon v. Superior Court** (1998) 67 Cal.App.4th 424, 431 . . . . "A trial judge's perceptions on such matters, inherently factual in nature at least in part, must not be lightly disturbed".

146. The Plaintiff in pro per went beyond modest efforts by emailing Mr. Coleman Esq. more than one time. The Judge Keosian abused its discretion in determining that the Plaintiff in pro per did not satisfy a reasonable and good faith attempt to Meet and Confer. The Order denying lawful discovery in this legal matter must be disturbed because the Record does not support the Judge Keosian's conclusion and is thus an abuse of discretion, demeans the integrity of the legal system, and is harmful.

THE DECLARATION OF LUKE EDWARD DUMAS ESTABLISHED GOOD FAITH ATTEMPTS TO "MEET AND CONFER" WITH THE DEFENDANT COUNTY GOVERNMENT'S COUNSEL OF RECORD BUT WAS DISREGARDED BY THE JUDGE KEOSIAN SUPERIOR COURT IN FAVOR OF THE DEFENDANT COUNTY GOVERNMENT

147. The Plaintiff in pro per in pro per made many efforts to resolve the dispute out of court in order to seek the Defendant County Government to be compelled to properly respond to all of the Judicial Council's Form Interrogatories for Unlimited Civil Case. In the Plaintiff in pro per's Declaration, the Plaintiff in pro per set forth the facts in line paragraphs numbers 6, 8, 9, 11, 12, 13, and 14 that he did his duty in properly attempting several times to meet and confer with Mr. Coleman in good faith.

148. The Plaintiff in pro per did in fact satisfy the meet and confer requirements as is required by California law. Therefore, the Plaintiff in pro per expressly fulfilled the legal prerequisite to meet and confer' with the Defendant's counsel of record but the Judge Keosian abused its discretion in ignoring the Plaintiff in pro per's Declaration and content in his emails that were sent to the Defendant County Government.

THE JUDGE KEOSIAN SHOULD HAVE DISCLOSED IF HE HAD RECIEVED UNLAWFUL COMPENSATION FROM THE DEFENDANT COUNTY

149. Pursuant to **Sturgeon I and II**, the appellate court found that the County of Los Angeles was issuing unlawful payments to Los Angeles County Judges as part of their scheme to control the local judiciary, pure judicial branch corruption.

If the Judge Keosian has taken unlawful supplemental benefit payments from the Defendant, then he surely should have disclosed the potential conflict of interest in this case.

150. Also, if the Judge Keosian has taken unlawful supplemental benefit payments from the County of Los Angeles as a Defendant, just as in this instant case, and the Judge Keosian has not disclosed it to the public in the course of litigation against the Defendant County of Los Angeles, then certainly the Judge Keosian and the Defendant appears to have a conflict of interest and it is a legal question that was not addressed in **Sturgeon v. County of Los Angeles** (2011) 191 Cal.App.4th 344 ("**Sturgeon I**") and in **Sturgeon v. County of Los Angeles** (2015) 242 Cal.App.4th 1437("**Sturgeon II**").

151. The Court has noted that the County of Los Angeles had provided unlawful "supplemental judicial benefit payments" ("payments") to trial judges in the County of Los Angeles since about 1998, and the payments were disguised as "supplemental judicial benefits" that the Los Angeles County Board of Supervisors unlawfully paid out an estimated $24.6 million per year, see **Sturgeon I & II**.

152. The Court predicted in **Sturgeon I** that the California ". . . Legislature would soon enact a more permanent 'uniform statewide system of judicial compensation'. (Id. at p. 356.) And as the Court has noted: *"it has not"*, see **Sturgeon II**. Therefore, the Judge Keosian in this legal case against the County of Los Angeles, should have disclosed to the Plaintiff if they he received the unlawful payments by the County because it presents a conflict of interest in litigation against the County in this case.

JUDGE KEOSIAN INTENTIONALLY FAILED TO READ AND PROPERLY CONSIDER AND WEIGH EVIDENCE BECAUSE OF HIS PREJUDICE AND THE PLAINTIFF IN PRO PER CANNOT RECEIVE A FAIR TRIAL

153. The Judge Keosian Hon. Gregory Keosian has not administered justice with fairness and impartiality in this case of false arrest and imprisonment of the Plaintiff by the Defendant County. The Judge Keosian is extremely prejudiced and did not care to hide it in the court on August 10, 2016. In the law and motion hearing, Plaintiff informed the Judge Keosian that he did in fact file an "Opposition to the Defendant's Motion to Strike". The Plaintiff informed the Judge Keosian that in his tentative decision, the Judge Keosian failed to consider his opposition pleading.

154. While sitting on the bench, the Judge Keosian looked through the case file and stated, "here it is", then took the Plaintiff's Opposition pleading out of the file, very quickly flipped through it in less than one minute, and then literally threw it down on his honor's desk. The Judge Keosian intentionally failed to consider and read the Plaintiff's opposition pleading in the law and motion hearing because he is prejudiced against the Plaintiff. The Judge Keosian did not provide the Plaintiff with a fair and impartial hearing.

155. The Judge Keosian purposefully failed to read and consider the Plaintiff's pleading and the Plaintiff has not nor will not receive a fair and impartial trial before the Judge Keosian Hon. Judge Gregory Keosian.

THE JUDGE KEOSIAN HAS MISCARRIAGED JUSTICE IN FAVOR OF THE DEFENDANT

156. The Judge Keosian allows attorneys to lie under oath against pro per litigants in violation of the rule of law and under the rules of ethics. The Judge Keosian has intentionally and completely ignored the Plaintiff's pleadings in this case including his lawful declarations. The Judge Keosian has set aside the rule of California law so that the Defendant and their attorneys can bully the Plaintiff in pro per in denying him due process.

157. The Judge Keosian is abusing, and has abused, his judicial branch governmental power and has stained the trust in the judiciary because he is prejudiced against the Plaintiff in pro per. The Plaintiff has not nor will not receive a fair and impartial trial before this Judge Keosian.

158. The Defendant's attorney of record had committed perjury in his Declaration on January 31, 2017.

159. The Plaintiff fully fulfilled the spirit and letter of California law but the Judge Keosian with evil intent had denied the Plaintiff his lawful right to discovery via judicial council form - interrogatories for unlimited civil case.

160. At this current rate, the Judge Keosian had unlawfully blocked all access to lawful discovery based on the Defendant's counsel of record Mr. Scott M. McIntosh's perjury in his Declaration.

161. The Judge Keosian knew or should have known and was even made aware of the fact that the Plaintiff did in fact fulfill his legal duty by attempting to meet and confer with the Defendant's attorney of record.

162. The Judge Keosian has aided the Defendant and the Defendant's attorney to lie under penalty of perjury. This type of judicial corruption reduces the State of

California to some type of third world county ruled by bribes and dictatorships but and this should not be so in the State of California.

163. For the Judge Keosian Hon. Judge Gregory Keosian to permit the and misprison a felony.

THE PLAINTIFF CANNOT RECEIVE A FAIR AND IMPARTIAL TRIAL FROM JUDGE KEOSIAN

164. A California judge just not has to be fair but has to appear to be fair under California law. The Judge Keosian has not treated, acted, nor ruled fairly, impartially, and legally in this case. For example, the Judge Keosian intentionally ignores the Plaintiff's pleadings such as his Opposition papers and Declarations.

165. The Judge Keosian cannot and will not provide the Plaintiff with a fair and impartial trial in this case because he allows the Defendant's.

THE JUDICIAL DISQUALIFICATION OF JUDGE KEOSIAN

166. The Judge Keosian Hon. Judge Gregory Keosian permits attorneys to lie in declarations and to violate to prosper in his courtroom, aid in the denial of due process of law, and has acted against self-represented litigants such as Plaintiff exercising a legal action for civil rights.

167. Stanley Mosk is certainly turning in his grave at the injustice's that have been brought about by the Judge Keosian at the Honorable Stanley Mosk Courthouse.

168. The judicial branch of government in this case, the Los Angeles Superior Court - Central District, has been stained by the appearance of impropriety, denial

of due process, prejudicial rulings, unlawful rulings, invasion of privacy, and allowing the Defendant and their attorney to slander the Plaintiff in this case.

COURT RELIEF REQUESTED:

WHEREFORE, for Good and Just Cause under the California **Code of Civil Procedure §170.1, § 170.3 and §170.6**:

1. That this Court, the Hon. Judge Gregory Keosian,

(a) To automatically disqualify himself from the *Complaint* and hearing and or trial set for February 13, 2018, at 8:30AM, or thereafter.

(b) For this Unlimited Civil Complaint be transferred accordingly under **Code of Civil Procedure §170.1, §170.3 and §170.6** to another duly qualified Judge Keosian without bias or prejudice as is required by law**.**

DATED: January 18, 2018

Respectfully submitted,

By: _____

Luke Edward Dumas,

Plaintiff in pro per in pro per

VERIFICATION

I, Luke Edward Dumas, am the Plaintiff in pro per in the above-entitled action.

I have read the foregoing Statement of Disqualification and know the contents thereof. The same is true of my own knowledge, except as to those matters which are therein alleged on information and belief, and as to those matters, I believe it to be true. I declare under penalty of perjury under the laws of the State of California that the foregoing is true and correct, in Los Angeles, California, on January 18, 2018, Long Beach, California.

_____

Luke Edward Dumas, declarant

MEMORANDUM OF POINTS AND AUTHORITIES

1. The Los Angeles County Board of Supervisors frequently retains a number of law firms that engage in "scorched earth litigation tactics" in the civil cases involving their civil rights violations, see **County of Los Angeles Board of Supervisors v. ACLU of Southern California** (2017) 12 Cal.App.5th 1264.

2. The Defendant Los Angeles County Board of Supervisors has indeed employed private lawyers John Coleman and Scott McIntosh to employ "slime ball litigation tactics" in this case and Judge Keosian has aided them in employing such tactics.

3. A judicial officer may be legally disqualified in three ways under California law: One, a judge may recuse her or himself for reasons set forth under the **Code of Civil Procedure**; or by the parties challenging a judicial officer for good cause; or by a party filing a timely peremptory challenge to a judicial officer, see **People v. Superior Court** (Mudge) (1997) 54 Cal.App.4th 407.

4. In the interests of justice a reasonable person may doubt whether the trial judge was impartial or where the trial court's rulings suggest the "whimsical disregard" of a statutory scheme, see **Hernandez v. Superior Court** (2003) 112 Cal.App.4th 285. When a judicial officer such as Judge Keosian fails to consider and pass upon the evidence produced before him, and when the evidence is in conflict, in order to resolve that conflict, the judge must find in favor of the party whose evidence outweighs that of the opposing party, see **Moulton Niguel Water Dist. v. Colombo** (2003) 111 Cal.App.4th 1210.

5. Under California law a judge is disqualified regardless of sufficiency of statement of disqualification irregardless if a judge strikes nor files an answer

within the ten-day period admitting or denying allegations in statement, see **Urias v. Harris Farms Inc**. (1991) 234 Cal.App.3d 415. Also, orders of disqualified judges such as Judge Gregory Keosian are void and must be vacated under California State law, **Christie v. City of El Centro** (2006) 135 Cal.App.4th 767. Statutes governing disqualification of a judge for cause are intended to ensure public confidence in the judiciary and to protect the right of the litigants to a fair and impartial trial judge, see **Peracchi v. Superior Court** (2003) 30 Cal.4th 1245. Although no case so holds, the time reasonably required to have a disqualification for cause determined should be good cause for trial delay, see **Bryant v. Superior Court** (1986) 186 Cal.App.3d 483, 500-502.

6. The right to file a motion for disqualification of a judge is a substantial right and an important part of California's system of due process. The doctrine of judicial disqualification promotes fair and impartial trials and confidence in the judiciary; and Courts must refrain from any tactic or maneuver that has the practical effect of diminishing this important right, see **Daniel V. v. Superior Court** (2006) 139 Cal.App.4th 28.

7. Therefore, there is a requisite for judges to remain impartial; and as a remedial statute, the statutory right to disqualify a judge is liberally construed, see **Bravo v. Superior Court** (2007) 149 Cal.App.4th 1489; it is a settled truism that the trial of a case should not only be fair in fact but appear to be fair, see **In re Marriage of Tharp**.

8. It is illogical and a false assumption of the appellate institution of the judicial branch of Government to entertain a presumption that no bias or prejudice actually exist in this instant case as was presumed under **Golish v. Feinstein** (1932) 123 Cal.App. 547, 549. Especially when the concrete facts demonstrate that the

Plaintiff is afforded no legal rights to due process, discovery, free from defamatory statements such as committing a crime. For the Judge Keosian as an agent of the judicial branch of Government paid for by the taxpayers, does in fact help suppress civil rights of the Plaintiff in pro per in order for the County Government to prevail is unconstitutional and inhumane.

9. Filing the statement of disqualification for cause temporarily suspends the judge's jurisdiction until the statement is stricken or decided, see **Oak Grove School District v. City Title Insurance Co**. (1963) 217 Cal.App.2d 678.

DATED: January 18, 2018

Respectfully submitted,

_____

Luke Edward Dumas, Plaintiff in pro per

Trial Court & Appeal: False Arrest, Imprisonment, and Civil Rights Violations By L.A. County

Dumas v. Los Angeles County Board of Supervisors et al. 45 Cal. App. 5th 348

PLAINTIFF'S REQUEST FOR COPIES – LOS ANGELES SUPERIOR COURT FORM

Copyright. © 2021. Paralegal Publishing Group.

Trial Court & Appeal: False Arrest, Imprisonment, and Civil Rights Violations By L.A. County
<u>Dumas v. Los Angeles County Board of Supervisors et al</u>. 45 Cal. App. 5th 348

Case No. B283557

Related Case No. B286369

IN THE COURT OF APPEAL
OF THE STATE OF CALIFORNIA
SECOND APPELLATE DISTRICT
DIVISION ___

LUKE EDWARD DUMAS,

Petitioner,

vs.

THE LOS ANGELES SUPERIOR COURT OF THE STATE OF CALIFORNIA FOR THE COUNTY OF LOS ANGELES,

Respondent;

LOS ANGELES COUNTY BOARD OF SUPERVISORS ET AL.,

Real Party in Interest,

Writ Regarding Order by the Los Angeles County Superior Court, Case No. BC618191, Department 61, Phone: (213) 633-1061, The Honorable Gregory Keosian, Presiding

PETITION FOR WRIT OF MANDAMUS, PROHIBITION, OR OTHER EXTRAORDINARY RELIEF (CCP §1085) OR (CCP §1094.5) "STAY REQUESTED"

Luke E Dumas, Petitioner in pro per
5462 E. Del Amo Blvd.
Long Beach, California, 90808
(562) 356-0492

Copyright. © 2021. Paralegal Publishing Group.

Certificate of Interested Persons

Attachment 2

Full Name of Interested entity or person	Nature of Interest (Explain):
(6) Hilda Solis	Supervisor for County
(7) Mark Ridley Thomas	Supervisor for County
(8) Sheila Kuehl	Supervisor for County
(9) Janice Hahn	Supervisor for County
(10) Kathryn Barger	Supervisor for County

TABLE OF CONTENTS

Page

TABLE OF AUTHORITIES 4

PETITION FOR WRIT OF MANDAMUS.. 13

I. INTRODUCTION 13

    A. The Parties to this Verified Petition for an Extraordinary Writ 14

    B. The Basis for Writ Review for the Denial of Discovery 14

    C. Petitioner has Good Cause and Reasonable Explained Delay 16

        i. In Propria Persona 16

        ii. Confidential Medical Condition & Disability 16

        iii. The Petitioner is in Forma Paupris 17

        iv. The Limitation of relying on Clerk Copies 17

    D. Authenticity of Exhibits Volume 1 & Volume 2 18

II. PROCEDURE AND FACTS 18

    A. Chronology of Pertinent Events to this Petition for a Writ 18

    B. Absence of Other Remedies 19

    C. No Prejudice to Opposing Party in Issuing a Writ 20

    D. An Alternative Writ of Mandate can be used to seek Compliance for the Statutory Right to Obtain Truthful Answers to Official Interrogatories 21

III. LEGAL DISCUSSION 21

A. The Respondent Superior Court had a duty to Act in accordance with The Civil Discovery Act 21

    B. Case of First Impression? 23

        1. Judicial Council Form Interrogatories 23

        2. Pro Per Litigants 24

3. The County of Los Angeles 24

　C. The Basis for Relief, Beneficial Interest of the Petitioner, and the Capacities of the Respondent Superior Court and the Real Party in Interest County of LA 24

　D. The Petitioner's Motion to Compel Further Discovery Responses to Official Interrogatories was completely disregarded by the Respondent ... 26

　E. The Declaration of Luke Edward Dumas established good faith attempts to "Meet and Confer" with the Real Party's Counsel of Record but was disregarded by the Respondent Superior Court in favor of the Real Party in Interest County of LA 27

　F. The Declaration of W. Scott McIntosh Esq. was a Sham Declaration and not truthful but the Respondent Superior Court permitted Mr. McIntosh to play fast and loose with the discovery process and showing prejudice 27

　G. The Respondent Tentative Ruling was a Clear Abuse of Discretion and not one Single Word from the Petitioner's pleadings were cited; the Respondent abused its discretion in favor of the Real Party 30

　H. The Real Party's Opposition to Plaintiff's Good Faith Meet and Confer Requests to Mr. John M. Coleman Esq. was based on a sham declaration by his associate Counsel of Record Mr. McIntosh Esq. 31

REQUEST FOR RELIEF 33

MEMORANDUM OF POINTS AND AUTHORITIES 34

I. INTRODUCTION 34

II. THE STANDARD OF REVIEW 36

　A. Writ Review is proper for the denial of the discovery of Official Interrogatories 36

III. CASE OF FIRST IMPRESSION 37

A. Pursuant to the Judicial Council's rule-making power, are "Form Interrogatories" primary authority in and of itself, and generally "Objection-Proof" notwithstanding the instructive and statutory legal exceptions? 37

IV. ARGUMENT 39

A. The Respondent's abuse of discretion resulted in the denial of discovery with no legal justification 39

B. California Judicial Council's Form Interrogatories are inherently primary Authority thus Commanding a proper and complete Response to each unanswered interrogatory 39

C. The Separate Statement Rule Does Not Limit the Respondent's Discretion to Compel Further Answers & Responses Notwithstanding even in its absence 42

D. The Petitioner is Entitled to Propound and Obtain Lawful Discovery Responses by using Official Form Interrogatories 43

E. The Petitioner has a broad right to obtaining lawful discovery from the Real Party using the Judicial Council Form Interrogatories 44

F. The Real Party was using Boilerplate Objections to Evade Lawful Discovery via Judicial Council Form Interrogatories and the Respondent abused its Discretion in denying the Petitioner's Motion to Compel Further Discovery Responses 45

G. The Real Party's Objections must be deemed waived by Operation of California law and the Respondent abused its Discretion in not Considering the Petitioner's Evidence 47

H. The Respondent abused its discretion and deprived the Petitioner a Statutory Right to Lawful Discovery via Judicial Council Form Interrogatories on its face 48

I. The Respondent has failed to perform a mandatory duty by California Law and the Respondent has not Acted in the Spirit of California Law and should be Mandated to do so or the Petitioner will be harmed at the upcoming jury trial 48

CONCLUSION 49

VERIFICATION 50

CERTIFICATE OF WORD COUNT 50

TABLE OF AUTHORITIES

                                                                                                      Page(s)

State Cases

Anderson v. Superior Court (1989) 213 Cal.App.3d 1321 49

Bailey v. Taaffe (1886) 29 Cal. 422, 424 49

Bockrath v. Aldrich Chem. Co. (1999) 21 Cal.4th 71 30

Boyer v. City of Long Beach (1920) 47 Cal.App. 617 35

Bryant v. Superior Court (1936) 16 Cal.App.2d 556, 561 .... 34, 35

Cantanese v. Superior Court (1996) 46 Cal.App.4th 1159, 1164 38

Carlson v. Superior Court (1961) 56 Cal.2d 431 .... 26, 39

Cellphone Termination Fee Cases (2009) 180 Cal.App.4th 1110 36

Chembrook v. Superior Court (Sterling Drug, Inc.) (1961) 56 Cal.2d 423 45

Coito v. Superior Court (2010) 182 Cal.App.4th 758 38

Colonial Life & Accident Ins. Co. v. Superior Court
(1982) 31 Cal.3d 785, 790 44

Coy v. Superior Court (1962) 58 Cal.2d 210, 220 46

Deyo v. Kilbourne (1978) 84 Cal.3d 771 .... 23, 46, 47

Eneaji v. Ubboe (2014) 229 Cal.App.4th 1457, 1463 36

Estate of Dupont (1943) 60 Cal.App.2d 276 49

Estate of Glassgold (1950) 97 Cal.App.2d 859, 863-864 34

Estate of Wickersham (1908) 153 Cal. 603 45

Farrar v. Farrar (1919) 41 Cal.App. 452 48

First Nat'l Bank v. Superior Court of Los Angeles County
(1925) 71 Cal.App. 64 22

Gamet v. Banchard (2001) 91 Cal.App.4th 1276 49

Gray v. Justice's Court of Williams Judicial Township
(1937) 18 Cal.2d 420 13

Greyhound Corp. v. Superior Court (1961)
56 Cal.App.4th 1559, 1612... 36, 38, 39, 42

Golden Gate Tile Co. v. Superior Court (1911) 159 Cal. 474 22

Gonzalez v. Munoz (1997) 156 Cal.App.4th 1110, 1113 36

Gonzalez v. Superior Court (1995) 33 Cal.App.4th 1539, 1546 44

Guzman v. General Motors Corp. (1984) 154 Cal.App.3d 438 45

Hellings v. Wright (1916) 29 Cal.App. 649 48

Hernandez v. Superior Court (Acheson Industries, Inc.)
(2003) 112 Cal.4th 285.. 22, 47

Ingalls v. Superior Court of Los Angeles County
(1932) 121 Cal.App. 453... 48

InHauk v. Superior Court (Demott) (1964) 61 Cal.2d 295 49

Irvington-Moore, Inc. v. Superior Court
(1993) 14 Cal.App.4th 733, 738-739 45

Johnson v. Superior Court (2000) 80 Cal.App.4th 1050 .... 23, 36

Kadelback v. Armal (1973) 31 Cal.App.3d 814, 822, 823 38

Korea Data Systems Co. v. Superior Court
(1997) 51 Cal.App.4th 1513, 1516 .... 23, 45

Lampley v. Alvares (1975) 50 Cal.App.3d 124, 128 42

Lehman v. Superior Court (1986) 179 Cal.App.3d 558, 562-563 .... 23, 34, 39

Liberty Mut. Fire Ins. Co. v. LcL Adm'rs, Inc.
(2008) 163 Cal.App.4th 1093 42

Lincoln v. Superior Court (1943) 22 Cal.2d 304, 311 34

Lipton v. Superior Court (1996) 48 Cal.App.4th 1599, 1611 44

Lombardi v. National Trust & Savings Bank of Los Angeles
(1995) 137 Cal.App.2d 206 45

McElhaney v. Cessna Aircraft Co. (1982) 134 Cal.App.3d 285, 289 32

Mobile Oil Corp. v. Superior Court (1961) 59 Cal.App.3d 293, 303 .... 36, 37

Monastero v. Los Angeles Transit Co. (1955) 131 Cal.App.2d 156 13

Moore v. Panish (1982) 32 Cal.3d 535 42

Nacht & Lewis Architect, Inc. v. Superior Court
(1996) 47 Cal.4th 214 .... 38, 39

Obregon v. Superior Court (1998) 67 Cal.App.4th 424, 431 .... 32, 42, 45

Oceanside Union School Dist. v. Superior Court
(1962) 58 Cal.2d 180, 185-186 ....23, 37

Pacific Tel. & Tel. Co. v. Superior Court of San Diego County (Duke)
(1970) 2 Cal.3d 161, 172-173 ....37, 39

Palma v. U.S. Industrial Fasteners, Inc. (1984) 36 Cal.3d 171 .... 20, 33, 39

Phelan v. Superior Court of the City and
County of San Francisco (1950) 35 Cal.2d 363 34

People v. Boehm (1969) 270 Cal.App.2d 13... 38

People v. Municipal Court (Mercer) (1979) 99 Cal.App.3d 749 34

People ex rel. Department of Transportation v. Superior Court
(1980) 26 Cal.3d 744 41

People v. Robinson (1883) 64 Cal. 372, 373 34

People v. Romero (1994) 8 Cal.4th 728, 742-743 34

People v. Superior Court (Duran) (1978) 84 Cal.App.3d 480, 489 34

Professional Career Colleges, Magna Institute, Inc. v. Superior Court
of Riverside (Stewart) (1989) 207 Cal.App.3d 490, 493 ....41, 43

Popelka, Allard, McCowan & Jones v. Superior Court of Santa Clara County
(H. Costner Enterprises) (1980) 107 Cal.App.3d 496 34

Regency Health Services, Inc. v. Superior Court (Settles)
(1998) 64 Cal.App.4th 1496 25

Reynolds v. Superior Court (1883) 64 Cal. 372, 373 35

R & B Auto Ctr., Inc. v. Farmers Group, Inc. (2006) 140 Cal.4th 327 21

Reid v. Superior Court of Trinity County (1919) 44 Cal.App. 349 35

Robinson v. Superior Court of Los Angeles County
(1950) 35 Cal.2d 379 .... 13, 22

Rodriquez v. Menjivar (2015) 243 Cal.App.4th 816, 821 36

Rodriquez v. McDonnell Douglas Corp. (1978) 87 Cal.App.3d 626, 647-648 38

Sav-on Drugs, Inc. v. Superior Court (1975) 15 Cal.3d 1, 5 39

San Diego v. Andrews (1924) 195 Cal. 111 22

Scheiding v. Dinwiddle Const. Co. (1999) 69 Cal.4th 64 .... 14, 21

Scott v. Municipal Court (1974) 40 Cal.App.3d 995, 996 34

Sentry Ins. Co. v. Superior Court (1989) 207 Cal.App.3d 526, 529-530 16

Shrimpton v. Superior Court of Los Angeles County (1943) 22 Cal.2d 562 14

Simons v. County of Kern (1965) 234 Cal.App.2d 362, 367 45

Sinaiko Healthcare Consulting, Inc. v. Pacific Healthcare Consultants
(2007) 148 Cal.App.4th 390, 402 .... 31, 42, 44, 47

Smith v. Kern County Land Co. (1958) 51 Cal.2d 205 45

Smith v. Superior Court (1893) 97 Cal. 348 35

State Market of Avenal, Inc. v. Superior Court of Kings County
(1959) 172 Cal.App.2d 517 14

Stewart v. Colonial Western Agency, Inc.
(2001) 87 Cal.App.4th 1006 .... 31, 32, 44

Sturgeon v. County of Los Angeles (2011) 191 Cal.App.4th 344 15

Sturgeon v. County of Los Angeles (2015) 242 Cal.App.4th 1437 .... 15, 24

Townsel v. Superior Court of Madera County (People)
(1999) 20 Cal.4th 1084, 1087 34

Townsend v. Superior Court (1998) 61 Cal.App.4th 1431, 1434 45

Union Bank v. Superior Court (Demetry) (1995) 31 Cal.4th 573 25

Volkswagen of Am. v. Superior Court of the City and County of San Francisco
(Adams) (2001) 94 Cal.App.4th 695, 701... 35

Wagner v. Superior Court (General Motors) (1993) 12 Cal.App.4th 1276 49

Waicis v. Superior Court (1990) 226 Cal.App.3d 283, 286-287 23

West Pico Furniture Co. v. Superior Court (1961) 56 Cal.2d 407, 419, fn.4 43

Walters v. Weed (1988) 45 Cal.3d 1, 9 42

California State Constitution
Article VI, §10 34

Statutes
Business and Professions Code
§6068(d) 30
§6106 30
§6128 30
§6067 30

Code of Civil Procedure
§128.7(b) 30
§425.12 30
§452 45
§1068 subd. (a) 14, 19
§§1085, 1086 .... 14, 19, 20
1088 33
§1094.5 .... 14, 33
§1102 14
§1103 19
§1105 33
§2016.010 et seq. 24, 44
§2016.040 .... 26, 31, 48
§2017.010 .... 43, 44
§2017.020(a) 46
§2019.030(a)(1) 47
§2019.030(a)(2) 48
§2019.030(b) 47, 48
§2023.010(f) 21
§2024.050 43
§2024.050 subd.(a) 43
§2025.420 subd. (g) 43

§2030.010 subd. (k) 43
§2025.420 subd. (n) 43
§2030.010 subd. (o) 32
§2030.090 48
§2030.010, §2030.020 15
§§ 2030.010 - 2030.070 23
§2030.010 - §2030.410 21
§2030.220 45
§2030.220(a), (b) 21
§2030.220(c) 26
§2030.240(a) 46
§2030.290(a) 47
§2030.290(b) 47
§2030.300 (a), (1)-(3) 48
§2030.300 (b) 42
§2030.300 (c) 48
§2031.010 (e) 43
§2031.310 (a), (1)-(3) 48
§2031.310 (b)(2) 48
§2031.310 (c) 48
§2031.060 48
§2033.710 .... 21, 40
§2033.740 (a), (b), (c) 41
The Civil Discovery Act 1986 .... 41, 42
Government Code §68511 .... 40, 41
§68070 44

Court Rules

California Rules of Court
1.5 (a) 42
1.5 (b)(1) 42
1.5 (c) 42
3.1020 .... 42, 48
3.501(3) 22
Los Angeles Superior Court Rule 3.25, Appendix 3.A(g)(3) 46

Miscellaneous "Advanced California Civil Procedure", Cerritos College, (August 2012) PowerPoint presentation on Interrogatories by the Hon. Judge Daniel S. Murphy, page 6 titled "Propounding Interrogatories" 46

Chief Justice Phil S. Gibson "For Modern Courts" (1957) 32 Cal.St.B.J. 727 .... 39, 40

Los Angeles Lawyer, (October 2008), "Will Someone Please Clean Up the Form Interrogatories Mess?", Paul Eisner Esq. 41

John Greacen, "Self-Represented Litigants: Learning from Ten Years of Experience in Family Courts", 44 Judges' Journal 24, 26, ABA Winter 2005 13

Weil & Brown, supra, at §6:105, page 6 - 24 41

Trial Court & Appeal: False Arrest, Imprisonment, and Civil Rights Violations By L.A. County

<u>Dumas v. Los Angeles County Board of Supervisors et al</u>. 45 Cal. App. 5th 348

<u>VERIFIED PETITION FOR WRIT OF MANDAMUS AND/OR PROHIBITION OR OTHER APPROPRIATE RELIEF</u>

TO THE HONORABLE PRESIDING JUSTICE AND ASSOCIATE JUSTICES OF THE COURT OF APPEAL OF THE SECOND APPELLATE DISTRICT FOR THE STATE OF CALIFORNIA:

"Sunshine is said to be the best of disinfectants; electric light is the most efficient policeman " - U.S. Chief Justice Louis Brandeis (1914)[8]

I. INTRODUCTION

A trial court is under a duty to hear and determine the merits of all matters properly before it which are within its proper jurisdiction and Mandamus may be used to compel the performance of this duty, see **Robinson v. Superior Court of Los Angeles County** (1950) 35 Cal.2d 379; the job of the judge is to call the ball and strikes, not to throw the pitches, see (John Greacen, "**Self-Represented Litigants: Learning from Ten Years of Experience in Family Courts**", 44 Judges' Journal 24, 26, ABA Winter 2005).

This lawsuit is not a game inwhere the party with a lawyer, the cleverest lawyer, or no lawyer prevails regardless and or irregardless of the merits, and the function of the trial judge is to be a fair umpire, see **Monastero v. Los Angeles Transit Co**. (1955) 131 Cal.App.2d 156. The trial court has unlawfully denied the Petitioner access to discoverable information by way of Judicial Council Form Interrogatories as a lawful discovery device; and he will be harmed and not fairly have his day before a jury trial. The Petitioner in pro per, as any litigant has a right to act as one's own 'attorney', see **Gray v. Justice's Court** (1937)18 Cal.App.2d

---

- [8] Brandeis, Louis D. (1914). <u>Other People's Money and How the Bankers Use It</u>. New York: Frederick A. Stokes.https://archive.org/stream/otherpeoplesmone00bran#page/n5/mode/2up

Copyright. © 2021. Paralegal Publishing Group.

420. Therefore, by this Verified Petition, the Petitioner in pro per alleges as follows:

A. The Parties to this Verified Petition for an Extraordinary Writ

1. The Petitioner is Luke Edward Dumas (herein "Petitioner"), an individual and in propria persona and in forma paupris, a resident of the County of Los Angeles ("County") and domiciled in the State of California. The Respondent is, and at all times herein incorporated by reference as the Los Angeles Superior Court - Central District ("Respondent"). The Respondent for purposes of this Verified Petition for Writ of Mandamus, is an inferior lower tribunal in where the Petitioner has no other plain, nor speedy remedy in the ordinary course of law. The Judge is the Hon. Judge Gregory Keosian of the Los Angeles Superior Court - Central District in Department 61, located at 111 N. Hill Street, Los Angeles, California, 90012. The Real Party in Interest is the "County of Los Angeles" ("Real Party"), named in this civil lawsuit as the "Defendant Los Angeles County Board of Supervisors", a local public entity, located at 500 W. Temple Street, Los Angeles, California, 90012.

B. The Basis for Writ Review for the Denial of Discovery

2. The ancient office of the "Writ of Mandamus" provides in essence that "One of the fundamental aims of the law [is] . . . to secure a litigant a judgment on the merits of a matter properly brought before the court, and . . . was used to compel courts to hear and decide merits of matters within its jurisdiction", see **State Market of Avenal, Inc. v. Superior Court of Kings County** (1959) 172 Cal.App.2d 517. The **Code of Civil Procedure Section §1068 subd. (a)** provides that "A writ of review may be granted by any court when an inferior tribunal, . . .

or officer, exercising judicial functions, has exceeded the jurisdiction of such tribunal, . . . or officer, and there is no appeal, nor, in the judgment of the court, any plain, speedy, and adequate remedy", see also **Shrimpton v. Superior Court of Los Angeles County** (1943) 22 Cal.2d 562; the **Code of Civil Procedure Section §1085**; and for abuse of discretion under the **Code of Civil Procedure Section §1094.5**; see also **Code of Civil Procedure Section §1102** for writs of prohibition.

    3. For the Respondent to have abused its discretion in denying the Petitioner's propounded "Judicial Council Form Interrogatories - General" ("Official Interrogatories") based on a sham declaration by the Real Party's counsel of record was inequitable, in Vol. 1 of Rec. at p. 000004[9]. A Notice of Appeal would be inadequate because this would harm the Petitioner in the upcoming jury trial against the Real Party because he was denied lawful discovery in the first instance because of Respondent's abuse of discretion, and the Respondent has thrown a pitch that essentially strikes him out from litigating his case properly before a jury trial, see Vol. 1 at p.000279; p.0000281; p. 0000285.

    4. Official Interrogatories have been designed by the *Judicial Council* of California to specifically aim at discovering the truth, see **Code of Civil Procedure Section §2030.010, §2030.020**: Vol. 1 at p.000050 - 000058. The Petitioner had a clear legal right to the truth, the whole truth and nothing but the truth from the Real Party in properly answering the because the Real Party has a duty to provide complete answers, see **Scheiding v. Dinwiddle Const. Co**. (1999) 69 Cal.4th 64; Vol.1 at p.000183.

---

[9] Volume 1 of the Petitioner's Record in Support of Writ of Mandamus, pages 000001 - 000291.

5. The Respondent appears to have a conflict of interest and it is a legal question that was not addressed in **Sturgeon v. County of Los Angeles** (2011) 191 Cal.App.4th 344 ("**Sturgeon I**") and in **Sturgeon v. County of Los Angeles** (2015) 242 Cal.App.4th 1437("**Sturgeon II**"). The Court has noted that the Real Party had provided unlawful "supplemental judicial benefit payments" ("payments") to trial judges in the County of Los Angeles since about 1998, and the payments were disguised as "supplemental judicial benefits" that the Los Angeles County Board of Supervisors unlawfully paid out an estimated $24.6 million per year, see **Sturgeon I & II**. The Court predicted in **Sturgeon I** that the California ". . . Legislature would soon enact a more permanent 'uniform statewide system of judicial compensation'. (Id. at p. **356**.) And as the Court has noted: *"it has not"*, see **Sturgeon II**. Therefore, should trial judges in the County of Los Angeles, disclose to if they had received the unlawful payments by the County because it presents a conflict of interest in litigation against the County?

C. Petitioner has Good Cause and Reasonable explained Delay

6. Although there ". . . is no absolute deadline for filing a Petition for Writ of Mandamus . . . the equitable doctrine of laches may bar relief when the Petitioner has unreasonably delayed in filing the Petition to the prejudice often opposing party. (**Sentry Ins. Co. v. Superior Court** (1989) 207 Cal.App.3d 526, 529-530". No such delay has been unreasonable given the current circumstances in this legal case. The Petitioner provides reasonable grounds and good cause for the waiver for the untimeliness of this Petition for a Writ of Mandate compelling the Real Party to answer in full Official Form Interrogatories. The reasons for the delay are as follows:

//

i. In Propria Persona

7. The Petitioner is in propria persona and not a licensed attorney at law and is not using advanced legal software as would a legal assistant(s) in a boutique law firm. The Petitioner does not specialize in Writ law and has no real-world experience in drafting writs presented to the Court of Appeal for review. Writs drafted for extraordinary relief are usually taken up by skilled attorneys, that specialize in that area of law and design their work to be officiated in the appellate courts. Therefore, the Petitioner must conduct his own legal research and draft his own legal formulations which takes large amounts of time. The Petitioner has other litigation pending, and in other matters, see Declaration of Luke Edward Dumas. Therefore, the Petitioner has been burdened with other legal matters and needed additional time to present this Writ, in which has caused delay in this filing before the 60-day rule on Writs.

ii. Confidential Medical Condition & Disability Issue

8. The Petitioner, without waiving confidential medical information herein, attaching a Confidential Judicial Council Form for "Request for Accommodation by Persons with Disabilities and Response" to this Court only. The Petitioner request that this Court please find it reasonable to accommodate him in the delay in filing this Petition.

iii. The Petitioner is in Forma Paupris

9. For good cause, the Petitioner is in forma paupris and does not have readily available financial resources due to his indigent status and "blacklisting" by his very own government. The Petitioner often has to obtain personal loans and is unable to hire an attorney at law to represent him in this legal matter.

The Petitioner cannot easily afford to buy office supply items such as ink, paper, postage, binding, copying, bates stamping, and color paper needed to present for Writ review in a timely manner. The Petitioner has had to buy and obtain each item at different times in order to gather the necessary materials to properly assemble this Petition which has caused delay. The Petitioner relies on public transportation to have to conduct the business needed to prepare the legal research at the law library, office supply store, post office, and other places of business necessary to prepare the materials needed for this Petition. Therefore, the Petitioner does not have readily available adequate resources because of his indigent status. The Petitioner cannot afford to hire a process server to serve this Writ but will make every good faith attempt in finding someone to help serve the Writ as is required under California law as expeditiously as possible. The Petitioner has had to rely on the court clerk for making copies and certifying the copies in order to package together and to present the Record, please see Vol. 1 at p. 000289-000290.

D. The Limitation of relying on Clerk Copies

10. The Petitioner has had to request from the court clerk to make copies pursuant to a fee waiver, please see Vol. 2 at p.000015-000016. The court clerk has limited the number of copies and certifications of each Exhibit filed herein pursuant to his fee waiver and department policy. The court clerk charges $25.00 for certification; and .50¢ per page for each copy and limits certification and copies under fee waiver requests. In order to able to compile the necessary number of copies needed to properly file this Petition along with Exhibits, the Petitioner has had to order the certified court clerk copies at different times. The Petitioner has had to borrow money to be able to complete all necessary copies that were not

available through the court clerk, and other needed costs in order to present this Petition and Exhibits.

D. Authenticity of Exhibits Volume 1 & Volume 2

11. All Exhibits accompanying this Petition are true copies of original documents on file with the Respondent with some certifications. Exhibits No. 1, 5, 6, 8, 9, 10, 11, and 12, which is a true copy of each Exhibit are not certified by the clerk due to the policy limits. Volume 1 & 2 of the Petitioner's Exhibits are bates stamped and paginated in order consecutively for each volume.

II. FACTS & PROCEDURE

A. Chronology of Pertinent Events to this Petition for a Writ

12. On April 26, 2016, the Petitioner in pro per filed an Unlimited Civil Complaint ("Complaint") against the Los Angeles County Board of Supervisors ("County of Los Angeles"), Sheriff Jim McDonnell, the Los Angeles County Sheriff's Department, and DOES 1-10, Vol. 2[10] at p.000018 - 000042. On July 1, 2016, the Real Party filed a Demurrer to the Petitioners Complaint with the Plaintiff. A law and motion hearing was held August 10, 2016, and the Respondent unjoined named Defendants "Sheriff Jim McDonnell, in his official and individual capacity" and the "Los Angeles County Sherriff's Department" in this legal matter. On August 21, 2016, the Real Party was served with the Petitioner's Judicial Council Official Form Interrogatories for an Unlimited Civil Case, Vol. 1 at p.000050 - 000057. On September 26, 2016, the Real Party provided to the Petitioner all boilerplate objections to the Official Interrogatories

---

[10] Volume 2 of the Petitioner's Record in Support of Writ of Mandamus.

Copyright. © 2021. Paralegal Publishing Group.

with no Verification with the exception of Interrogatories No. 1.1 in part and incomplete; No. 4.1, 4.2; No. 12.1 in part and incomplete; No. 14.1 and No. 14.2 in part and incomplete; and did not properly respond to No. 17.1 Vol. 1 at Vol 1. at p. 000060 - 000108.

13. On November 4, 2016, the Real Party served "Further Responses" and on November 9, 2016, Vol. 1 at p. 000135 - 000172. The Real Party served their Verification as a supplemental response, Vol. 1 at p. 000181. The Petitioner contacted in good faith the Real Party's counsel of record four times; such as on November 28, 2016, December 2, 2016, December 6, 2016, and on December 8, 2016, see Vol. 1. at p.000183 - 000192. The Petitioner did in fact consistently requested to "meet and confer" with Mr. Coleman Esq. in order to discuss the improper responses as evidenced by his correspondences. On December 8, 2016; and on December 14, 2016; the Petitioner emailed the Real Party's counsel of record a copy of a draft of a Separate Statement that included all the Interrogatories that the Real Party failed to properly answer and respond to, see Vol. 1at p. 000192 - 000221. Therefore, the Real Party's counsel of record failed to properly "meet and confer" in good faith to discuss narrowing the issues they have with the Official Interrogatories.

B. Absence of Other Remedies

14. Writ review is herein warranted because there is no current adequate remedy at law pursuant to the **Code of Civil Procedure §§ 1068, §1086, §1103**. The Petitioner will suffer irreparable injury if this Writ is not granted to command the Respondent to set aside its abusive Order denying the Petitioner the right to lawful discovery via Official Interrogatories. Substantial justice and fair play cannot be achieved nor corrected by a later appeal because the Petitioner is already

harmed in this case by not being able to discover the information being sought for the jury trial. The Petitioner will be harmed by not being able to present to the jury at the trial the discoverable information and complete full responses to the Official Interrogatories as is required under California law. The relevance and good cause for this Writ is that the *Code of Civil Procedure* has been followed by the Petitioner to the letter and the spirit of the law. Therefore, it was unjust and an abuse of discretion for the Respondent to have denied the Petitioner's "Notice of Motion & Motion to Compel Further Discovery Responses & for Monetary Sanctions" (herein "Motion"), see Vol.1 at p.000002 - 000011. In the pending legal proceeding the Petitioner will be harmed at jury trial if not being able to utilize the discovery device by way of Official Interrogatories.

C. No Prejudice to Opposing Party in Issuing a Writ

15. The opposing parties would not be prejudiced in this Petition for a Writ in seeking compliance with answering the Official Interrogatories because the trial date is set for February 13, 2018. Good cause exists in the best interest of justice and pursuant to the notion of substantial justice and fair play to allow the Petitioner to obtain lawful discovery in this case. Since the 60 days has run since the trial court issued its "Minute Order" Plain. Vol.1 at p.000281-000282; and the Real Party's "Notice of Ruling" was filed thereafter, Plain. Ex. Vol.1 p.000284-000285. Therefore, if determined by this Court for good and just cause; that there should be no prejudice to the opposing parties given the facts and issues at law in order to compel lawful discovery in this legal matter.

//

//

D. An Alternative Writ of Mandate can be used to seek Compliance with the Petitioner's Statutory Right to obtain Truthful Answers to Official Interrogatories

16. With respect to Alternative Writs, authorized under **Code of Civil Procedure Section §§1085, §1086**, if the Petition appears sufficient on its face, the Court may issue an Alternative Writ and the Alternative Writ commands the Respondent either to do the Act required to be performed, or to show cause before this Court as to why she or he has not done so. A Writ of Mandate may issue from any Court to any inferior tribunal, . . . or person to compel the performance of an act that the law specifically enjoins as a duty from an office, trust, or station, or to compel the response of a party to the use an enjoyment of a right or office to which the party is entitled and from which the party is unlawfully precluded. This Writ should be issued on the Verified Petition of the Petitioner beneficially interested, especially because there is no plain, speedy, and adequate remedy in the ordinary course of the law, under **Code of Civil Procedure Section §§1085, §1086; Palma v. U.S. Industrial Fasteners, Inc**. (1984) 36 Cal.3d 171.

17. Therefore, the Respondent had a duty to compel the Real Party in Interest to provide complete answers and responses to the Official Interrogatories. So there is no harm or prejudice to the Real Party in commanding the Respondent to set aside its decision and issue an order consistent with this statutory construction of lawful discovery specifically with regard to upholding the authority inherent in the Official Interrogatories.

III. LEGAL DISCUSSION

A. The Respondent Superior Court had a duty to Act in accordance with The Civil Discovery Act

18. The Petitioner did in fact seek from the Respondent to Act in accordance with The **Civil Discovery Act** and **Code of Civil Procedure Section §2030.010-§2030.410; §2033.710** by filing a timely Motion. The Real Party failed to provide full and complete answers to the Official Form Interrogatories as is required under California law. So, each answer in the response to the Official Interrogatory must be complete and straightforward as the information is reasonably available to the responding party as the truth permits. And if an Official Interrogatory cannot be answered completely, then it shall be answered to the fullest extent as possible under the **Code of Civil Procedure Section §2030.220(a), (b)**. Also, "false and evasive answers" are improper, and an answer that supplies only a portion of the information sought to a specific question is improper, see **Scheiding**. It is also improper to provide "conclusionary answers" designed to evade a series of questions, see **Deyo v. Kilbourne** (1978) 84 Cal.3d 771. As such in evading Official Interrogatories, the Real Party's evasive responses are grounds for sanctions under **Code of Civil Procedure Section §2023.010(f)**.

19. Official Interrogatory Numbers 12.1, 12.2, 12.3; 12.6; 16.6; 16.7; 16.8; 16.9; 16.10; and 17.0 asks the names of persons and witnesses to the event in this case. So even where an Interrogatory asks the names of all witnesses to a particular event that is known to the Real Party, then their response omitting the name of a known witness could and may subject the Petitioner to unfair surprise at trial, see **R & B Auto Ctr. Inc. v. Farmers Group, Inc**. (2006) 140 Cal.4th 327.

20. The Real Party referenced other documents such as "Responding party filed a general denial to an unverified complaint", see Vol.1 at p.000147. Responding to these Official Interrogatories that have required the Real Party to identify documents such as Interrogatory No. 12.1, 12.2, 12.3, 12.4, 12.5, 12.6, 13.2, 15.0, 16.1, 16.2, 16.3, 16.8, 16.9, 17.0. Thus, the mere existence of a privileged document is not generally privileged. Therefore, an adequate response must include a description of the documents even if the Real Party has the right to object to their production, see **Hernandez v. Superior Court** (Acheson Industries, Inc.) (2003) 112 Cal.4th 285. The Respondent, as the "judicial officer assigned for all purposes", see **Cal. Rules of Court, rule 3.501(3)** and is under the duty to hear and determine the merits of all matters properly before the court which are within its jurisdiction, and mandamus may be used to compel the performance of this duty, see **Robinson v. Superior Court of Los Angeles County** (1950) 35 Cal.2d 379.

21. The Respondent allowed the counsel of record Mr. McIntosh Esq. for the Real Party to misrepresent the facts in his Declaration, in which should have been found to be a sham, see Vol. 1 at p. 000277. The Respondent intentionally ignored the evidence, then failed to perform the mandatory duty of compelling the Real Party to provide full and complete answers to Judicial Council's Official Interrogatories, see Vol. 1 at p. 000277 - 000279. Therefore, Mandamus lies to compel the Respondent to proceed and exercise its functions why it has neglected or refused to do so, see **First Nat'l Bank v. Superior Court of Los Angeles County** (1925) 71 Cal.App. 64; see also **Golden Gate Tile Co. v. Superior Court** (1911) 159 Cal. 474.

22. The Respondent should be compelled by a Writ of Mandate to proceed with the issues at law by requiring a full and complete response to each of the Official Interrogatories that have been evaded in this legal matter, see Vol. 1 p.000049 - 000058. There is no current plain nor speedy remedy before the Respondent, especially if the Respondent refuses to do so without legal reason, see **San Diego v. Andrews** (1924) 195 Cal. 111.

B. Case of First Impression?

23. Under California law written interrogatories are governed and authorized for use in legal proceedings for lawful discovery under **Code of Civil Procedure Section §§ 2030.010 - 2030.070** as part of the **Civil Discovery Act. Ultimately in Johnson v. Superior Court** (2000) 80 Cal.App.4th 1050, at the top of page 1061,

"As a result, Writ review of discovery rulings are limited to situations where (1) the issues presented are of first impression and of general importance to the trial courts and to the profession (**Oceanside Union School Dist. v. Superior Court** (1962) 58 Cal.2d 180, 185-186, fn. 4 [23 Cal.Rptr. 375, 373 P.2d 439]), (2) the order denying discovery prevents a party from having a fair opportunity to litigate his or her case (**Waicis v. Superior Court** (1990) 226 Cal.App.3d 283, 286-287 [276 Cal.Rptr. 45]; **Lehman v. Superior Court** (1986) 179 Cal.App.3d 558, 562-563 [224 Cal.Rptr. 309, 508 P.2d 309]; **Korea Data Systems Co. v. Superior Court** (1997) 51 Cal.App.4th 1513, 1516 [59 Cal.Rptr.2d 925])".

Therefore, here are the issues in question presented of first impression and of general importance to the courts and legal industry, based on the Respondent's Order in denying the Petitioner discovery to Judicial Council Official Form Interrogatories:

1. Judicial Council Form Interrogatories

24. Are Judicial Council Form Interrogatories inherently authoritative, such as the "Form Interrogatories for Unlimited Civil Case"? Are the Judicial Council Form Interrogatories generally "objection proof" with established statutory exceptions, and as to their form and subparts? Are the Judicial Council Form Interrogatories for any civil case inherently authoritative thus automatically triggering the responding party to bear the burden of proving that the Interrogatories in question must be answered notwithstanding the legal doctrines and statutory exceptions to Judicial Council Official Interrogatories? Are trial judges allowed to disregard "Judicial Council Form Interrogatories for Unlimited Civil Cases" and treat them as having no primary authority in a Plaintiff's Separate Statement? Are Judicial Council Form Interrogatories "Instructions", in and of itself as primary authority, a compelling a legal reason for compelling a proper response?

2. Pro Per Litigants

25. Simply, are self-represented litigants such as pro per's "'officers of the court" for civil litigation purposes Pursuant to the **Code of Civil Procedure Section 2016.010 et seq**. similarly to a "guardian ad litem is considered[11]"? If a licensed attorney as an "officer of the court" acts unethically against a self-represented litigant ("pro per") by submitting a sham declaration and the judicial officer permits it, what remedy does the pro per litigant have in a court of law?

3. The County of Los Angeles

---

[11] In Regency Health Services v. Superior Court (1998) 64 Cal.App.4th 1496, "A guardian ad litem is an officer of the court . . ." and "Every litigant has a legal obligation to comply with the provisions of the Civil Discovery Act of 1986".

Copyright. © 2021. Paralegal Publishing Group.

26. Pursuant to the aftermath of: **Sturgeon I** and **Sturgeon II**. Did the unethical payments create a conflict of interest amongst LA Superior Court judges in providing fair and impartial court proceedings in lawsuits against the County of Los Angeles? Should Los Angeles County Superior Court judges disclose if they had received the unlawful "supplemental benefit payment" from the County of Los Angeles, and if so does this trigger a procedure to Disqualify or Recuse the judge in these type of legal matters for good cause and or a conflict of interest? When the County of Los Angeles, acting through its Board of Supervisors issued an unethical payment of $24.6 million dollars, about $57,000.00 per judge in 2013, did it leave intact a biased judicial system built in favor for the County of Los Angeles? Did the County of Los Angeles through fixing judicial compensation created a conflict of interest when it comes to suing the Real Party in Interest the County of Los Angeles?

C. The Basis for Relief, Beneficial Interest of the Petitioner, and the Capacities of the Respondent Superior Court and the Real Party in Interest County of LA

27. The Petitioner has no other plain, speedy, nor ordinary remedy in the course of law to compel the Real Party in Interest County of Los Angeles to provide total complete answers and responses to the Petitioner's properly served Official Interrogatories. This Petition, for good cause, should be permitted for review. The Petitioner will be further harmed by not being able to move for summary judgment because the incomplete answers to the Official Interrogatories cannot be used to satisfy the moving party's burden, see **Union Bank v. Superior Court** (Demetry) (1995) 31 Cal.4th 573.

And the Petitioner will further be harmed by not being able to narrow the issues and proffer all the relevant evidence being withheld by the Real Party before a trial by jury.

28. The Respondent had a duty to compel the Real Party and ensure that the Petitioner was able to obtain complete and truthful answers to the Official Interrogatories. However the Real Party obtained a "discovery exemption" based on a sham declaration by the Respondent, Vo. 1 at p. 000260 - 000262. In the case of **Regency Health Services, Inc. v. Superior Court** (Settles) (1998) 64 Cal.App.4th 1496, the Court noted that no party is exempt from lawful discovery and a party has a duty to conduct a reasonable investigation to obtain the competent information propounded by interrogatories. Therefore, the Real Party with the assistance of counsel, is under the duty to investigate or search out information propounded in the Official Interrogatories.

29. As for Interrogatories, unlike depositions, interrogatory answers are prepared with the assistance of counsel; the party must furnish all the information under his or her control; if the responding party does not have personal knowledge sufficient to respond fully to an interrogatory that party shall so state, but shall make a reasonable and good faith effort to obtain the information by inquiry to other natural persons or organizations, except where the information is equally available to the propounding party see **Code of Civil Procedure Section 2030.220(c)**; also in Regency Health Services Inc.

30. The Petitioner *has not and will not get a fair trial before the Respondent* because it has abused its discretion and has failed to perform the mandatory duty to compel the Real Party to comply with California law by evading lawful discovery vis-a-vis Judicial Official Interrogatories. The Petitioner will be harmed before a

jury by not being able to present the facts, information, and proper responses discovered, answered, and or admitted from the Official Interrogatories. The Petitioner's remedy at law is inadequate because he is not being permitted to access lawful discoverable information; the lawful discoverable information will not be available to the Petitioner because of the Respondent's abuse of discretion. The Real Party has the capacity to perform the duty of obtaining the discoverable information being sought.

31. The Petitioner has a beneficial interest in these legal proceedings because he is the Plaintiff suing for damages, see Vol. 2 at p. 000042; and therefore, has a beneficial interest in being made whole again. The Respondent has the capacity and legal duty and obligation to perform the Act sought to be compelled by this Verified Petition for Writ of Mandamus and/or Prohibition. The Petitioner in this legal case had a clear and beneficial right to the performance of that Act, the truth via Official Interrogatories. If the Respondent allows a duly licensed attorney at law to misrepresent the truth in their declarations in order to help the Real Party evade lawful discovery, what remedy does a self-represented litigant have against the Respondent and Real Party in order to not be harmed at trial?

D. The Petitioner's Motion to Compel Further Discovery Responses to Judicial Council Form Interrogatories was completely disregarded by the Respondent

32. The Petitioner properly set forth a Notice of Motion & Motion to Compel Defendant's Further Discovery Responses and for Monetary Sanctions", see Vol. 1 at p. 000002 - 000011. The Motion included a Memorandum of Points and Authorities, see Vol. 1 pgs. 000006 - 000007; and the Declaration of Luke

Edward Dumas, see Vol. 1 at p. 000004 - 000005 thus setting forth the facts. Therefore, the Petitioner did in fact show a reasonable good faith effort and attempt at an informal resolution to discuss the issues in the propounded Official Interrogatories. The Petitioner's Declaration, in Vol. 1 at p 000004 - 000005, was in substantial compliance with the **Code of Civil Procedure Section 2016.040**; in that he attempted to meet and confer in good faith with the Real Party's counsel of record Mr. John M. Coleman Esq., State Bar. No.79602 ("Mr. Coleman Esq.") several times, see Vol. 1 pgs 000183 - 000203. Mr. Coleman Esq. failed to participate in good faith in the meet and confer process and failed to discuss in good faith with the Petitioner whether by email or phone, Vol. 1 at p. 000005; 000188. The Respondent abused its discretion by ignoring these facts and unjustly denied the evidence before it, see Vol. 1 at p. 000004 - 000005; 000041 - 000221.

E. The Declaration of Luke Edward Dumas established good faith attempts to "Meet and Confer" with the Real Party's Counsel of Record but was disregarded by the Respondent Superior Court in favor of the Real Party in Interest County of LA

34. The Petitioner in pro per made many efforts to resolve the dispute out of court in order to seek the Real Party to be compelled to properly respond to all of the Judicial Council's Form Interrogatories for Unlimited Civil Case, Vol. 1 pgs. 000004 - 000005. In the Petitioner's Declaration, the Petitioner set forth the facts in line paragraphs numbers 6, 8, 9, 11, 12, 13, and 14 that he did his duty in properly attempting several times to meet and confer with Mr. Coleman Esq. in good faith, Vol. 1 at p. 000005. The Petitioner did in fact satisfy the meet and confer requirements as is required by California law. Therefore, the Petitioner expressly fulfilled the legal prerequisite to meet and confer' with the Defendant's

counsel of record but the Respondent abused its discretion in ignoring the Petitioner's Declaration and content in his emails that were sent to the Real Party.

F. The Declaration of W. Scott McIntosh was a sham declaration and not truthful but the Respondent Superior Court permitted Mr. McIntosh to play fast and loose with the discovery process and showing prejudice against the Petitioner

35. Mr. W. Scott McIntosh Esq., State Bar. No. 304124 ("Mr. McIntosh Esq."), an associate attorney at law working on behalf of Mr. Coleman Esq. The Real Party in Interest the County of Los Angeles had hired "Coleman & Associates" to represent them in this legal matter. Mr. McIntosh Esq. is playing fast and loose with the rules of discovery; and in fact has set forth a sham declaration in support of the Real Party's Opposition. Mr. McIntosh Esq. had declared under penalty of perjury that some mysterious "Office Staff[er]" contacted the Petitioner via telephone: "On Thursday, September 22, 2016, I directed Coleman & Associates' Office Staff to contact Plaintiff via telephone at the number Mr. Dumas has on file with the Court ((562)-356-0492), and request an extension in order to respond to Plaintiff's Discovery, as COUNTY's investigation was still ongoing. Mr. Dumas did not answer or respond to our telephone call and did not contact anyone at Coleman & Associates in response to that telephone call". As a matter of fact, no one from "Coleman & Associates' Office Staff" contacted the Petitioner at his telephone number as Mr. McIntosh Esq. so vaguely claims, see Vol. 1 pgs. 000260 - 000261.

36. The Petitioner informed the Respondent of this fact but the Respondent completely disregarded this disputed fact with prejudice and injustice so the Petitioner never submitted to the tentative decision, see Vol. 1 at p. 000281. Mr. McIntosh Esq. does not specifically identify by name exactly who in from

the 'Coleman & Associates' Office Staff" contacted the Petitioner, see Vol. 1 at p. 000260. Why did not Mr. McIntosh Esq. attach a supporting declaration of that mysterious Office Staff person? It simply was not truthful and in fact irrelevant. It was irrelevant because this alleged contact was made in connection with compelling discovery, not further discovery. Therefore, the Respondent abused its discretion in permitting this so-called 'evidence' as even being relevant to 'Further Discovery' in this case.

37. On November 4, 2016, the Real Party provided "Further Responses", therefore, Mr. McIntosh Esq. was misrepresenting the fact that this was satisfying a "meet and confer" pursuant to the supplemental response, see Vol. 1 at p. 000119; 000122-000130. The Respondent should have known of its irrelevancy and misrepresentation as fraudulent. The Petitioner did in fact inform the Respondent at the law and motion hearing that no one from the "law offices of John M. Coleman" had called him and the Petitioner verified that fact in his lawful Declaration, see Vol 1. at p. 000004 - 000005. The Respondent completely ignored this fact and abused its discretion by favoring Mr. McIntosh's fraudulent declaration in opposition over the Petitioner's truthful declaration.

38. Mr. McIntosh Esq. further claims under penalty of perjury that "On Friday, September 23, 2016, one day later, I called Mr. Dumas. . .". "No one answered or responded to my September 23, 2016 phone call . . . and I left a voicemail detailing County's request for an extension of time to responds to Plaintiff's Discovery and required Mr. Dumas contact Coleman & Associates to discuss. Plaintiff failed to respond to my September 23, 2016 voicemail". The fact of this legal matter is that no such voicemail was left by Mr. McIntosh Esq. on the Petitioner's voicemail and the Respondent was made aware of this

specific fact in the law and motion hearing, see Decl. of Luke Edward Dumas; and see Vol. 1 at p.000188; 000269. The Respondent abused its discretion by ignoring the disputed facts and simply failed by not asking Mr. McIntosh Esq. to simply prove it and or to provide rebuttable evidence to the Petitioner's.

39. As the Petitioner specifically demonstrates herein, there are two emphatic problems that the Respondent failed to note in its unjust tentative decision: The dates of "September 22" and "September 23" only relate to the Petitioner compelling discovery responses not the *further discovery responses*. Secondly, the two alleged "phone calls" made do not relate to the meet and confer requirements set forth in this disputed law and motion hearing.

40. Mr. McIntosh Esq. claims in his declaration, which should be found as a sham, starting in line paragraph number 13 in Vol. 1 at p. 000261:

> "On November 28, 2016, and December 2, 2016, Plaintiff sent emails purporting to 'Meet and Confer' re COUNTY's responses to Plaintiff's Form Interrogatories, Set One." "14. The November 28, 2016 emails failed to identify any discrete reason(s) why COUNTY"s Responses were allegedly deficient, and instead generally concluded the Responses were "incomplete" and /or 'evasive," without identifying which Interrogatory Response(s) Plaintiff was referring to". . . Plaintiff's purported 'Meet and Confer' efforts . . . contained any substantive discussion of any of COUNTY'S Responses to Interrogatories, Set One, but instead vaguely concluded COUNTY's Responses were 'incomplete' or 'evasive'. Plaintiff offered no basis for his positions as to any specific Form Interrogatory Response to Meet and Confer. As such, COUNTY was and is unable to address Plaintiff's suggestions that the Interrogatory Response is deficient".

41. The Attorneys of Record for Real Party intentionally distort the truth, such as Mr. McIntosh Esq. for Real Party in fact violated California **Code of Civil Procedure Section §128.7(b)**, by presenting to the Respondent false information by signing, filing, submitting, and later advocating their sham pleadings and

papers. The Real Party acting through their Attorney of Record did in fact certify to the best of their knowledge, information, and belief, allegedly formed after "an inquiry reasonable under the circumstance", that all of the following conditions have been met: (1) It is not being presented primarily for an improper purpose, such as to harass or to cause unnecessary delay or needles increase in the cost of litigation. (2) The claims, defense, other legal contentions therein are warranted by existing . . . , or reversal of exiting law or the establishment of new law"; see **Bockrath v. Aldrich Chem. Co**. (1999) 21 Cal.4th 71.

 42. Mr. McIntosh Esq. not only violated California's rules of ethics for state licensed lawyers but violated California law by perjuring himself. The Petitioner informed the Respondent that Mr. McIntosh Esq. was in fact lying and misleading Respondent in his declaration and it was disturbing that "his Honor" would rubberstamp it; see Decl. of Luke Edward Dumas.; **Business and Professions Code Section §6068(d)**; **Business and Professions Code Section §6106**; and **Business and Professions Code Section §6128**. Under **Business and Professions Code Section §6067**, the requirement for a lawyer is to "faithfully to discharge the duties of any attorney at law to the best of [their] knowledge and ability". The Real Party has acted above the rule of law without consequence in regard to this legal matter and is an institutional problem.

G. The Respondent Tentative Ruling was a Clear Abuse of Discretion and not one Single Word from the Petitioner's pleadings were cited; the Respondent abused its discretion in favor of the Real Party in Interest County of LA

 43. How can a trial judge completely disregard a pro per's pleadings, not even cite the moving party in a tentative decision, and not be an abuse of discretion? The Respondent is allowing the Real Party to evade lawful discovery

by making all blanket objections. However, at **footnote 14** in **Sinaiko**, in which the Respondent cited in the tentative ruling, to the effect that even absence a separate statement, a trial court can still rule to continue the law and motion hearing.

The Respondent abused its discretion in giving a discovery exemption to the Real Party, and this type of impropriety is cause for disqualification, and raises serious doubt as to if the Respondent is in fact impartial to the Petitioner's claims against the County of Los Angeles.

H. The Real Party's Opposition to Plaintiff's Good Faith Meet and Confer Requests to Mr. John M. Coleman Esq. was based on a sham declaration by his associate Counsel of Record Mr. William Scott McIntosh Esq.

44. A number of factors identified in the Petitioner's "Statement of Evidence to be Introduced" was completely disregarded by the Respondent, thus leading to its abuse of discretion. The Petitioner has presented this to the Respondent as direct evidence, but they have neglected to include it into the record, thus showing substantial prejudice. The Real Party is allowed to declare that "someone" made a phone call not even related to the Motion. . . . The Real Party, acting through their attorney Mr. Coleman Esq., contend that in their reason for not compelling further responses to Judicial Council Form Interrogatories are because: "Plaintiff failed to properly 'Meet and Confer' as required by case law, statute, and Local Court Rules, as set forth in the "Declaration of W. Scott McIntosh". The purpose of the 'Meet and Confer' requirement contained **California Code of Civil Procedure §2016.040** is to force the parties to reexamine their positions and narrow discovery disputes. **Stewart v. Colonial Western Agency, Inc**. 87 CA4th 1006, 1016-1017 (2001). As Plaintiff's 'Meet and Confer' letters did not identify any specific

issue(s) with County's Response, Plaintiff's 'Meet and Confer' efforts were therefore not a good faith attempt to resolve this discovery issue".

45. The Real Party only purports that the Petitioner ". . . failed to properly 'Meet and Confer' as required . . ." but does not establish any factual or legal basis for this conclusion. The Respondent ignores the Declaration of Luke Edward Dumas set forth in the Motion, Vol. 1 at p. 000004 - 000005. The Respondent in its tentative ruling abusively re-asserted the Real Party's statement as a conclusion but not as a matter of fact thus abusing its discretion, see page 000277. The Real Party, in citing **Stewart v. Colonial Western Agency, Inc**. (2001) 87 Cal.App.4th 1006, misapplies the case and the Respondent abuses its discretion in disregarding the caselaw presented before it, see Vol. 1 of p. 000278.

46. The Petitioner did exactly what the Court said to do in Stewart, "The Discovery Act requires that, prior to the initiation of a motion to compel, the moving party declare that he or she has made a serious attempt to obtain 'an informal resolution of each issue.' **(§2025, subd. (o))**. This rule is designed 'to encourage the parties to work out their differences informally so as to avoid the necessity for a formal order . . .' (**McElhaney v. Cessna Aircraft Co**. (1982) 134 Cal.App.3d 285, 289. . .". Further in **Stewart**, the Court noted that:

> "A determination of whether an attempt at informal resolution is adequate . . . involves the exercise of discretion. The level of effort at informal resolution which satisfied the 'reasonable and good faith attempt' standard depends upon the circumstances. in a larger, more complex discovery context, a greater effort at informal resolution may be warranted. In a simpler, or more narrowly focused case, a more modest effort may suffice. The history of the litigation, the nature of the interaction between counsel, the nature other issues, the type and scope of discovery requested, the prospects for success and other similar factors can be relevant. A judge has broad powers and responsibility to

determine what measure and procedures are appropriate in varying circumstances." (**Obregon v. Superior Court** (1998) 67 Cal.App.4th 424, 431 . . . . "A trial judge's perceptions on such matters, inherently factual in nature at least in part, must not be lightly disturbed".

47. The Petitioner went beyond modest efforts by emailing Mr. Coleman Esq. more than one time, see Vol.1 at p. 000004 - 000005. The Respondent abused its discretion in determining that the Petitioner did not satisfy a reasonable and good faith attempt to Meet and Confer. The Order denying lawful discovery in this legal matter must be disturbed because the Record does not support the Respondent's conclusion and is thus an abuse of discretion, demeans the integrity of the legal system, and is harmful.

RELIEF REQUESTED:
WHEREFORE, PETITIONER prays as follows:

1. That this Court issue a Writ of Mandate ordering Respondent:

(a). Issue a peremptory writ of mandate and or prohibition in the first instance (**Code Civ. Proc., §§ 1088, §1094.5, §1105**), directing respondent court to vacate its order granting defendants' motion denying the petitioner's motion to compel further discovery responses to the official judicial council form interrogatories and granting the motion to compel further discovery responses;

(b). Issue an alternative writ directing respondent superior court to act as specified in Paragraphs 2(a) of this prayer, or to show cause why it should not be ordered to do so, and upon return to the alternative writ issue a peremptory writ as set forth in paragraph 2(a) of this prayer or such other extraordinary relief as is warranted.

(c) To issue a stay of the trial scheduled to commence on February 13, 2018, in the Los Angeles Superior Court - Central District Court Case Number BC618191, with the stay to remain in effect pending final disposition of this Petition.

2. To issue a "Palma Writ" in the first instance, and in its discretion and for good cause issue an alternative writ, and grant Petition as an ex parte application without notice or service of this Petition as an application as provided in Palma at fn. 7.

3. For costs of Petition herein incurred; for such other and further relief as the court may deem proper.

Dated: 6/20/2017   Respectfully submitted,

Trial Court & Appeal: False Arrest, Imprisonment, and Civil Rights Violations By L.A. County
Dumas v. Los Angeles County Board of Supervisors et al. 45 Cal. App. 5th 348

MEMORANDUM OF POINTS AND AUTHORITIES

I. INTRODUCTION

The Writ requested herein is the appropriate method of judicial review because the Respondent abused its discretion in denying the Petitioner lawful discovery. As based on such, the Court noted, "The prerogative writ is an appropriate method of review when an abuse of discretion results in a denial of discovery, see **Lehman v. Superior Court** (1986) 179 Cal.App.3d 558, 562.

The **California Constitution in Article VI**, **§10**, grants the Supreme Court, the Courts of Appeal, and the superior courts original jurisdiction in issuing writs of mandate and prohibition in special proceedings for extraordinary relief; see **Townsel v. Superior Court of Madera County** (People) (1999) 20 Cal.4th 1084, 1087; see also **People v. Romero** (1994) 8 Cal.4th 728, 742-743. In the case of **Popelka, Allard, McCowan & Jones v. Superior Court of Santa Clara County** (H. Costner Enterprises) (1980) 107 Cal.App.3d 496, "An appellate court may consider a petition for an extraordinary writ at any time (**Bryant v. Superior Court** (1936) 16 Cal.App.2d 556, 561 . . . but has discretion to deny a petition filed after the 60-day period applicable to appeals, but should not do so if "extraordinary circumstances" justified the delay as in this legal matter, see **Reynolds v. Superior Court** (1883) 64 Cal. 372, 373; **People v. Municipal Court** (Mercer) (1979) 99 Cal.App.3d 749; **People v. Superior Court** (Duran) (1978) 84 Cal.App.3d 480, 489; **Scott v. Municipal Court** (1974) 40 Cal.App.3d 995, 996; **Estate of Glassgold** (1950) 97 Cal.App.2d 859, 863-864.).

Copyright. © 2021. Paralegal Publishing Group.

"There may be some difference in time under present practice between the calendaring of writs and appeals since it may take longer for records and briefs to reach this court on appeal in a writ proceeding, but this difference in time should not exceed 90 days in any case", see **fn. 3** in **Phelan v. Superior Court of the City and County of San Francisco** (1950) 35 Cal.2d 363. In the case of Phelan, the Petitioner must show some special reason as to why the remedy of appeal is inadequate in this particular circumstance, see **Lincoln v. Superior Court** (1943) 22 Cal.2d 304, 311.

The Respondent abused its discretion in denying lawful discovery and the remedy of appeal is inadequate and inequitable. The remedy of appeal is inadequate because it does not serve substantial justice and fair play, and is a waste of judicial resources, especially if a Notice of Appeal is taken and the case is remanded back to Respondent for further proceedings raised in this Writ. Therefore, it is not enough to wait to file a notice of appeal after disposal of this case when the Respondent abuse of discretion which shall result in immediate harm to the Petitioner at jury trial because the Respondent is permitting the Real Party to abuse the discovery process by fairly adjudicating this case at taxpayer expense, given the fact that both parties are hereby exempt by way of fees waived under California law.

"It is well established that a petition for writ of mandamus must be filed within the same statutory period as prescribed for appeals. As the Supreme Court put it in **People v. Robinson** (1883) 64 Cal. 372, 373, 'Unless circumstances of an extraordinary character be shown to have intervened, the remedy through a writ of certiorari should be held to be barred by the lapse of the same length of time that bars an appeal from a final judgment.' A Petition may also be rejected as untimely if not filed for review within 60 days from the date of the order being challenged herein, please see **Volkswagen of Am. v. Superior Court of the City and County of San Francisco** (Adams) (2001) 94 Cal.App.4th 695, 701. The Petitioner has shown good cause for the delay in seeking this writ of mandate such as being in propria persona, in forma paupris, as well as needing an accommodation. In **Bryant**, at page 561, the Court stated that:

> "There is no statutory provision placing a limitation on the time
> within which a petition for writ of review must be filed.
> The remedy of may be barred by laches, although 'there is no
> hard-and-fast rule by which to determine whether laches has
> barred the remedy'. (**Reid v. Superior Court**, 44 Cal.App. 349 . . . .
> Where there has been an unreasonable, unexplained delay in
> seeking the writ, the courts have considered the time allowed by
> law within which to appeal from a final judgment as sufficient,
> and, by analogy, have held that the remedy through certiorari
> should be held barred by the lapse of the same length of time.
> (**Reynolds v. Superior Court**, 64 Cal. 372; **Smith v. Superior Court**,
> 97 Cal. 348; **In Boyer v. City of Long Beach**, 47 Cal.App. 617
> . . . the court stated that 'the time within which certiorari . . .
> may be instituted is determined by the equities of the case'.

II. THE STANDARD OF REVIEW

A. Writ Review is proper for the denial of the discovery of Official Form Interrogatories

The Respondent abused its discretion in unjustly denying Judicial Council Official Form Interrogatories as primary authority based on the sham declaration of Mr. McIntosh Esq. Also, the subject of Judicial Council Form Interrogatories as being generally "objection-proof" and as to its inherent primary authority should be considered of great importance to the profession and judiciary. In the case of

Rodriquez v. Menjivar (2015) 243 Cal.App.4th 816, at page 821, "The question of whether a trial court applied a correct legal standard to an issue in exercising its discretion is a question of law. . .", see **Gonzalez v. Munoz** (1997) 156 Cal.App.4th 413, 420-421, requiring de novo review; see **Cellphone Termination Fee Cases** (2009) 180 Cal.App.4th 1110, 1118; see **Eneaji v. Ubboe** (2014) 229 Cal.App.4th 1457, 1463.

In **Johnson**, at page **1061**, the Court analyzes the Standard of Review, and stated that "Management of discovery lies within the sound discretion of the trial court. Consequently, appellate review of discovery rulings is governed by the abuse of discretion standard", see also **Greyhound Corp. v. Superior Court** (1961) 56 Cal.App.4th 1599,1612. The Respondent's determination should be set aside only when it has been demonstrated that there was 'no legal justification' for the order granting or denying the discovery in question (Ibid., citing **Carlson v. Superior Court** (1961) 56 Cal.2d 431, 438. The Court further noted in **Johnson**, "We are reminded, however, that in passing on orders denying discovery, appellate courts 'should not use the trial court's discretion argument to defeat the liberal policies of the statute.' (**Greyhound Corp. v. Superior Court**, (1961). . . 56 Cal.2d 355, 378-379.)". In **Mobil Oil Corp. v. Superior Court** (1976) 59 Cal.App.3d 293, at page 303 the Court stated: "(1) Orders either compelling an interrogatory or sustaining an objection to an interrogatory are reviewable by extraordinary writ **Greyhound Corp. v. Superior Court**, 56 Cal.2d 355. 368-369, fn. 1[15 Cal.Rptr. 90, 364 P.2d 266]) but such writs will not be issued routinely or as a matter of course even where the trial court's order is erroneous **Oceanside Union School Dist. v. Superior Court**, 58 Cal.2d 180, 185-186, fn.4 [23 Cal.Rptr. 375, 373 P.2d 439]). Generally, the prerogative writ should only be used in discovery matters to review questions of first impression that are of general importance to the trial courts and to the profession". The Court further noted in **Mobile Oil Corp**. that discovery in mandamus proceeding is not well defined and the complexity of the subject matter of rulings depending, can provide a compelling reason for consideration of this Writ. The Court, continuing further in **Mobile** at page **304** further guides us in interpreting California law:

> ". . . but the appellate court should not use the rule giving the trial court wide discretion to defeat the liberal policies of the statutes with respect to orders which limit or deny discovery. The Supreme Court in the **Pacific Telephone and Telegraph** Company case has given the broadest possible interpretation of relevance, namely, relevance of the subject matter, in defining the scope of discovery, stating: "Matters sought are properly discoverable if they will aid in a party's preparation for trial [Citations.] In addition, because all issues and arguments that will come to light at trial often cannot be ascertained at a time when discovery is sought, court may appropriately give the applicant substantial leeway, especially when the precise issues of the litigants of the governing legal standards are not clearly established [citation]; a decision of relevance for purposes of discovery is in no sense a determination of relevance for purposes of trial.' (**Pacific Tel. & Tel. Co. v. Superior Court**, supra, 2 Cal.3d 161, 172-173.)".

III. A CASE OF FIRST IMPRESSION?

A. Pursuant to the Judicial Council's rule-making power, are "Form Interrogatories" primary authority in and of itself, and generally "Objection-Proof" notwithstanding the instructive and statutory legal exceptions?

The issue of first impression in this legal case is as follows: Should the Judicial Council Form Interrogatories used in civil cases be considered "objection-proof"? According to a secondary source, the Hon. Judge Daniel S. Murphy of the Los Angeles Superior Court currently a duly elected Judge, whom is also an Adjunct Professor at the Cerritos College ABA-approved Paralegal Program in Norwalk, California, has theorized and is of the school of thought that the Official Interrogatories are indeed "objection-proof.", and "Not subject to Rule of 35", see Cerritos College, ABA-approved paralegal program, Adjunct Professor Hon. Judge Daniel S. Murphy, "**Advanced California Civil Procedure**" (August 2012), PowerPoint presentation on Interrogatories, page 6 titled "Propounding Interrogatories").

In the case of **Nacht & Lewis Architect, Inc. v. Superior Court** (1996) 47 Cal.4th 214, which the third district court of appeal for California found that Form Interrogatory 12.2 was objectionable on and if, only on the grounds of work product, if there were a list of potential witnesses interviewed by opposing counsel, already identified in defendant's response to interrogatory no. 12.1, and if counsel deemed it important enough to interview. The Court noted at page **217** to **218** in **Nacht & Lewis Architects, Inc**.:

> "On the other hand, a list of potential witnesses who turned over to counsel their independently prepared statements would have no tendency to reveal counsel's evaluation of the case. Such a list would therefore not constitute qualified work product. Moreover, unlike interview notes prepared by counsel, statements written or recorded independently by witnesses neither reflect an attorney' evaluation of the case nor constitute derivative material, and therefore are neither absolute nor qualified wok product. (See, e.g., **Rodriguez v. McDonnell Douglas Corp**. (1978) 87 Cal.App.3d 626, 647-648 [151 Cal.Rptr. 399]; **Kadelback v. Amaral** (1973) 31 Cal.App.3d 814, 822-823 [107 Cal.Rptr. 720]; **People v. Boehm**, supra, 270 Cal.App.2d 13".

In the case of **Coito v. Superior Court** (2010) 182 Cal.App.4th 758, the fifth district court of appeal for California ruled that form interrogatory number 12.3 was not protected by the work product privilege. The court stated at page **768** and **769**, in that common questions are clearly proper in written interrogatories because answers to interrogatories are prepared with the assistance of counsel, see **8:898 ff** and certain objections are generally not appropriate for other discovery devices such as interrogatories; **Greyhound v. Superior Court** (Clay); for rule of 35 see **Catanese v. Superior Court** (1996) 46 Cal.App.4th 1159, 1164. For work product, under **Nacht & Lewis Architect, Inc**. and unlike the **Coito** case which was fully briefed case, the **Nacht & Lewis** was decided as a peremptory "**Palma**" writ, meaning the court of appeal decided it only based on the papers of the party filing the appeal, without receiving full briefing of the case, Id. at p. **218** in **Palma v. U.S. Industrial Fasteners, Inc**. (1984) 36 Cal.3d 171. Is there any case in where a court of appeal in any district in California has ever found the actual form as inherent authority including the definitions "objectionable"? Pursuant to the Judicial Council's rule-making power, is a nonsensical result to construe lawful interrogatories as entirely objectionable without a clear showing of statutory exceptions or by judicial doctrine.

IV. ARGUMENT

A. The Respondent's abuse of discretion resulted in the denial of discovery with no legal justification

In **Lehman v. Superior Court** (Lehman) (1986) 179 Cal.App.3d 558, at page 560,

> "[1] Ordinarily the prerogative writ is not a favored method of obtaining review of discovery orders (**Sav-on Drugs, Inc. v. Superior Court** (1975) 15 Cal.3d 1, 5 [123 Cal.Rptr. 283, 538 P.2d 739]), but it is appropriate where an abuse of discretion results in a denial of discovery.
> (**Pacific Tel. & Tel. Co. v. Superior Court** (1970) 2 Cal.3d 161, 170, fn. 11 [84 Cal.Rptr. 718, 465 P.2d 854].) Though broad, the trial court's discretion in discovery matters is not unlimited.
> (**Greyhound Corp. v. Superior Court** (1961) 56 Cal.2d 355, 380 [15 Cal.Rptr. 90, 364 P.2d 266].) "[I]f there is no legal justification

for such exercise of discretion it must be held that an abuse occurred." (**Carlson v. Superior Court** (1961) 56 Cal.2d 431, 438 . . . . "

B. California Judicial Council Form Interrogatories are inherently primary authority thus commanding a proper and complete response to each unanswered interrogatory

The rule making power and the modernization of the Judicial Council was comprehensively noted in the California's State Bar Journal in 1957, by Hon. Chief Justice Phil S. Gibson, please see (Chief Justice Phil S. Gibson "**For Modern Courts**" (1957) 32 Cal.St.B.J. 727, 728, 730, 731); I have attached this highly valued secondary authority in Vol. 2 at pgs. 000003 - 000013. The Hon. Chief Gibson notes in Vol. 2 at page 00005,

> "Since its establishment, the Council has had the power to adopt rules of practice and procedure not inconsistent with our codes, and, accordingly, for more than 30 years it has supplemented the statues with such rules for all our courts. In 1941 the Legislature gave the Council authority to make all rules governing appellate practice, and in 1955 it gave the Council the power to make rules governing pretrial conference procedure. The proposed measure would round out this development by placing in the Council compete rule-making power over all practice and procedure".

In Vol. 2 at p. 000006 , the Hon. Chief Gibson briefly describes this modern perspective, "The modern approach is to give to a special body of judges, or judges and lawyers, aided by a skilled staff and the cooperation of the profession, the responsibility of formulating flexible rules adaptable to changing needs".

The California Legislature had indeed codified the Judicial Council's rule-making power and its authority to prescribe forms for use in California courts, pursuant to **Government Code Section §68511** which states: "The Judicial Council may prescribe by rule the form and content of forms used in the courts of this state. When any such form has been so prescribed by the Judicial Council, no court may use a different form which as its aim the same function as that for which the Judicial Council's prescribed form is designed". The Judicial Council has inherent authority to have designed and approved these forms for use in unlimited civil cases as an official discovery device. Therefore, the form itself is a primary authority and the Instructions commanding proper and complete responses to the form is mandatory and not permissive.

The **Code of Civil Procedure Section § 2033.710**, states that "The Judicial Council shall develop and approve official form interrogatories . . . of the genuineness of any relevant documents or of the truth of any relevant matters of fact for use in any civil action in a state court based on personal injury, property damage, . . . or . . . for any other civil action the Judicial Council deems appropriate". Therefore, pursuant to California law, the Judicial Council has inherent authority to develop and approve Official Interrogatories. Thus, Judicial Council form interrogatories are statutorily authorized to obtain the truth of any relevant matters of fact for their use in any civil action in the Respondent's court. Pursuant to **Code of Civil Procedure Section §2033.740**: **Subdivision (a)** - "Use of the form interrogatories . . . approved by the Judicial Council shall be optional"; "subdivision (b) The form interrogatories . . . shall be made available . . ." and subdivision (c) provides that, "[t]he Judicial Council shall promulgate any necessary rule to govern the use of the form interrogatories. . .". This brings this Petition to an interesting point, "Since there are only two types of interrogatories - attorney drafted, specially prepared interrogatories and Judicial Council form interrogatories . . .". (Los Angeles Lawyer, (October 2008), "**Will Someone Please Clean Up the Form Interrogatories Mess?**", Paul Eisner Esq.). The Respondent diverged from the Judicial Council's rule-making power by disallowing Official Interrogatories as a discovery device.

In **People ex rel. Department of Transportation**, the Court discusses how **Government Code Section §68511** authorizes the Judicial Council to prescribe by rule the form and content of forms used in the courts of this state, see also **Code of Civil Procedure Section §425.12**. "The Judicial Council pleading forms have simplified the art of pleading and have made the task of drafting much easier. Nevertheless, in some cases more is required than merely placing an 'X' in a box. (**Weil & Brown, supra, at § 6:105, p. 6-24**.) 'Adoption of Official Forms for the most common civil actions has not changed the statutory requirement . . .". The court further notes, that "In some cases, merely checking a box on a Judicial Council form . . .will be sufficient". With regard to Official Interrogatories only, the Respondent should have found that placing a 'X' in a box of the Official Interrogatory is sufficient.

C. The Separate Statement Rule Does Not Limit the Respondent's Discretion to Compel Further Answers & Responses Notwithstanding even in its absence

In **Professional Career Colleges**, **Magna Institute, Inc. v. Superior Court of Riverside County** (Stewart) (1989) 207 Cal.App.3d 490, the Court noted the well-established rule that, ". . . in construing a statute the task of the court is to ascertain the legislative intent so as to effectuate the purpose of the law. (**Walters v. Weed** (1988) 45 Cal.3d 1, 9; **Moore v. Panish** (1982) 32 Cal.3d 535 . . .Where language is susceptible of two meanings, the one leading to mischief or absurdity is to be avoided, and the meaning according to justice and common sense adopted. (**Lampley v. Alvares** (1975) 50 Cal.App.3d 124, 128 . . .". Therefore, it makes no sense as to why the Respondent would deny the Petitioner the statutory right to discoverable information via Judicial Council Official Form Interrogatories. Pursuant to the California **Rules of Court, rule 1.5 (a)** "The rules and standards of the California Rules of Court must be liberally construed to ensure the just and speedy determination of the proceedings that they govern". Under the California **Rules of Court, rule 1.5 (b) (1)**, "'Must' is mandatory;".

Therefore, under **subd. (c)** "Standards are guidelines or goals recommended by the Judicial Council. The Respondent failed to perform its mandatory duty and must be compelled to do so.

In **Sinaiko Healthcare Consulting, Inc. v. Pacific Healthcare Consultants** (2007) 148 Cal.App.4th 390, at page **409**, in the **fn.14**, states: "Normally, to compel further responses, the trial court would need to find that the propounding party made an effort at informal resolution sufficient to satisfy the "meet and confer" requirement of **Section §2030.300, subdivision (b)**. Although the court rule requiring a separate statement on a motion to compel further responses (**Cal. Rules of Court, rule 3.1020**) would permit the trial court to continue or deny a motion to compel when no separate statement is provided, it does not limit a trial court's discretion to compel further answers notwithstanding the absence of a separate statement". The Respondent even cited **Sinaiko** it one its authorities in its tentative ruling, see Vol.1 at p. 000277.

The conclusion in **Greyhound** apply equally to the new discovery statutes enacted by the **Civil Discovery Act of 1986** which retain the expansive scope of discovery, see **Obregon v. Superior Court** (Cimm's, Inc.) (1998) 67 Cal.App.4th 424, 434. For example, even when a statute requires a showing of good cause to obtain discovery this term is liberally construed-to permit, rather than to prevent, discovery whenever possible, see Greyhound; see **Liberty Mut. Fire Ins. Co. v. LcL Adm'rs, Inc**. (2008) 163 Cal.App.4th 1093. The Respondent prevented lawful discovery rather than to liberally allow it, thus abusing its discretion in violation of California law.

D. The Petitioner is Entitled to Propound and Obtain Lawful Discovery Responses by using Judicial Council's Official Form Interrogatories

There are several limitations on the time when discovery may be sought, firstly, a pending action is required, see **Code of Civil Procedure Section §2017.010**. The "**Code of Civil Procedure Section §2024.050** provides, in part, that "any party shall be entitled as . . . a matter of right to complete discovery proceedings on or before the 30th day...before the date initially set for trial of the action." (**Code Civ. Proc., §2024.050, subd. (a)**, italics added.)"
In **Professional Career Colleges, Magna Institute, Inc**. at page **493**:

> "The **Civil Discovery Act of 1986** made sweeping changes in the methods by which the parties to a lawsuit may obtain formal discovery. Most notably, it imposed severe restrictions on the use of written interrogatories by lifting the number of questions which could be asked. (See **§ 2030, subd. (c)**.) Provisions with respect to sanctions were redrafted with the effect that a refusal to comply with a discovery request, or an unsuccessful motion to compel further response, is subject to mandatory sanctions unless the court specifically finds that the refusal or motion was either substantially justified or excused by other equitable considerations. (See **§ 2030, subd. (k)** (interrogatories): **§ 2025, subd. (g)** (depositions); **§ 2031, subd. (e)** (requests to produce).) In some cases, the party seeking to compel discovery must show that he has made an effort to resolve the dispute out of court. (See, e.g. **§ 2025, subd. (n)**.)".

The fact that a triable issue has not yet been determined cannot bar the disclosure of information sought for the very purpose of trying that issue, see **West Pico Furniture Co. v. Superior Court** (1961) 56 Cal.2d 407, 419, fn.4. Although broad, the right to discovery is not absolute, there are several important limitations to consider and some contained in the **Discovery Act** itself, and others resulting from other laws: such as the information sought must be (1) not privileged, (2) relevant to the subject matter" of the action, and (3) either itself admissible to "reasonably calculated to lead to the discovery of admissible evidence", see **Code of Civil Procedure Section §2017.010**. The Respondent has no authority to make restrictions under **Government Code Section §68070(a)** and abused its discretion by adopting a tentative ruling inconsistent with the law and rules adopted by the Judicial Council. The Respondent ultimately imposed a penalty by upon the Petitioner by denying Judicial Council Official Interrogatories, Vol. 1 pgs. 000277-000279.

It is a central precept of the California **Civil Discovery Act**, see **Code of Civil Procedure Section §2016.010 et seq**., and that discovery be self-executing. Discovery is to be allowed whenever consistent with justice and public policy. The statutory provisions must be liberally construed in favor of discovery and the courts must not extend the statutory limitations upon discovery beyond the limits expressed by the Legislature. Civil discovery is intended to operate with a minimum of judicial intervention. For the exact purposes of lawful discovery via Judicial Council Form, the information being sought is and must be considered relevant if that information might reasonably assist a party in evaluating the case, preparing for trial, or facilitating settlement thereof, see **Gonzalez v. Superior Court** (1995) 33 Cal.App.4th 1539, 1546; **Lipton v. Superior Court** (1996) 48 Cal.App.4th 1599, 1611; **Stewart v. Colonial Western Agency** (2001) 87 Cal.App.4th 1006, 1013. Rules are liberally applied in favor of discovery, **Colonial Life & Accident Ins. Co. v. Superior Court** (1982) 31 Cal.3d 785, 790.

E. The Petitioner has a broad right to obtaining lawful discovery from the Real Party in Interest County of LA using the Judicial Council Form Interrogatories

In fact, the Court of Appeal for the Second District in stated in **Sinaiko Healthcare Consulting, Inc**. at page **402** states :

"The **Civil Discovery Act** provides litigants with the right to broad discovery. In general, 'any party may obtain discovery regarding any matter, not privileged, that is relevant to the subject matter involved the pending action or to the determination of any motion made in that action, if the matter either is itself admissible in evidence or appears reasonably calculated to lead to the discovery of admissible evidence.' (**§2017.010**.)' In establishing statutory methods of obtaining discovery, it was the intent of the Legislature that discovery be allowed whenever consistent with justice and public policy. [Citation.]
The statutory provisions must be liberally construed in favor of discovery...' (**Irvington-Moore, Inc. v. Superior Court** (1993) 14 Cal.App.4th 733, 738-739... Civil discovery is intended operate with a minimum of judicial intervention. '[I]t is a 'central precept' of the **Civil Discovery Act** ... that discovery 'be essentially self-executing'.' (**Obregon v. Superior Court** (1998) 67 Cal.App.4th 424, 434..., quoting **Townsend v. Superior Court** (1998) 61 Cal.App.4th 1431, 1434".

Furthermore, it is not the duty of the Respondent to assist a pro per litigant but it is the duty of the Respondent to show the appearance of objectivity and impartiality which are so important to public confidence in the administration of justice, see **Lombardi v. National Trust & Savings Bank of Los Angeles** (1955) 137 Cal.App.2d 206. The Respondent failed in showing the appearance of objectivity and impartiality. The Respondent must have liberally construed the Petitioner's pleadings in the Notice of Motion to Compel Further Discovery Responses but did not. The Respondent failed in committing itself to the rule of liberal construction of pleadings with a view of substantial justice between the parties, see **Simons v. County of Kern** (1965) 234 Cal.App.2d 362, 367; **Estate of Wickersham** (1908) 153 Cal. 603; **Smith v. Kern County Land Co**. (1958) 51 Cal.2d 205; see **Code of Civil Procedure Section §452**.

F. The Real Party was using Boilerplate Objections to Evade Lawful Discovery via Judicial Council Form Interrogatories and the Respondent abused its Discretion in denying the Petitioner's Motion to Compel Further Discovery Responses

An answer to Official Interrogatories must be made as completely and straightforwardly as possible given the information available to it, under **Code of Civil Procedure §2030.220**. This duty has been described as follows: "Parties must state the truth, the whole truth, and nothing but the truth in answering written interrogatories", see **Guzman v. General Motors Corp**. (1984) 154 Cal.App.3d 438. Boilerplate objections are in and of itself sanctionable conduct, see **Korea Data Systems Co., Ltd. v. Superior Court** (1997) 51 Cal.App.4th 1513, 1516; furthermore under **Chembrook v. Superior Court** (1961) 56 Cal.2d 423, the court has held that with regard to discovery requests, it is not proper ground for objection that the request is ambiguous unless it is so ambiguous that the responding party cannot in good faith frame an intelligent reply. An Interrogatory may be objectionable in part or in full and if an interrogatory is objectionable only in part, the portion should be answered pursuant to **Code of Civil Procedure Section §2030.240(a)**; Similarly, objections to interrogatories should be based on a good faith belief in their merit and not be made for the purpose of withholding relevant information. If an interrogatory is objectionable only in part, the unobjectionable portion should be answered, see **Los Angeles Superior Court, Rule 3.25, Appendix 3.A(g)(3)**. When responding to Official Interrogatories, the answering party, as the Real Party in Interest owed a duty to respond to the Petitioner's Official Form Interrogatories in good faith as best as they can, see **Deyo**. By the Respondent falsely finding without any reasonable inference, that the Petitioner did not meet and confer with the Real Party's attorney of record, it essentially sustained all of the boilerplate objections forthwith.

Objections on the ground of over breadth of undue burden or lack of merit under the burden expense or intrusiveness of that discovery clearly outweigh the likely that the information sought will lead to the discovery of admissible evidence, see **Code Civil Procedure §2017.020, subd. (a)**. If not using the proper objection can lead a trial court to view the Real Party as misusing the discovery process and subject to sanctions, the wrong use of the discovery process.

G. The Real Party's Objections must be deemed waived by Operation of California law and the Respondent abused its Discretion in not Considering the Petitioner's Evidence

The Petitioner sets forth the fact that the Real Party as the Defendant in this case has a duty to answer the Official Interrogatories, see Plaint. Ex. Vol.1 p. 000004-000005.

The burden of proof, on the propounding party's motion to compel a further response, the responding party has the burden of establishing a valid objection, see **Coy v. Superior Court** (1962) 58 Cal.2d 210, 220. The Respondent's decisions were not supported by the pleadings filed in the Noticed Motion to Compel Further Discovery Responses. The Respondent has the authority to grant a motion to compel interrogatory responses under **Code of Civil Procedure Section §2030.290, subdivision (b)**, especially after the Petitioner set forth the evidence of the Real Party's all blanket objections were in noncompliance with California law, see Vol. 1 at p. 000006-000007.

The Petitioner set forth evidence that the responses provided by the Real Party were in fact evasive, Vol. 1 at p. 000004-000005. If a party fails to serve a timely response to the interrogatories, as the Defendant County did, Vol. 1 at p. 000006; then by operation of law, all objections that it could assert to those interrogatories are waived **(§2030.290, subdivision (a)**. So, unless the Real Party had obtained relief from its waiver, the propounding party, the Petitioner and Plaintiff in pro per, is entitled to move under the **Code of Civil Procedure Section §2030.290, subd. (b)** for an order compelling the response to which the propounding party is entitled. In **Deyo**, at page **782**, where the question is specific and explicit the answer which supplies only a portion of the information sought is wholly insufficient; and the Court noted that the responding party is required to provide information not only based on their own personal knowledge, but also on knowledge that they may acquire through a reasonable inquiry.

H. The Respondent abused its discretion and deprived the Petitioner a Statutory Right to Lawful Discovery via Judicial Council Form Interrogatories on its face

Moreover, the scope of permissible discovery is broad and the purpose of pretrial discovery is to obtain all of the facts relative to a claim or defense, see **Hernandez v. Superior Court** (2003) 112 Cal.App.4th 285 301. The Court further notes in **Sinaiko**:

> "When discovery disputes arise as to interrogatories and document requests, the trial court may intervene in the discovery process in three circumstances. First, a responding party may move for a protective order to challenge a discovery demand. To prevail it bears the burden **(§2019.030, subd. (b)**) to demonstrate that the 'discovery sought is unreasonably cumulative or duplicative or is obtainable from some other source that is more convenient, less burdensome, or less expensive' **(§2019.030, subd. (a)(1)**), or that the 'selected method of discovery is unduly burdensome or expensive' **(§2019.030, subd. (a)(2)**; see **§§2030.090** [motion for protective order on interrogatories], **§2031.060** [motion for protective order

on inspection demands]). The responding party must also demonstrate that it made 'reasonable and good faith attempt at a formal resolution of each issue presented' by the motion for a protective order. (**§2016.040**; see **§§2019.030, subd.(b)**, **§2030.090, subd. (a),§2031.060, subd. (a)**.) This is sometimes referred to as an obligation to "meet and confer" (**§2016.040**.)".

The Court continues its analysis in **Sinaiko**:

"Second, if a propounding party is not satisfied with the response served by a responding party, the propounding party may move the court to compel further responses. (**§§2030.300** [fn. omitted] [interrogatories], **§2031.310** [inspection demands].) The propounding party must demonstrate that the responses were incomplete, inadequate or evasive, or that the responding party asserted objections that are either without merit to too general. (**§§2030.300, subd. (a)(1)-(3)**; **§2031.310, subd. (a)(1)-(3)**.) The propounding must bring its [notice of] motion to compel further response within 45 days of the service of the response (**§§2030.300, subd. (c), §2031.310, subd. (c)**), and must demonstrate that it complied with its obligation to 'meet and confer.' (**§§2016.040, §2030.300, subd. (b), 2031.310, subd.(b)(2)**.) (Also required is a separate statement as specified in **Cal. Rules of Court, rule 3.1020**.)".

Where a court has jurisdiction of a case, it should not be permitted by an arbitrary or erroneous order to divest itself of jurisdiction but should be compelled by mandamus to proceed with the case, **Ingalls v. Superior Court of Los Angeles County** (1932) 121 Cal.App. 453 [9 P.2d. 266].

I. The Respondent has failed to perform a mandatory duty by California Law and the Respondent has not Acted in the Spirit of California Law and should be Mandated to do so or the Petitioner will be harmed at the upcoming jury trial

It is the duty of a trial judge to see that a cause is not defeated by: Firstly, by 'merely inadvertence', see **Hellings v. Wright** (1916) 29 Cal.App. 649; Secondly, by the evidence or defects in the pleadings' which are likely to result in a decision other than on the merits, see **Farrar v. Farrar** (1919) 41 Cal.App.452; and Thirdly, by failing to within reasonable limits to clearly bring out the facts so that the important functions of the Respondent's office may be fairly and justly performed, see **Estate of Dupont** (1943) 60 Cal.App.2d 276. The Respondent must conform to the spirit of the law and not defeat the ends of substantial justice. A trial court's discretion is not absolute, the Court noted: "The discretion intended, however, is not a capricious or arbitrary discretion, but an impartial discretion, guided and controlling its exercise by fixed legal principles. It is not a mental discretion, to be exercise ex gratia, but a legal discretion, to be exercised in conformity with the spirit of the law and in a manner to subserve not to impede or defeat the ends of substantial justice.' (**Bailey v. Taaffe** (1886) 29 Cal. 422, 424.)", see **Gamet v. Banchard** (2001) 91 Cal.App.4th 1276.

The Respondent cutoff the Petitioner's right to discovery contrary to California law, the Petitioner in pro per, as a litigant had a right to lawful discovery, see **Wagner v. Superior Court** (General Motors) (1993) 12 Cal.App.4th 1315; **InHauk v. Superior Court** (DeMott) (1964) 61 Cal.2d 295, the Supreme Court did in fact issue a writ in InHauk, and concluded that ". . . the trial court acted in excess of its jurisdiction because there was no factual or legal basis supporting its exercise of discretion." Therefore, the trial court nor the opposing party can prevent the disclosure of lawful information sought in this case for the very purpose of trying this case. In **Anderson v. Superior Court** (1989) 213 Cal.App.3d 1321, although there are well recognized limits on the availability of prerogative writs, the intervention of an appellate court may be required to consider instances of a grave impression and general importance to the bench and bar where general guidelines can be laid down for future cases.

V. CONCLUSION

The Respondent has abused its discretion by unlawfully cutting off discovery, may have an undisclosed conflict of interest, and has issued a ruling inconsistent with California law. Therefore, this Court should issue a Writ of Mandate compelling the Respondent to set aside its Order denying discovery via Official Interrogatories.

Dated: 6/20/2017

Respectfully submitted,

_____

Luke E. Dumas, Petitioner in pro per

VERIFICATION

I, Luke Edward Dumas, am the Petitioner in the above-entitled action. I have read the foregoing Petition for Writ of Mandamus and know the contents thereof. The same is true of my own knowledge, except as to those matters which are therein alleged on information and belief, and as to those matters, I believe it to be true. I declare under penalty of perjury under the laws of the State of California that the foregoing is true and correct, in Los Angeles, California, on June 20, 2017, Los Angeles, CA.

_____

Luke E. Dumas, Petitioner in pro per

CERTIFICATE OF WORD COUNT

(Cal. Rules of Court, rule 8.204(c)(1))

The total number of words in this Petition and Points and Authorities (excluding the caption page, table of contents and authorities, verification, certificates, and exhibits) is 13,533.

Copyright. © 2021. Paralegal Publishing Group.

Trial Court & Appeal: False Arrest, Imprisonment, and Civil Rights Violations By L.A. County

Dumas v. Los Angeles County Board of Supervisors et al. 45 Cal. App. 5th 348

Case No. B288554

IN THE COURT OF APPEAL
OF THE STATE OF CALIFORNIA
SECOND APPELLATE DISTRICT
DIVISION FOUR

LUKE EDWARD DUMAS,

Plaintiff & Appellant,

vs.

The Los Angeles County Board of Supervisors et al,

Defendants & Respondents;

APPEAL FROM FINAL ORDER OF DISMISSAL AND SUBSEQUENT ORDERS FOR ABUSE OF DISCRETION, DENIAL OF DUE PROCESS, & DISQUALIFICATION

Luke Edward Dumas, in pro per
5462 E. Del Amo Blvd.
Long Beach, California, 90808
(562) 356-0492

Copyright. © 2021. Paralegal Publishing Group.

Trial Court & Appeal: False Arrest, Imprisonment, and Civil Rights Violations By L.A. County

Dumas v. Los Angeles County Board of Supervisors et al. 45 Cal. App. 5th 348

TO BE FILED IN THE COURT OF APPEAL — APP-008

COURT OF APPEAL, SECOND APPELLATE DISTRICT, DIVISION FOUR	COURT OF APPEAL CASE NUMBER: B288554
ATTORNEY OR PARTY WITHOUT ATTORNEY: STATE BAR NUMBER: NAME: LUKE EDWARD DUMAS FIRM NAME: N/A STREET ADDRESS: 5462 E. DEL AMO BLVD CITY: LONG BEACH STATE: CA ZIP CODE: 90808 TELEPHONE NO.: (562) 356-0420 FAX NO.: E-MAIL ADDRESS: ATTORNEY FOR (name): PLAINTIFF IN PRO PER	SUPERIOR COURT CASE NUMBER: BC618191

APPELLANT/PETITIONER: LUKE E. DUMAS

RESPONDENT/REAL PARTY IN INTEREST: Los Angeles County Board of Supervisors et al.

CERTIFICATE OF INTERESTED ENTITIES OR PERSONS

(Check one): [X] INITIAL CERTIFICATE   [ ] SUPPLEMENTAL CERTIFICATE

Notice: Please read rules 8.208 and 8.488 before completing this form. You may use this form for the initial certificate in an appeal when you file your brief or a prebriefing motion, application, or opposition to such a motion or application in the Court of Appeal, and when you file a petition for an extraordinary writ. You may also use this form as a supplemental certificate when you learn of changed or additional information that must be disclosed.

1. This form is being submitted on behalf of the following party (name): LUKE EDWARD DUMAS, PLAINTIFF & APPELLANT

2. a. [ ] There are no interested entities or persons that must be listed in this certificate under rule 8.208.

   b. [X] Interested entities or persons required to be listed under rule 8.208 are as follows:

Full name of interested entity or person	Nature of interest (Explain)
(1) LOS ANGELES COUNTY GOVERNMENT	County Government controls, operates, and compensates Trial Courts
(2) LOS ANGELES SUPERIOR COURT	Trial Court of Claim & Dismissal; Property/Payee of County Govern.
(3) HILDA L. SOLIS, First District Supervisor	Party to action in official capacity; pecuniary and financial and legal
(4) MARK RIDLEY-THOMAS, Second Dist. S.	Party to action in official capacity; pecuniary, financial, and legal
(5) SHEILA KUEHL, Third Dist. Supervisor	Party to action in official capacity; pecuniary, financial, and legal

[X] Continued on attachment 2.

The undersigned certifies that the above-listed persons or entities (corporations, partnerships, firms, or any other association, but not including government entities or their agencies) have either (1) an ownership interest of 10 percent or more in the party if it is an entity; or (2) a financial or other interest in the outcome of the proceeding that the justices should consider in determining whether to disqualify themselves, as defined in rule 8.208(e)(2).

Date: June 5, 2019

LUKE E. DUMAS, PLAINTIFF & APPELLANT
(TYPE OR PRINT NAME)   (SIGNATURE OF APPELLANT OR ATTORNEY)

Form Approved for Optional Use
 Judicial Council of California
 APP-008 [Rev. January 1, 2017]

CERTIFICATE OF INTERESTED ENTITIES OR PERSONS

Cal. Rules of Court, rules 8.208, 8.488 <br> www.courts.ca.gov

---

Copyright. © 2021. Paralegal Publishing Group.

"ATTACHMENT 2"

FULL NAME:	NATURE OF INTEREST:
JANICE HAHN, SUPERVISOR	Party to action in official capacity, pecuniary, financial and legal interest in appeal outcome; respondeat superior
KATHERYN BARGER, SUPER.	Party to action in official capacity, pecuniary, financial and legal in appeal outcome; respondeat superior
LOS ANGELES COUNTY SHERRIFF'S DEPARTMENT	Party to action in official capacity, pecuniary, financial and legal in appeal outcome; respondeat superior
SHERRIFF FOR LOS ANGELES COUNTY	Successor in interest; Party to action in official capacity, pecuniary, financial and legal interest in appeal outcome; chief law enforcement officer for Los Angeles County
2ND COURT OF APPEAL	Judicial Branch of Government for the State of California; Beneficiaries and recipients of Los Angeles County monetary and supplemental benefits
ATTORNEY GENERAL OF CALIFORNIA	Chief law enforcement officer for the State of California; responsible for litigating civil and criminal rights violations by and against the Defendants; Legal review of California's anti-discrimination laws in civil appeals

Copyright. © 2021. Paralegal Publishing Group.

TABLE OF CONTENTS

Certificate of Interested Persons

Table of Contents

Table of Authorities

I. Introduction

II. Good and Just Cause Exists for the Legal Reasons of Why the Final Order Dismissing Plaintiff's Case Should Be Reversed & Assigned a New Judicial Officer

III. Plaintiff is Entitled to Due Process of Law & the Trial Court Abused its Discretion Throughout the Legal Process of this Case Against the Government

IV. Summary of Facts and Procedural History

V. The Court Order dismissing the Plaintiff's Case against the Defendant County Government Should and or Must be Reversed and Remanded

VI. The Trial Judge Made a Harmful Error by not Disqualifying himself and or for Calendaring a Hearing before the Presiding Judge

VII. The Trial Court made a Harmful Error by sustaining the Defendants Demurrer to the Plaintiff's Complaint, the final Order must be reversed, and is null and void

VIII. The Trial Court made a Harmful Error by Sustaining the Defendant's Motion to Strike and a Disqualified Judge's Order is null and void

IX. The Trial Court made a Harmful Error by Failing to Disclose his Potential Conflicts of Interests involving the County of Los Angeles

X. The Trial Court's Order Violated the Plaintiff's right to privacy in his medical records, the trial court violated the Plaintiff's Rights in disclosing medical information to the Government and police, who are now using and misusing his medical conditions against him

CONCLUSION

CERTIFICATE OF WORD COUNT

Copyright. © 2021. Paralegal Publishing Group.

TABLE OF AUTHORITIES

Federal Constitution

US Constitution, Art. III

Federal Codes

42 USC 666

42 USC 18

Federal Cases

EEOC v. Consol Energy Inc. (2017) 4th Circuit, No. 16-1406

Scott v. Sanford (1857) 60 US 393

Mendez v. Westminster (1946) 161 F.2d 774 [64 F.Supp.544]

Brown v. Board of Education (1954) 347 US 483

Miranda v. Arizona (1966) 384 US 436

Bates v. Arizona (1977) 433 US 350

California Constitution

Cal. Const. Art. 1, Sec. 1

California State Cases

Garza v. Delano Union Elementary District (1980) 110 Cal.App.3d 306

Roman v. County of Los Angeles 85 Cal.App.4th 316

California State Codes

Government Code 820.4

Government Code 815.2 & 851.5

Code of Civil Procedure 170.3

Code of Civil Procedure 430.41(a)

California Court Rules

Cal. Rules of Court, rule 8.100

Cal. Rules of Court, rule 8.104

Additional Citations

Psalms 82:6

Jonah 1:17

Daniel 3 & 6

Revelations 13 & 17

APPEAL FROM FINAL ORDER OF DISMISSAL AND SUBSEQUENT ORDERS FOR ABUSE OF DISCRETION, DENIAL OF DUE PROCESS, & DISQUALIFICATION

TO THE HONORABLE JUSTICES OF DIVISION FOUR:

I.

INTRODUCTION

This appeal is authorized under California's **Rules of Court, rule 8.100** & **rule 8.104**; **Garza v. Delano Union Elementary District** (1980) 110 Cal.App.3d 306; **Roman v. County of Los Angeles** (____) 85 Cal.App.4th 316; and under California law and US Constitutional law inclusive.

The Appellant and Plaintiff in pro per appeal the Final Order and subsequent Orders (CT-000175-000181, in Vol. 1 of 3; see CT-000463-000466, in Vol. 2 of 3; and see CT-000534-00535; CT-000590; 000627;000688 in Vol. 3 of 3) made throughout the legal process of this unlimited civil case against the Defendant and Respondent Los Angeles County Board of Supervisors, the Los Angeles County Sherriff's Department, the Sherriff, and DOES 1 – 3, otherwise known as "COLA".

The California court system is not immune to making mistakes of law and fact and in this legal case at the trial court level, has shown bias and prejudice against self-represented litigant in favor of the Defendant COLA.

We know that lawyers and judges are ordinary humans but have been endowed with god-like powers, indeed, lawyers and judges have the power to decide one's life and death. As the psalm's states, "ye are gods" (Psalms 82:6). Not the Supreme God, but the contrast is made because of the power of the judicial branch of Government, see **US Constitution, Art. III**.

And as the modern saying goes: "it is what it is". But it should not be so though, and if most people do not vote, then the result is the fate that legal affairs get decided by elite group of persons[12]. Our Government professes Courts to be the check and balance in the Government.

In this legal case, no justice can be adequately achieved in the State of California when it comes to the civil rights, the right to privacy in medical records, and in derailing the Plaintiff's right to petitioning the Government for its grievances. Especially for self-represented litigants such as the Plaintiff in this case.

When going against the Government, the ordinary self-represented individual litigant, as a citizen and taxpayer, no matter how rich or poor, is comparable to the likes of an ant; and the Government (city, county, state, and federal) is comparable to the likes of a "Godzilla".

Without any other choice, the Appellant comes to the belly of this beast in order to appeal for his legal rights, see *Jonah 1:17; Daniel 3 & 6; Revelations 13 & 17*; **42 USC 666**; **42 USC 18**; **EEOC v. Consol Energy Inc**. (2017) 4th Circuit, No. 16-1406[13].

II.
GOOD AND JUST CAUSE EXISTS FOR THE LEGAL REASONS OF WHY THE FINAL ORDER DISMISSING PLAINTIFF'S CASE SHOULD BE REVERSED & ASSIGNED A NEW JUDICIAL OFFICER

This unlimited civil case raises legal issues relating to Federal Constitutional and Statutory laws. A notice of appeal should be liberally construed and in favor of pro per litigants (CT-000689-000701, in Vol. 3 of 3), **Cal. Rules of Court, rule 8.100**.

These legal Brief outlines and describes how the trial court acted with extreme prejudice, intentionally made errors, disregarded the Plaintiff's legal rights, and violated the rules of law in order to appease the Defendant County who pays him extra money aside from his State Government salary.

---

[12] https://www.courts.ca.gov/documents/judicial-branch-overview.pdf
[13] http://www.ca4.uscourts.gov/Opinions/Published/161230.P.pdf

Copyright. © 2021. Paralegal Publishing Group.

Under California's **Code of Judicial Ethics**, it is a conflict of interest for a judicial branch government official, to get paid from the State Government and County Government and then claim "objectivity" in a case inwhere either public entity is a party. Nothing could be more illogical and unreasonable in the public eye; a judge has a serious conflict of interest if it is collecting money from a party and then that same judge gets to decide the fate of that party's legal dilemma. Denial is not proof nor does offer a proof of anything.

Rarely, as a matter of statistic, do appellate courts overturn trial courts. Therefore, most statutory appeals get denied as a matter of custom and policy, not as a matter of fact and law. This is the breakdown of our legal system as we know it. Some of the lawyers officiating this Government in the California courts have no value for the letter nor the spirit of the laws for and by the People. By designing a failed trial court system, disregarding the facts and law are the ultimate abuse of discretion.

III.
PLAINTIFF IS ENTITLED TO DUE PROCESS OF LAW & THE TRIAL COURT ABUSED ITS DISCRETION THROUGHOUT THE LEGAL PROCESS OF THIS CASE

This case also involves civil rights violations and an interest to the general public because it involves the unlawful expenditure of taxpayer dollars by the Respondent/Defendant Government; the Defendants have unlawfully surveilled me during the time pending this lawful appeal and is misusing your and my taxpayer dollars to do it illegally.

Plaintiff and Appellant has been under continuing harassment, surveillance, and sabotage by the Defendants and Respondents.

As the trial court abused its discretion, the Plaintiff was and still is entitled to due process of law but may not get any justice (CT-000619, Vol. 3 of 3). Appellate Courts are reluctant to reverse lower court decisions and blindly presume that all lower court decisions are presumed valid unless shown otherwise.

This type of legal reasoning may lead to support unconstitutional and unlawful orders and judgments such as the ones in this case. Are the California appellate courts subscribing to the fallacy of authority in their logic by blindly presuming all judgments are correct unless shown otherwise. As if after being smashed by a Godzilla like an ant, the judicial branch embodies authoritarianism and not democracy.

In this legal case it would be a false and fallacious presumption to assume that just because the lower court made a judgment that that judgement is always true and correct (**Scott v. Sanford** (1857) 60 US 393; **Mendez v. Westminster** (1946) 161 F.2d 774 [64 F.Supp.544]; **Brown v. Board of Education** (1954) 347 US 483; **Miranda v. Arizona** (1966) 384 US 436; **Bates v. Arizona** (1977) 433 US 350). These types of historical cases have a common legal reasoning and such a custom or policy is illogical, unconstitutional, and undemocratic.

This appeal must and should be treated on an individual case by case basis, and when it comes to petitioning the government, *the Plaintiff as an ordinary American citizen has an inalienable legal right to petition his government for grievances* according to the **US Constitution**.

This Court should solicit supplemental briefing on the legal principle and argument that as such, the individual American citizen taxpayer's legal rights are superior to any form of Government, regardless whether city, county, state, and or federal. No form of Government is superior or overrides the **US Constitution**, as such the **US Constitution** is the supreme law of this land is settled law. The trial court judge failed to uphold the US Constitutional principles and words proscribing the right to due process, truthfulness, and privacy.

The trial court failed to uphold the spirit and letter of the law, especially the Plaintiff's constitutional rights in this case. The Plaintiff's legal rights were discarded and diminished as the case progressed through the trial court level.

IV.
SUMMARY OF FACTS AND PROCEDURAL HISTORY

On April 26, 2016, the Plaintiff in pro per filed a timely Complaint for Damages against and naming the following Defendants: the "Los Angeles County Board of Supervisors", the "Los Angeles County Sherriff's Department", the former "Sherriff Jim McDonnell", and "DOES 1 to 10" (CT-000013, Vol. 1 of 3). The Plaintiff alleged nine causes of action in the Complaint for Damages against all Defendants (CT-000009-000045, Vol. 1 of 3):

1) **False arrest & imprisonment** under **Government Code 820.4** conspiracy (CT-00028-000030, Vol. 1 of 3)
2) **Denial of Civil Rights & Discrimination** (CT-000030-000031, Vol. 1 of 3)
3) **Violation of Cal. Const. Art. 1, Sec. 1** (CT-000031-000032, Vol. 1 of 3)
4) Gross Negligence (CT-000032, Vol. 1 of 3)
5) Failure to Discharge Mandatory Duty under **Government Code 815.2 & 851.5** (CT-000032-000033, Vol. 1 of 3)
6) Delay in Processing & Releasing (CT-000033, Vol. 1 of 3)
7) Malicious Prosecution (CT-000033-000034, Vol. 1 of 3)
8) Conspiracy (000034-000035, Vol. 1 of 3)
9) **Unruh Civil Rights** Conspiracy (000035, Vol. 1 of 3)

The Defendants hired a private law firm, headed by an attorney named John M. Coleman who was also assisted by licensed attorney Scott McIntosh as the counsel of record for all Defendants in this case (CT-000063; 000088; 000108; 000117; 000182; 000230 – 000234, in Vol. 1 of 3) and see (CT-000244 – 000249; 000251; 000280, in Vol. 2 of 3).

The Defendants demurred and moved to strike Plaintiff's Complaint (CT-000063-000074; 000076-000111, in Vol. 1 of 3). The Plaintiff opposed the demurrer with motion to strike (CT-000120-000172, Vol. 1 of 3). The trial court granted the Defendants motion to demurrer in part by dismissing the Defendants Los Angeles Sherriff's Department and Jim McDonnell (CT-000175-000181, Vol. 1 of 3).

The trial court Ordered the remaining named Defendant Los Angeles County Board of Supervisors to file an Answer but failed to order Plaintiff to amend his Complaint. The dismissal of the named police Defendants was improper, prejudicial, and discriminatory (CT-000181, Vol. 1 of 3).

V.

The Court Order dismissing the Plaintiff's Case against the Defendant County Government Should and or Must be Reversed and Remanded

If the trial court's Final Order found in (CT-000688, in Vol. 3 of 3) is not reversed and remanded for its legal errors or any error at all, then real justice surely is not designed to be obtained in the industrial legal complex administered in California courts. The trial court made several technical legal errors as a matter of law and civil procedure throughout the progress of the case (CT-000181, Vol. 1 of

3); and see (CT-000463-000466, in Vol. 2 of 3); and see, CT-000534-000535; 000590; 000592-000625; 000654; 000678-000681; 000688, in Vol. 3 of 3). The trial court was covertly prejudicial and allowed the Defendants to abuse the legal process in this legal case because:

1) the Plaintiff appeared in pro per and was not a licensed attorney (CT-000013-000045, Vol. 1 of 3).
2) The trial court made and ordered technical legal errors in the motion to demurrer (CT-000175-000181).
3) in the motion to compel plaintiff's deposition (CT-000590, Vol. 3 of 3)
4) in the motion to quash subpoena of medical records dating back to about 20 years ago (CT-000475-00482; 000534-000535, Vol. 3 of 3), allowing the Defendant to obtain the Plaintiff's confidential medical records in violation of California and Federal law [code], and
5) the motion to compel discovery was not granted prejudicially in favor of Defendant County because they are a government entity and provide annual monetary compensation directly to the trial court judge in the form of payments of money and benefits.
6) The trial judge was legally disqualified under **Code of Civil Procedure 170.3**; and avoided setting the Plaintiff's statement of disqualification for a hearing thus denying him due process under Constitutional law.
7) The Defendants counsel of record were allowed and permitted to sidestep proper legal procedure in its demurrer in violation of **Code of Civil Procedure 430.41(a)**,
8) The trial court judge allowed the Defendant County to illegally obtain Plaintiff's medical records by making an Order that is normally criminal and unlawful [code];
9) The trial court judge allowed the Defendant County acting through their counsel to lie under penalty of perjury in their declarations, make secret orders, intentionally make legal errors in support of the defendant government.

VI.
The Trial Judge Made a Harmful Error by not Disqualifying himself and or for Calendaring a Hearing before the Presiding Judge

After the Plaintiff set forth substantial facts in his verified statement of disqualification (CT-000592-00626, Vol. 3 of 3), the trial court never sent a copy of the Order (CT-000627-000631, in Vol. 3 of 3). The fact is that the trial court "filed" its responsive pleading but never served the court's response to the Plaintiff or Defendants, and never issued a minute order; as is required by law (code, caselaw). This proof of fact is demonstrated in lack of proof of service in the certified record (CT-000627, Vol. 3 of 3) because the Order was never properly and legally served.

The trial court judge was supposed to set the duly verified filed statement of disqualification under **CCP 170.3** for a law and motion hearing as set forth by civil procedure under **CCP 170.3 et seq**. but failed to do so. And as a result of this action the Plaintiff was not afforded the right to due process and must have been allowed a hearing on the legal issues presented in the verified statement of disqualification, that much was owed to the Plaintiff. And as a result, the Plaintiff was denied the due process of law under the **US Constitution** and California Constitutions.

Although the remedy is mandate at the trial court level, the right to review an error of due process cannot be denied on appeal. The fact of the matter is that the Plaintiff was never given the proper legal required notice of the trial court's Order (CT-000627, found in Vol. 3 of 3) and the judicial officer secretly filed his responsive pleading in this case and derailed the Plaintiff from filing a writ of mandate against the trial court. The Plaintiff had filed two writs in this Court of Appeal and although discretionarily denied, the Plaintiff would have filed another one anyway. This trial court knew that the Plaintiff would probably draft and file a third writ but intentionally avoided its duty of serving the Order (CT-000627, in Vol.3 of 3) with prejudice.

The Plaintiff was denied due process of law under the US Constitution on its face, as such the conclusive Final Order dismissing the Plaintiff complaint is void of law; the judicial officer's decision in this case is highly questionable. A judicial officer that is disqualified cannot make any valid legal order and any previous order in the case must be vacated and reversed.

If the trial court had cared and did the proper legal procedure, then the Plaintiff would have filed for a petition for mandate in the court of appeal. The Plaintiff previously filed two writs in this court of appeal known as case numbers "**B283557 & B286369**" (Appellant has duly filed an application for an extension of time to augment record to include the Documents from the two Writs related to this case).

The trial court failed to perform its duty under the law, has acted with abuse of discretion, and has ultimately denied the Plaintiff due process of law under the **US Constitution** and California Constitution. The trial court was prejudiced and in favor of the defendant government for no valid legal reason, and whether a petition for a writ of mandate or prohibition was filed or not, the Plaintiff was still denied due process of law under the **US Constitution** and California Constitutional protections. And as such, the due process of law denied to the Plaintiff by this trial court. The legal issues raised and demonstrated herein must be reversed as matter of law and fact, if not then Plaintiff is denied true justice.

Mandate is the only remedy at the trial court level but as a matter of fact and custom, appellate courts in the state of California typically deny writs of mandate because they are discretionary and not mandatory. This loophole makes it nearly impossible for courts to fulfill its duties by law, produces paperwork waste, and fails the citizen taxpayer who pays for it all. But raised on appeal, the lack of due process of law under the **US Constitution** and California Constitution is a reversible error on appeal. If this court states otherwise then it is not being uniform nor being consistent with the rule of law.

VII.
The Trial Court made a Harmful Error by sustaining the Defendants Demurrer to the Plaintiff's Complaint, the final Order must be reversed, and is null and void

The Defendant's counsel of record, on its face of the pleadings, never complied with the legal procedure required to truly satisfy **Code of Civil Procedure 430.41(a)** "meet and confer requirements". On that correct and plain statutory language, the trial court should have never sustained any objection raised in the Defendant's Demurer.

Accordingly, the **Code of Civil Procedure 430.41(a)** clearly mandates and plainly states:

The Defendant did not follow the required legal procedure and instead choose to take his own route, and clearly erred as a matter of California statutory law, see **Code of Civil Procedure 430.41(a)**;

The Defendants' counsel of record filed and served his declaration claiming that he fully complied with the legal requirements explained in the code, but he did not. In fact, the code expressly states and requires by California legislative law, that in order to meet and confer as required, the meet and confer between counsel of parties must be in person or by telephone, see **Code of Civil Procedure 430.41(a)**.

The fact in the record clearly states and by the Defendant's counsel of record own 'declaration', that Mr. John M. Coleman only made an unlawful attempt to meet and confer with the Plaintiff by letter, in which he did. The fact of this case is, as the record demonstrates and reflects, Mr. Coleman Esq. never properly complied with the statutory meet and confer requirements and must have filed a declaration as to such, in order to be granted an automatic 30-day extension.

And as the law explains, if the counsel of parties still cannot properly meet and confer after the extension has been filed and served in the court and on all parties, ONLY then will the defects in a meet and confer requirement can be disregarded, but not before an extension has been filed. Instead, the Defendant's filed the improper declaration and must have filed a declaration in compliance with the statute. Therefore, the trial court made a harmful error by overlooking the statutory requirement.

Sustaining such an improper and unlawful motion to demurer and motion to strike concurrently in the same hearing was a harmful error of law and prejudiced the Plaintiff's case. Further, the trial court never ordered nor required to amend the complaint as regularly practiced in Californian courts.

VIII.
The Trial Court made a Harmful Error by Sustaining the Defendant's Motion to Strike and a Disqualified Judge's Order is null and void

The trial judge never read the Plaintiff's opposition, just looked at it for a couple of seconds and then dropped it back onto his judge's desk. **What a fraud**. The trial court judge lied with an intent to deny the Plaintiff the exercise of his legal right to petition his Government for their grievances against his under the US Constitution but was not.

The trial court judge was prejudiced and made an intentional error and knew for a fact that the Plaintiff had filed an Opposition to their Motion to Strike but blatantly disregarded it and lied about it in his Order on the motion to Strike. The trial court made intentional prejudicial errors in favor of the Defendant County and against the self-represented Plaintiff.

In the hearing and decision on the motion to strike (CT-000181, Vol. 1 of 3) the trial judge completely and purposefully disregarded the Plaintiff's pleadings in the form of his Opposition to Defendants motion to strike his Complaint CT-000602;000606;000609-000610, Vol. 3 of 3).

The trial court completely ignored the Plaintiff's opposition to the Defendants motion to strike (CT-000602; 000606, Vol. 3 of 3). For example, the Plaintiff observed and verified that "63. The Judge Koonsian has intentionally acted with bias by disregarding the fact that the Plaintiff did submit timely Opposition to the Defendant's Motion to Strike on July 28, 2016", see CT-000602, in Vol. 3 of 3).

The trial court judge falsely claimed and wrote in his tentative ruling on the motion, that "Plaintiff has not filed an Opposition . . . That is a lie from the pit of hell because the devil is the father of all liars. Unfortunately, the devil is the trial judge's father and that is why the Plaintiff was doomed to fail and trapped in Keosian's courtroom. Keosian claims to be religious but promotes and writes lies, how tragic, hypocritical, and unethical.

IX.
The Trial Court made a Harmful Error by Failing to Disclose his Potential Conflicts of Interests involving the County of Los Angeles

The trial court judicial officer harbored his prejudice and was indeed prejudiced against the Plaintiff in pro per (CT-000591-00625, Vol. 3 of 3) and had an unethical conflict of interest that must have been disclosed but was never properly disclosed to the parties in this case (CT-000618-000619, Vol. 3 of 3). Professional Superior Court Judges typically disclose if one has a relative or spouse working for the County Government as an ethical practice.

If Judge Keosian has or had a relative working for the County Government as an attorney, and now that relative is working as a partner in their law firm, under the Code of Ethics, that should have been disclosed to the parties at the initial onset of the case. The trial court made a harmful error of law and the appearance of impropriety and the lack of transparency suggests that Judge Keosian may have a potential conflict of interest.

And if the Judge owns or manages a law firm that has partners or employees whom work for the County Government, have worked, and or still advise the County Government on its legal matters, then it is reasonable to infer that the trial court had a serious conflict of interest. The trial court attempted to conceal it and intentionally failed to disclose it to the parties. But the error was not harmless and could have been avoided by the trial court's obligatory disclosure by going on the Record.

Los Angeles County Superior Court judges are paid extra money from the Los Angeles County Board of Supervisors every year, in which were considered unlawful but then the California Legislative branch of Government decriminalized and legalized the practice for County Government. Although it is legal to pay judges extra money aside from state funds, the trial judge had a duty to disclose it to the parties but did not. There is nothing wrong nor unethical to accept compensation as a government official or employee per se.

However, it is wrong and unethical for a trial court judge to not disclose the fact that he receives extra compensation from the County Government. The fact of the matter is that a civil lawsuit against the County Government in where a trial judge receives extra compensation from that same County Government may be recused on its own motion or a parties' motion, or even to transfer the lawsuit to a change of venue for a potential conflict of interest.

Every year lawsuits are filed against the Los Angeles County in Superior Court and rarely anyone wins against the County Government, that is a fact. Without a state licensed attorney working on such a civil case, a Plaintiff in pro per such as myself is often "dead in the water". The statistics prove, that race and ethnicity is often a factor in the outcome of the legal settlements filed and made against the County of Los Angeles.

These outcomes are facts, and factual and undisputable statistics prove, that private individuals filing lawsuits against the county is a failed cause designed by the Government themselves. So, such a cause, like this one, is not a failure per se, but the trial court system administered in Los Angeles County is inherently designed to fail someone like the Plaintiff in pro per. And not only did the Los Angeles Superior Court for the County of Los Angeles fail the Plaintiff, but they allowed the Defendant Government to invade his privacy, lie in declarations, and evade rules of law.

The fact of the matter and breakdown of this case is because the County controls the Superior Court judges through a scheme of unnecessary and extra compensation paid for by California taxpayers such as the Plaintiff in pro per. The fact of the matter is that tax dollars are being wasted and the very dollar that the citizen tribute to this Government, the Government uses that very same dollar against him or her.

Now as some in the public has coitized this custom and practice, the County Board of Supervisors has the trial court judges in their pocket*. The judiciary of the Court of Appeal do not call themselves judges, but "justices", and this custom and practice is to inherent and embody the product of American and Californian justice. None has ever been had since the Plaintiff has filed this legal case against the Defendant County.

X.
The Trial Court's Order Violated the Plaintiff's right to privacy in his medical records, the trial court violated the Plaintiff's Rights in disclosing medical information to the Government and police, whom are now using and misusing his medical conditions against him

The Defendant government never liked this lawsuit, never attempted to investigate as claimed, and has probably spent millions of taxpayer dollars unlawfully surveilling me during the time pending this Appeal. The Defendants used the trial court to rubberstamp an Order for his medical records that would normally be denied by a reasonable judicial officer. A 20-year-old medical record has no relation to this case and the Defendant illegally obtained the information, the Plaintiff properly objected, but the judge knowingly authorized an illegal search and seizure of his medical records, which has probably been distributed throughout the Government in order to ***Target*** the Plaintiff misusing taxpayer dollars. A proper and truthful disclosure will reveal that Plaintiff describes the truth, and the Defendant government, like a monster, has 24-hour target on a disabled person such as the Plaintiff.

The Plaintiff never waives any of his medical information nor consents to it by describing his class as disabled, and the Plaintiff never sued the Defendant Government for disability discrimination, and the Defendant waived their right to any relevant medical records to this case by failing to compel discovery of their Interrogatory.

The Defendants and their counsel of record demanded the Plaintiff's medical records stemming from 20 years ago. The false arrest by the Defendants was done only four years ago. So why would a 20-year-old medical records be relevant to this legal case? Why would any fair and impartial judge make such an irrelevant, arbitrary, and illegal order? Why would any government official be so careless and act so unlawfully?

The Plaintiff was and still is entitled to the right to privacy in his medical records and the trial court conspired by common design or by actual fraud to ensure that the defendant government and police could have unauthorized use but intentionally failed to do so.

Copyright. © 2021. Paralegal Publishing Group.

XI.
CONCLUSION

If the trial judge had me as a client or campaign contributor then he would have to disclose it, so why did the trial judge fail to disclose that he receives extra money from the County of Los Angeles? What is the trial judge hiding? The fact is this trial judge operated similar "slime ball litigation tactics" that the County of Los Angeles is known for. And because the County Government pays your colleagues and subordinates, or pays for your "COLA", this institution could seemingly careless. The published and unpublished opinions tell it all, this power elite group can deny and play semantics, but the People know, and statistics show it. Now, here comes the Plaintiff to prove it, regardless if the authorities herein claim otherwise, the true story will be told beyond these chambers and walls. The spirit of free speech lives, and the World will know the truth:

This Government is corrupt and broken, this legal case is a snapshot and example of a crumbling system and waste of tax dollars.

In my experience in dealing with the Government after paying taxes since I was 16 and voting since I was 18; the current legal system is broken, corrupt, and avoids fact and law, the judicial system has failed the citizen taxpayer and benefits only a collegiate elite group of lawyer-made-judges. The Defendant County of Los Angeles is a corrupt public entity that may be unconstitutional and should be dismantled and reorganized.

Therefore, as a matter of procedure, historical fact, and in the evolution of this Democracy, this type of Brief details the history of an ordinary Mexican-American self-represented litigant, that is exercising one's right to Petition the Government for grievances. The problem with this institution is that the California courts operate it as a business for lawyers and the legal industry, not for the justice that they subscribe to in their mission statement. That is just government marketing and advertising. If the Government truly enforced the laws on the books then We, the Appellant, The Respondents, and this Court would not be here reading this right now. But you are because the legal system has failed to uphold the rule of laws, deprived vested rights, and perpetuate falsehoods for professional gain and political power.

Copyright. © 2021. Paralegal Publishing Group.

CERTIFICATE OF WORD COUNT

I hereby certify that this Brief was performed on Microsoft word and the true and correct word count minus caption, table of contents, table of authorities, certificate of interested persons and attachment 2, inclusive, is the number a total of 4,863.

Respectfully submitted,

Luke E. Dumas, Plaintiff & Appellant in pro per

Trial Court & Appeal: False Arrest, Imprisonment, and Civil Rights Violations By L.A. County

<u>Dumas v. Los Angeles County Board of Supervisors et al</u>. 45 Cal. App. 5th 348

Court of Appeal No. B288554

Superior Court No. BC618191

IN THE COURT OF APPEAL OF THE STATE OF CALIFORNIA

SECOND APPELLATE DISTRICT, DIVISION FOUR

―――――――――

LUKE EDWARD DUMAS,

Plaintiff & Appellant,

vs.

The Los Angeles County Board of Supervisors et al,

Defendants & Respondents

―――――――――

APPELLANT'S MOTION FOR JUDICIAL NOTICE

―――――――――

Luke Edward Dumas, in pro per
5462 E. Del Amo Blvd.
Long Beach, California, 90808
(562) 356-0492

Appellant in pro per

LUKE E. DUMAS

Copyright. © 2021. Paralegal Publishing Group.

Trial Court & Appeal: False Arrest, Imprisonment, and Civil Rights Violations By L.A. County

Dumas v. Los Angeles County Board of Supervisors et al. 45 Cal. App. 5th 348

TABLE OF CONTENTS

	PAGE
CAPTION	1
TABLE OF CONTENTS	2
TABLE OF AUTHORITIES	
I. INTRODUCTION	4
II. EXHIBITS TO BE JUDICIALLY NOTICED	4
III. ARGUMENT	5
IV. CONCLUSION	7

EXHIBIT 1

EXHIBIT 2

BLANK PAGE

Copyright. © 2021. Paralegal Publishing Group.

TABLE OF AUTHORITIES

PAGE

California State Codes

Evidence Code Section §451   5

Evidence Code Section §452   6

Copyright. © 2021. Paralegal Publishing Group.

APPELLANT'S MOTION FOR JUDICIAL NOTICE

TO THE HON. JUSTICES OF DIVISION FOUR:

I. **INTRODUCTION**

This Motion for Judicial Notice is made on the following grounds for:

1. For this Court to permit the Appellant to be granted judicial notice of documents that have been filed and related to this legal matter. This Motion is made further to support the Appeal for proper judicial review in support of my Opening Brief, Respondent's Reply Brief, and my Reply to Respondent's Reply Brief.

2. This Motion is brought into compliance with and modeled after in support of an Appeal filed by persons not represented by an attorney.

II. EXHIBITS TO BE JUDICIALLY NOTICED

3. Appellant requests that the Court permit the judicial notice of the following court documents and papers in the case to be a part of the appellate record attached to this motion herein:

Exhibit No. 1: "MINUTE ORDER" of the original true and correct certified copy of proof that I was scheduled for trial on February 5, 2018, at 8:30AM, on the exact same date and time that I was also scheduled for trial on February 5, 2018, at 8:30AM in this legal case in which caused extreme conflict thus resulting in a Final Order of Dismissal.

Exhibit No. 2: "OBJECTION TO NOTICE OF TAKING DEPOSITION OF LUKE EDWARD DUMAS" in which is the true and correct copy and includes a true and correct copy of the "PROOF OF SERVICE".

III. ARGUMENT

    3. This Reviewing Court should take judicial notice of legal matters listed in **Evidence Code Section §451** and **Section §452**. Judicial Notice of matters listed in **Evidence Code §452** is left to the court's discretion.

    4. **Evidence Code Section §451** provides in full:

Judicial notice shall be taken of the following:

(a) The decisional, constitutional, and public statutory law of this state and of the United States and the provisions of any charter described in **Section 3, 4, or 5 Article XI** of the **California Constitution**.

(b) Any matter made a subject of judicial notice by **Section 111343.6, 11344.6, or 18576** of the **Government Code** or by **Section 1507 of Title 44** of the **United States Code**.

(c) Rules of professional conduct for members of the bar adopted pursuant to **Section 6076** of the **Business and Professions Code** and rules of practice and procedure for the courts of this state adopted by the Judicial Council.

(d) Rules of pleading, practice, and procedure prescribed by the United States Supreme Court, such as the Rules of the United States Supreme Court, the Federal Rules of Civil Procedure, the Federal Rules of Criminal Procedure, the Admiralty Rules, the Rules of the Court of Claims, the Rules of the Customs Court, and the General Orders and Forms in Bankruptcy.

(e) The true signification of all English words and phrases and of all legal expressions.

(f) Facts and propositions of generalized knowledge that are so universally known that they cannot reasonably be the subject of dispute.

Evidence Code Section §452 provides in full:

(a) The decisional, constitutional, and statutory law of any state of the United States and the resolutions and private acts of the Congress of the United States and of the Legislature of this state.

(b) Regulations and legislative enactments issued by or under the authority of the United States or any public entity in the United States.

(c) Official acts of the legislative, executive, and judicial departments of the United States and of any state of the United States.

(d) Records of (1) any court of this state or (2) any court of record of the United States and of any state of the United States.

(e) Rules of court of (1) any court of this state or (2) any court of record of the United States or of any state of the United States.

(f) The law of an organization of nations and of foreign nations and public entities of foreign nations.

(g) Facts and propositions that are of such common knowledge within the territorial jurisdiction of the court that they cannot be the subject of dispute.

(h) Facts and propositions that are not reasonably subject to dispute and are capable of immediate and accurate determination by resort to sources of reasonably indisputable accuracy.

IV. CONCLUSION

For all the reasons stated, this Reviewing Court should take judicial notice as requested.

Dated: 10/16/2019   Respectfully submitted,

_____
Luke E. Dumas, Plaintiff &
Appellant in pro per

Trial Court & Appeal: False Arrest, Imprisonment, and Civil Rights Violations By L.A. County
<u>Dumas v. Los Angeles County Board of Supervisors et al</u>. 45 Cal. App. 5th 348

Court of Appeal No. B288554

Superior Court No. BC618191

IN THE COURT OF APPEAL OF THE STATE OF CALIFORNIA

SECOND APPELLATE DISTRICT, DIVISION FOUR

LUKE EDWARD DUMAS,

Plaintiff & Appellant,

vs.

The Los Angeles County Board of Supervisors et al,

Defendants & Respondents

APPELLANT'S MOTION TO AUGMENT THE RECORD

Luke Edward Dumas, in pro per
5462 E. Del Amo Blvd.
Long Beach, California, 90808
(562) 356-0492

Appellant in pro per

LUKE E. DUMAS

Copyright. © 2021. Paralegal Publishing Group.

TABLE OF CONTENTS

	PAGE
CAPTION	1
TABLE OF CONTENTS	2
V. INTRODUCTION	3
VI. ARGUMENT	3
A. The administrative record should include all papers in the case	3
B. Good cause exists to grant the augmentation the legal papers to be part of the appellate record	6
III. CONCLUSION	7
LIST OF EXHIBITS	8
EXHIBIT 1	9
EXHIBIT 2	15
BLANK PAGE	88

Copyright. © 2021. Paralegal Publishing Group.

APPELLANT'S MOTION TO AUGMENT THE RECORD

TO THE HON. JUSTICES OF DIVISION FOUR:

I. INTRODUCTION

This Motion is made on the following grounds for:

1. For this Court to permit the Appellant to be granted to augment documents that were before the trial court. This Motion is made further to support the Notice of Appeal and Appeal for proper judicial review in support of my Brief and Reply to Respondent's Reply Brief.

2. This Motion is brought into support of an Appeal filed by persons not represented by an attorney and this Reviewing Court should augment the appellate record for good and just cause.

II. ARGUMENT

A. The administrative record should include all papers in the case

3. On June 12, 2017, I had a person over the age of 18 years of age personally serve "OBJECTION TO NOTICE OF TAKING DEPOSITION OF LUKE EDWARD DUMAS" in the attached "Exhibit 1" in which includes the original "PROOF OF SERVICE".

4. On November 17, 2017, I had filed a "PETITION FOR WRIT OF MANDAMUS, PROHIBITION, OR OTHER EXTRAORDINARY

RELIEF" in the Court of Appeal of the State of California, identified as "Exhibit 2", and should be augmented in the appellate record.

In the Petition for Writ includes inside a true and correct copy of the subpoenas that were in question and in dispute in the Motion to Quash in where a medical provider's information was illegally obtained by Mr. Coleman on behalf of the Respondent and Defendant Los Angeles County Board of Supervisors. The subpoenas in question and dispute provide for better examination of the issue raised in my Opening Brief, Respondent's Reply Brief, and in my Reply to their Reply Brief.

5. These legal documents should be included into the appellate record; including the documents, in Exhibits 1 to 2, therefore Appellant request that these documents be augmented to the appellate record.

6. The complete appellate record should and must include the pleadings, and the written evidence and any other papers in the case.

7. The documents in Exhibit 1 through 2 to be augmented are indeed other papers in the case, as is evidenced by the Designation of Transcript on Appeal.

8. Pursuant to California law which states all or part of the papers in the lower trial court's proceedings may be filed with this Motion to

Augment. In which true and correct copies of parts of the legal papers made were indeed made part of Respondent's legal papers.

9. California law also states that all or part of the appellate record may be filed with the Respondent, in which Respondent failed to do, nor did, as the law permits, therefore this Court should order the appellate record to be augmented in the best interest of justice.

10. The Appellant had indeed filed and served "Exhibit 2", in which are the true and correct copies of the legal papers and documents for the appellate record with the Court as expeditiously as possible as permitted by law. California law further permits the Respondent could have filed any part of the appellate record in opposition to the Petition but never did so.

11. The contents of the supporting documents have been accompanied before the time of briefing has expired.

12. Now comes Appellant in pro per pursuant to California law, herein depositing all documents and exhibits submitted, or other papers in the case in the lower trial court.

13. The Appellant, with regards to the form of supporting documents to be augmented in Exhibits 1 through 2.

14. If there be any issue with the noncompliance of any supporting documents with regards to this motion, the Appellant respectfully requests for the Court to allow the Appellant to bring the documents into compliance and cure them within the stated reasonable time of not less than five days.

B. Good cause exists to grant the augmentation the legal papers to be part of the appellate record

19. California law allows for order for the augmentation of the record to be complete as it should contain all written evidence and any other papers in the case pertinent to this Appeal.

Appellant requests that the Court permit the augmenting of the following written evidence and papers in the case to be a part of and lodged with the appellate record attached to this motion herein:

Exhibit No. 1: OBJECTION TO NOTICE OF TAKING DEPOSITION OF LUKE EDWARD DUMAS" in which includes the original "PROOF OF SERVICE".

Exhibit No. 2: PETITION FOR WRIT OF MANDAMUS, PROHIBITION, OR OTHER EXTRAORDINARY RELIEF".

III. CONCLUSION

1. For the reasons stated above, this Court should grant this motion, thus ordering the augmentation of the legal papers in this unlimited civil case for civil rights and proceedings for judicial review of the entire lower trial court's final order.

Dated: 10/16/2019

Respectfully submitted,

_____

Luke E. Dumas, Plaintiff &
Appellant in pro per

LIST OF EXHIBITS

EXHIBIT NO.	Document Name	Date Filed or Served	Pages
1	OBJECTION TO NOTICE OF TAKING DEPOSITION OF LUKE EDWARD DUMAS" & "PROOF OF SERVICE"	June 12, 2017	5
2	"PETITION FOR WRIT OF MANDAMUS, PROHIBITION, OR OTHER EXTRAORDINARY RELIEF"	November 17, 2017	71

Case No. B288554

IN THE COURT OF APPEAL
OF THE STATE OF CALIFORNIA
SECOND APPELLATE DISTRICT
DIVISION FOUR

LUKE EDWARD DUMAS,

Plaintiff & Appellant,

vs.

The Los Angeles County Board of Supervisors et al,

Defendants & Respondents

APPELLANT'S REPLY TO RESPONDENT'S REPLY BRIEF

Luke Edward Dumas, in pro per

5462 E. Del Amo Blvd.

Long Beach, California, 90808

(562) 356-0492

Copyright. © 2021. Paralegal Publishing Group.

APPELLANT'S REPLY BRIEF TO RESPONDENT'S REPLY

TO THE HON. JUSTICES OF DIVISION FOUR:

I. INTRODUCTION

As justices and judges, you are the epitome of "American Justice", hence your titles "Justices of the Court". But you are still not the Supreme God, but you possess certain "god-like-powers" over me as an ordinarily poor Mexican American male by deciding my fate for this American type of justice in this legal matter for Civil Rights under American and California laws. See **US Constitution**, in **Article III**; and under California's **Rules of Court, rule 8.100** & **rule 8.104**; **Garza v. Delano Union Elementary District** (1980) 110 Cal.App.3d 306; **Roman v. County of Los Angeles**, 85 Cal.App.4th 316; *Genesis 1*; *Revelations 22*).

II. ARGUMENT

1. THE TRIAL COURT ABUSED ITS DISCRETION AND DISREGARDED CALIFORNIA LAW BY GRANTING THE DEMURRER

Again, the facts of this legal case are not in question (CT-000001-000701, Volumes 1/3). Material allegations were factually accepted as true as a matter of California law pursuant to a Demurrer - (CT-000130; and 000136; and 000176; in Vol. 1 of 3). But the problem with the Demurrer as was only granted to the

Defendants and Respondents in part to dismiss their co-Defendant Los Angeles County Sherriff's Department and Sherriff Jim McDonnell from the Plaintiff's Complaint but not the Defendant and Respondent Los Angeles County Board of Supervisors (CT-000175; and 000181, in Vol. 1/3).

This Reviewing Court simply does not have to look no further but to the initial procedure of this unlimited legal case in how to see where I, the Appellant and Plaintiff in pro per, did not get a fair chance nor opportunity for my day in a court of law from the very start. In fact, the trial court made a very harmful and prejudicial error by granting any part of the Demurrer because the Defendants and Respondents never complied with the letter nor the spirit of the law as is required under the **Code of Civil Procedure Section 430.41**.

For example, in an article written by *Hon. Judge Richard L. Fruin Jr.* of the Los Angeles County Superior Court for the Daily Journal, titled "**New Law is Driving Down Motions**", the Hon. Judge Fruin Jr. writes:

"**Section 430.41** requires that a defendant meet and confer with plaintiff's counsel - - 'in person or by telephone' (not through letter or email) - - for the purpose 'of determining whether an agreement can be reached that would resolve the objections to be raised by demurrer.' The meet and confer is to occur at least five days 'before the date a demurrer must be filed,' but, if the parties are unable to meet, then the moving party is to file a declaration stating that a good faith attempt to meet and confer was made. The moving party is then granted a 30-day extension to complete the meet and confer and, if need be, to file the intended demurrer." [14]

The counsel of record Mr. John M. Coleman, has misrepresented the truth in litigation, overtly lies without conscious, and uses 'slime ball litigation tactics' again, even in this Court. Said counsel and author of the Reply Brief, Mr. Coleman, never filed nor properly complied with the legal mandate set forth in **Code of Civil Procedure Section 430.41** which clearly states:

> "Before filing a demurrer pursuant to this chapter, the demurring party shall meet and confer in person or by telephone with the party who filed the pleading that is subject to demurrer for the purpose of determining whether an agreement can be reached that would resolve the objections to be raised in the demurrer." (emphasis added).

In the Respondent's Reply Brief on page 16 (RB-16), Mr. Coleman states:

> "In this case, the Respondent's counsel filed a Declaration that complied with the Provisions of **Code of Civil Procedure Section 430.41** (C.T., pg. 00076-00079). In that Declaration he stated that he attempted to contact Appellant, but Appellant did not reply to his written attempt to meet with him to engage in the meet and confer process" (emphasis added).

The Respondent's counsel of record in the trial court in their Reply Brief, admit that it was only a "WRITTEN ATTEMPT". The California legislative law and mandate is clear as sunshine in a summer day. As the code states and remains

---

[14] https://www.dailyjournal.com/articles/345642-new-law-is-driving-down-motions

Copyright. © 2021. Paralegal Publishing Group.

operative, and as the *Hon. Judge Fruin Jr.* write in the article cited above recite the code in the *Daily Journal*, hence a "meet and confer" cannot be made by and through letter, the California legislature changed that practice of old.

Before the code was operative, that is how California lawyers and parties in civil matters used to "meet and confer" but for better or worse, the new legislative law mandating the meet and confer process to be made only by and through telephone or in person, not simply by letter as Mr. Coleman would like this Reviewing Court to believe. That is a fairy tale and unprofessional conduct by purposefully misrepresenting the facts and law.

The trial court was not legally authorized to even have scheduled, calendared, or even entertained the Defendants and Respondents' Demurrer because the new legislative law makes the following mandate of law:

"**(2)** The parties shall meet and confer at least five days before the date the responsive pleading is due. If the parties are not able to meet and confer at least five days prior to the date the responsive pleading is due, the demurring party shall be granted an automatic 30-day extension of time within which to file a responsive pleading, by filing and serving, on or before the date on which a demurrer would be due, a declaration stating under penalty of perjury that a good faith attempt to meet and confer was made and explaining the reasons why the parties could not meet and confer. The 30-day extension shall commence from the date the responsive pleading was previously due, and the demurring party shall not be subject to default during the period of the extension. Any further extensions shall be obtained by court order upon a showing of good cause" (emphasis added).

The appellate record, the Appellant's Brief, and the Respondent's Reply Brief all disclose the facts that the parties did not meet and confer as the **Code** requires by California law. The **Code** makes it mandatory to meet and confer in person or by telephone at least five days prior to the date the responsive pleading is due.

The Defendants and Respondents, as the demurring parties, were never granted an "automatic 30-day extension of time" within which to file their responsive pleading by filing and serving, on or before the date on which a demurrer would be due. Because a declaration stating under penalty of perjury that a good faith attempt to meet and confer in person or by telephone was supposed to be made but was never made by Mr. Coleman as the Defendants and Respondents' counsel of record. As Mr. Coleman admits in his declaration and his Reply Brief on page 16, he only "meet and conferred" by sending me a letter. Therefore, that was a sham declaration and a bogus "meet and confer" in which is now always denied as the *Hon. Judge Fruin Jr.* states in his article "New Law is Driving Down

Motions"[15]. But the trial court made a harmful error and pitfall in my legal case, and this was unjust and with an abuse of discretion as is reviewable under Roman.

And the counsel of record for the Defendants and Respondents, Mr. Coleman, never explained any of the reasons why the parties could not meet and confer in person or by telephone as is required under California law in any declaration that he filed and set forth. Mr. Coleman cannot and fails to even explain it at all in his Reply Brief, for the Respondent in which he misnamed as the "Los Angeles County Board of Supervisors Unified School District", as this case is not against the School District but for the County of Los Angeles.

Accordingly, the **Code of Civil Procedure 430.41(a)** clearly mandates and plainly demonstrates that none of the Defendants did not follow the required legal procedure, and the trial court clearly erred with an abuse of discretion as a matter of California statutory law, see **Code of Civil Procedure 430.41(a)**.

The Defendants' counsel of record filed and served his declaration claiming that he fully complied with the legal requirements explained in the code, but Mr. Coleman did not at comply with the law. In fact, the code expressly states and requires by California legislative law, that in order to meet and confer as required, the meet and confer between counsel of parties must be in person or by telephone,

---

[15] https://www.dailyjournal.com/articles/345642-new-law-is-driving-down-motions

Copyright. © 2021. Paralegal Publishing Group.

see **Code of Civil Procedure 430.41(a)**. Mr. Coleman admits that he only attempted by letter, and this Reviewing Court should and must not disregard this matter of fact and law. Therefore, for good and just cause, this Court should and must remand this case back to the trial court with instructions to comply with the code as it is applied amongst the trial courts.

The fact in the record clearly states and by the Defendant's counsel of record own 'declaration', that Mr. Coleman only made one unlawful attempt to meet and confer with the Plaintiff by letter, so is this Reviewing Court going to ignore my legal rights and the appellate record documenting this fact in black and white (CT-000076-000077; and 000139 in Vol. 1/3)? The fact of this case is, as the appellate record demonstrates and reflects, Mr. Coleman admits in his Reply Brief, that he never properly complied with the statutory meet and confer requirements and must have filed a declaration as to such, in order to be granted an automatic 30-day extension under **Code of Civ. Procedure 430.41(a)(2)** (CT-000136-00137 in Vol. 1/3). Will this Reviewing Court ignore the California law and disregard the law just as did the trial court of and for the County of Los Angeles?

So, the trial court made a very harmful error by entertaining, calendaring, and granting any part of the Defendants and Respondent's Demurrer as a matter of fact and law. Such failure to side-step the law in this case for civil rights was in noncompliance and unlawful. So, will this Reviewing Court ignore the legislative law and disregard my legal rights in the State of California and in the United States of America just as the trial court did in favor of the County of Los Angeles?

The due process requirement, setting forth a legally compliant Demurrer, was not properly complied with from the very beginning of my civil Complaint filed against the Defendants and Respondents as a whole. And this Reviewing Court should and or must for good and just cause, as a matter of issue at law, reverse the Order granting any portion of the Demurrer and send it back to the trial court for the proper procedure codified in **Code of Civil Procedure Section 430.41**.

III. APPELLANT'S REQUEST FOR JUDICIAL NOTICE

1. Evidence of Two Separate Trials on the Exact Same Day

I, the Plaintiff and Appellant, have for good and just cause, submit a request for judicial notice of the following legal court document. A minute order for proof of scheduling me for two trials on the same day and the trial court's administration knew or should have known, as is required by California law and under ethical standards, to not have scheduled me for two completely separate trials on the exact same day. This unlimited civil case was filed in April of 2016 and I had filed a completely separate limited civil action against the government in [date]. So, I had filed two separate government actions for civil rights on two very different dates but was scheduled and calendared to magically appear for trial on the exact same date and time. How does that happen in the Los Angeles Superior Court – Central District? How can that be and what are the chances of that happening? This is evidence of sabotage, unfair bias, and abuse of due process of law and abuse of the legal processes for persons like myself as a natural born Mexican-American whom is a self-represented litigant contending for Civil Rights.

This is clear and further evidence of government bullying in the Los Angeles Superior Court. This type of mistake, fraud, and sabotage can only be cured on Appeal for good and just cause. The evidence clearly shows that the Los Angeles Superior Court designed me for failure in both legal cases I had filed to secure my civil rights and intended to miscarry justice in a fashion meant to defeat my chances for civil rights. Apparently, I have no legal rights with the government and if this Reviewing Court upholds such errors and injustice made against me for my legal and civil rights to be had in a court of law then I certainly do not have any legal rights in the State of California and in the United States of America.

Therefore, this Reviewing Court should take judicial notice of the following facts at hand, I was sabotaged by the Los Angeles Superior Court for the County of Los Angeles because I was simultaneously scheduled for two trials on the same exact day. This was no accident and was an intentional destruction of my fight for civil rights in the State of California against various public entities. Please see my "Request for Judicial Notice" regarding the proof of a minute order issued in another civil case.

As I was and have been derailed, dealt with unjustly, and unfairly in violation of due process, improper court administration, and treated like nothing by the Los Angeles Superior Court – Central District, Stanley Mosk Courthouse. The late and great Honorable Stanley Mosk is turning in his grave as you read this, in spirit knowing that injustice continues to reign against ethnic minorities attempting to secure their constitutional legal rights in the State of California.

IV. PLAINTIFF HAD REASONABLE EXPECTATION OF PRIVACY IN HIS MEDICAL AND OR EMPLOYMENT RECORDS

1. Appellant Request this Reviewing Court to take Judicial Notice of Writ or alternatively to Augment Record of Writ

I, the Plaintiff in pro per, had a reasonable expectation of privacy in my medical records and or employment records. How did Mr. Coleman ever obtain that information because I never disclosed nor authorized that medical provider information to him in any course of this litigation? Mr. Coleman and his associates obtained that information of my medical provider from 20 years ago illegally!

Of course, the defendant's counsel of record is going to contend that the court did not error, but the fact is the medical records sought were never authorized by law nor were ever properly disclosed to the Defendant nor to defendant's counsel of record and were illegally obtained.

The Los Angeles County Superior Court denied (me) the Plaintiff, his right to Constitutional and Statutory privacy in his confidential medical records and information, and employment records in direct violation of California and Federal law inclusive (CT-000475-000482; and see 000534-000535, in Vol. 3/3).

The Los Angeles County Superior Court violated a set of California state laws such as **Code of Civ. Proc. 1987.1**; **1983.5**, the **California Constitution, Art. 1, Sec. 8, Privacy**; **City of Los Angeles v. Superior Court** (2003) 111 Cal.App.4th 883; **CIMA** under **Civ. Code 56 et seq**.

V. **APPELLANT MOTION TO AUGMENT THE CLERK'S TRANSCRIPT OR ALTERNATIVELY REQUEST FOR JUDICIAL NOTICE**

1. **Evidence of Plaintiff and Appellant's Objection to the Defendant and Respondent's Deposition Notice**

VI. **CONCLUSION**

This is not a case against the "Los Angeles County Board of Supervisors Unified School District" but is in fact against the Los Angeles County Board of

Supervisors, Los Angeles County Sherriff's Department, and former Sherriff Jim McDonnell, not the "Unified School District". That part of Mr. Coleman's Reply Brief is just plain flat out wrong and misidentified. There is no certificate of interested persons inserted in the Reply Brief as is required under **Cal. Rules of Court**.

There were two facts that were and have never been denied nor disputed in this legal matter: One, the Respondent and Defendants never denied or disputed being un-American and Fascist as reported in my trial court Complaint. Second, the Respondent and Defendants as interested persons have never denied or disputed illegally surveilling me by using unauthorized and unaccounted millions of taxpayer dollars and public funds in order to conduct illegal activities against me since about December 5, 2015 to date. Since then, now I have taken some of these issues to the Federal government and am dealing with it accordingly.

So much for Democracy and Civil Rights in the State of California and in the United States of America. **As a Mexican-American, I continue to be the victim of oppression, white supremacy, and racial attacks under the current government and the institutions that they control and operate**.

VII. CERTIFICATE OF COMPLIANCE

I hereby certify that this Brief was performed on Microsoft word and the true and correct word count minus caption, table of contents, table of authorities, certificate of interested persons and attachment 2, inclusive, is the number a total of ▇▇▇

Dated: 10/15/2019

Afterword

As Mr. Dumas believes and contends that this case in the trial court and in the court of appeal, he did not get a fair trial. In this case, it is possible that the judges were possibly bribed, blackmailed, and or simply racist against him as a "Mexican-American" male. And that is not an illogical statement to make at all as is evidenced in the entire appellate record. The California courts have secret files and reports on litigants, these secret reports are prejudicial and judgmental in civil litigation. The California courts are plagued with corruption and inside their "judicial system" exists a deep swamp of institutionalized racism, bribery, and or blackmail. Since the filing of Mr. Dumas' first government complaint, he has been the target of supremacists, crooked cops, and corrupt politicians.

Copyright. © 2021. Paralegal Publishing Group.

MORE ABOUT THE AUTHOR

Mr. Dumas has been politically active since the days of Long Beach City College from working on propositions to promoting political candidates; Dumas stayed involved in politics. As a student leader, Mr. Dumas was the President of the ASB Senate for two terms; he was also a Senator for the Native American Club, President of the Anthropology Club, and the Founder and President of the student hip hop club known at the time as "Culture Junction".

Mr. Dumas learned to fight for civil and human rights in total opposition to racism at every angle. As a child Mr. Dumas was targeted, bullied, and harassed by supremacists his whole life. And currently to date, there have been no exceptions. Now Mr. Dumas leads the fight against government corruption.

In this case, Mr. Dumas was the Plaintiff and L.A. County was the Defendant along with the Los Angeles County Sherriff's Department. It is no secret and fact that the L.A. County Sherriff's Department is corrupt, racist, and are in fact advent civil rights violators. That is the culture. The Los Angeles Superior Court has a history of taking "bribes" from the L.A. County Government. That is the fact. The California legislature granted special immunity to those "judges" for taking the 'bribes' as unlawful compensation. That is the history.

Copyright. © 2021. Paralegal Publishing Group.

Sample lawsuits against the Police & Government for False Arrest, Imprisonment, and Civil Rights Violations.

True Story.

Real Case.

(A Collection, Commentary, and Analysis of Pro Per Legal Documents under the case of **Dumas v. Los Angeles County Board of Supervisors** et al. 45 Cal. App. 5th 348)

"Can wicked rulers be allied with [GOD], by those who frame injustice by statute? They band together against the life of the righteous and condemn the innocent to death." - *Psalm 94:20-21.*

Thank You For Reading!

Copyright. © 2021. Paralegal Publishing Group.

www.ingramcontent.com/pod-product-compliance
Lightning Source LLC
Chambersburg PA
CBHW080539220526
45466CB00010B/2972